Praise for

MACHIAVELLI

"Machiavelli easily understood the motives behind the actions of people in the past and in the present."

—ADOLPH CASO

"A most extraordinary lover of liberty."

—GIOVANNI BATTISTA BUSINI

"I count religion but a childish toy, and hold there is no sin but ignorance."

—CHRISTOPHER MARLOWE

"Machiavelli was a teacher of evil."

—LEO STRAUSS

"The staying power of *The Prince* comes from . . . its insistence on the need for a clear-sighted appreciation of how men really *are* as distinct from the moralizing claptrap about how they *ought* to be."

—ALAN RYAN

"Here is the moral politician: 'it is by his dirty hands that we know him.'"

—MICHAEL WALZER

"What's distinctively shocking about Machiavelli is that he didn't care. He believed not only that politicians must do evil in the name of the public good, but also that they shouldn't worry about it. He was unconcerned, in other words, with what modern thinkers call the problem of dirty hands."

—MICHAEL IGNATIEFF

"Written, an Eng   ▒ger,' and put on Pope Paul IV's In      Machiavelli's little treatise would be   political ruthlessness in Europe ov   ast Henry VIII's dissolution of the   ▒. Bartholomew Day massacre in France in 1572. Very soon 'Machiavelli' would be a popular term of denigration; Mach Evil and Mach-a-villain, were typical English corruptions. By the end of the sixteenth century 'Machiavellian' was firmly established in the language as an adjective describing cold, clever, immoral calculation."

—TIM PARKS

"Niccolò Machiavelli is unworthy of the adjective he has given us. In horror at the unscrupulous politics of Cesare Borgia, at the start of the sixteenth century he orchestrated an armed rebellion that succeeded in defeating Pisa in 1509. But he didn't abuse power, nor did he have time to be disdainful of it, though he was an addicted womanizer. He ended up exiled from his hometown, Florence. From his estate near San Casciano in Val di Pesa, sober, reflective, he meditated on politics as a theatrical exercise of extremes. ('Everyone sees what you appear to be, few experience what you really are.') Machiavelli wasn't Machiavellian."

—ILAN STAVANS

"Machiavelli addresses all of his political writings to individuals in positions of power or ambitious to hold them. But in urging them to institute and maintain 'good government' by securing the lives, families and properties of their subjects or fellow citizens, he does not appeal to their sense of justice, mercy or public-spiritedness. On the contrary, he appeals to their ambition—their human desire for status and wealth. Machiavelli's debunking of traditional notions of virtue and vice was therefore a necessary part of his broader contention that government should not serve the interests of the few best, but that it should serve the more modest desires of the many. He does not expect ordinary people to understand the intricacies of military strategy or institutional design—that is, the means by which their basic desires can be satisfied. He is certain, however, that they are the best judges of the outcomes or effects."

—CATHERINE ZUCKERT

MACHIAVELLI

On Politics and Power

MACHIAVELLI

On Politics and Power

NICCOLÒ MACHIAVELLI

Translated from the Italian by
W. K. Marriott and Ninian Hill Thomson

Introduction by Jon Lee Anderson

Illustrations by Eko

Restless Classics

RESTLESS BOOKS
Brooklyn, New York

First published as *Machiavelli: On Politics and Power*
by Restless Books, Brooklyn, 2021

First Restless Books paperback edition March 2021

Paperback ISBN: 9781632062567
Library of Congress Control Number: 2019944002

Cover design by Jonathan Yamakami
Cover illustration by Eko
Set in Arno by Tetragon, London

Printed in Canada
1 3 5 7 9 10 8 6 4 2

Restless Books, Inc.
232 3rd Street, Suite A101
Brooklyn, NY 11215

www.restlessbooks.org

Contents

Introduction

In the art of things that humans do—exercising power, making love, and waging war—there are certain rules that transcend the ages. At times they are forgotten because of the conceits of a certain age, but they are, for better or worse, rules that have defined human behavior forever, and, one suspects, always will.

In early 2002, I visited the southern Afghan city of Kandahar. The recent Taliban ouster had left behind a power vacuum, and Kandahar, their longtime stronghold, was full of intrigue, as rival mujahedin warlords and various foreign powers, including the Americans, the Iranians, and the Pakistanis, jockeyed for influence.

One day, after a week spent shuttling between power centers in an attempt to ascertain where the new alliances and fault lines lay, my Afghan companion and interpreter asked me if I wished to become a warlord myself.

To be a warlord was the ultimate expression of power in Afghanistan, and to him, a young man of twenty-one, who had grown up in a country in a state of perpetual war, it must have seemed a logical aspiration for anyone with means to have. When I asked him what would be required for me to become a warlord, he responded excitedly. All I needed to get started was ten thousand dollars, he said: enough to hire one hundred fighters and to pay them each a salary of a hundred dollars for one month. It was a handsome sum at the time. As Afghans, he explained, they would already have their own weapons, so I wouldn't need to spend any money to arm them, but if I wished to appear more fearsome, I could also rent a few pickup trucks for my men and buy a couple of heavy machine guns and rocket-propelled grenade launchers. He looked at me hopefully.

"But what then?" I asked. How would I pay my little army their second month's salary?

Looking embarrassed at the obviousness of my question, my Afghan friend waved a hand in the direction of the Kandahar bazaar. "It's simple. You just go to the merchants, and the people, and they will give you money." After the first month, he explained, my only concerns would be to decide the terms of enforcement in the area under my sway, to maintain control over my fighters, and then, depending on the extent of my ambitions, to consider the possibilities for expansion. "How large do you want your army to be?" he asked.

A perennial battlefield of history, Afghanistan's political landscape has changed very little over the centuries, making its rough-and-tumble realities sharply reminiscent of the kinds of scenarios described five centuries ago by Niccolò Machiavelli, the Florentine diplomat, philosopher, and author, in *The Prince*, his epochal primer on the practical dos and don'ts of taking and holding power. Machiavelli's era was a convulsed one, in which European monarchies, city-states, and dueling religious armies pursued wars of territorial conquest using any means necessary, from alliances forged through marriage, to outright warfare waged between dukes and kings and popes employing vassal militias and mercenary armies. The rewards of victory could mean the acquisition of power that bordered on the absolute; the consequences of losing power could be equally dramatic, often involving death by torture for oneself and, sometimes, one's family, too.

In the contemporary age, things have moved on somewhat, here and there, but much is unchanged, not least, of course, in that the essential politics of power remain amoral, in the same way that the rules of chess are amoral. It is this immutable fact of life that has given *The Prince* its timeless currency and air of clairvoyant sensibility.

In the end, wisdom is wisdom; there is a fount at which all princes drink, where the waters of knowledge and experience mingle. Some come away with the despot's merciless cunning, while others find themselves incapable, unhappy with the ruthless behavior that is usually the key to unbridled power. Such princes may be better human beings, but, as Machiavelli pointed out, they do not necessarily make better leaders. "Everyone admits how praiseworthy it is in a prince to keep faith, and to live with integrity and not with craft. Nevertheless our experience has been that those princes who have done great things have held good faith of little account, and have known how to circumvent the intellect of men by craft, and in the end have overcome those who have relied on their word."

In such ways, Machiavelli's scrutiny of power feels astonishingly modern, with the personality traits he noticed then among leaders just as visible in the world of power today. During the modern-day American presidency of Donald Trump, for instance, it became common for certain political commentators to describe his approach to politics, to foreign policy, and to power itself as "transactional." The term afforded a polite neutrality to behavior that might otherwise have been described as ruthless, even inhuman, while less obsequious observers would almost certainly also call out Trump as a "Machiavellian," a definition that has come to mean someone possessing the traits of cunning and deceit. The same term is appropriate for several of Trump's more cynical contemporaries, such as Putin, Erdoğan, Xi, and Netanyahu.

If Machiavelli were alive today, however, he would probably demur, concluding that while Trump may have possessed the instincts to seek power and to wield it, his personal vanity usually overwhelmed his ability to use it effectively, while allowing others—including some of the leaders named above—to take advantage at his expense. One recalls the episode in which, following a phone conversation with Erdoğan, the foxy, ambitious Turkish leader, Trump ordered American troops to leave the battlefield in Syria, abandoning their Kurdish allies in the process, and giving up the territory they had won in battle to soldiers from Turkey and Russia, both rival powers. Later, when Trump rescinded his own order, it was too late; the battle space was now shared and infinitely more complicated, and he had lost the respect of his own generals as well as his adversaries.

In a chapter that feels as if it had been written with Trump in mind, "How Flatterers Should Be Avoided," Machiavelli issued an admonitory warning about the kind of prince who "is either over-thrown by flatterers, or so often changed by varying opinions that he falls into contempt." One such man, wrote Machiavelli scathingly, was Maximilian, the Holy Roman Emperor, whom he described as a leader who "does not communicate his designs to anyone, nor does he receive opinions on them. But as in carrying them into effect they become revealed and known, they are at once obstructed by those men whom he has around him, and he, being pliant, is diverted from them. Hence it follows that those things he does one day he undoes the next, and no one ever understands what he wishes or intends to do, and no one can rely on his resolutions."

Machiavelli was born in Florence in 1469, during the Italian Renaissance, at a time when much of Europe was in ferment. Italy itself was a warring mosaic of city-states, with the Medici family installed as the dynastic rulers of Florence, while the papacy and the kingdoms of France and Spain were engaged in unceasing military campaigns to invade and annex new territories. Little Portugal had recently embarked on maritime voyages of discovery, and before long Spain also joined the race for overseas possessions, after defeating and dislodging the Moors at Granada, following eight centuries of Islamic occupation. In 1494, two years after Columbus's first voyage to the Americas, the Medicis were also expelled from Florence, and the city's republican system of government restored after a sixty-year hiatus. The new order was a religious regime overseen by a charismatic Dominican priest, Savanarola, but in 1498, after a mere four-year tenure in office, he was toppled, tortured, and executed.

This was the dramatic turn of events that set the stage for Machiavelli's own professional career. Florence's representative body, the Great Council, named him Second Chancellor, handling its correspondence and internal reports. He was only twenty-nine years old, but evidently showed qualities that impressed those who met him because within a few short weeks he was also named as Secretary to the Great Council's war cabinet, a position that made him the aide-de-camp to Florence's new leader, Piero Soderini. Before long, Machiavelli had effectively become Florence's foreign secretary, and he travelled frequently on diplomatic missions—to Rome to meet with the pope, to other Italian city-states, and to the royal courts of Spain and France—to carry messages and to negotiate, and to observe and become informed on behalf of Florence. Long before the term "shuttle diplomacy" was conceived as a definition for Henry Kissinger's global missions by jet on behalf of the United States, Machiavelli was doing it for Florence on horseback.

While he was first and foremost a diplomat, as a man of his time, Machiavelli did not eschew violence as an aberration, but rather contemplated its political utility, and when he decided against it, he did so for its lack of value as a political tool. Citing the ancient Greek myth of the Centaur, Machiavelli believed that an effective prince must harness the fighting abilities of both man and beast, his respective terms for the law and the use of force: "but because the first is frequently not sufficient, it is necessary to have recourse to the second," he wrote. "So it is necessary for a prince to know how to make use of both natures, and that one without the other is not durable. A prince, therefore, being compelled knowingly to adopt the beast, ought to choose the fox and the lion; because the lion cannot defend himself against snares and the fox cannot defend himself against wolves. Therefore, it is necessary to be a fox to discover the snares and a lion to terrify the wolves."

Such memorable parables were the result of Machiavelli's close observation of the ways in which the princes he met with deployed their power. He had come away especially impressed by the fearsome duke, Cesare Borgia, whose proven determination and ability to outwit his adversaries and betray his friends—while also winning favor from his subjects—was, he suggested, a feat of near-perfection. He lauded Borgia in *The Prince*, writing: "Therefore, he who considers it necessary to secure himself in his new principality, to win friends, to overcome either by force or fraud, to make himself beloved and feared by the people, to be followed and revered by the soldiers, to exterminate those who have power or reason to hurt him, to change the old order of things for new, to be severe and gracious, magnanimous and liberal, to destroy a disloyal soldiery and to create new, to maintain friendship with kings and princes in such a way that they must help him with zeal and offend with caution, cannot find a more lively example than the actions of this man."

Living as he did in embattled times, Machiavelli's brief on behalf of Florence eventually extended beyond diplomacy to encompass the direct administration of warfare, and in 1506, in emulation of a practice he had seen Borgia implement in his conquered territories, he organized and trained a citizen's militia. Two years later, he put it to use and successfully commanded it himself in a battle that resulted in the surprise defeat of the rival city-state of Pisa. But in the end, Machiavelli's triumph was short-lived. In 1512, the members of that same Florentine militia turned and ran from a battle at Prato in an offensive that was backed by Pope Julius II and fought on the ground by hardened Spanish troops. Afterward, the Medicis returned to power in Florence, ending the Republic and dissolving its city-state. Fourteen years after becoming the city's indispensable man, Machiavelli, then forty-three, lost his job, while his boss, Soderini, fled into exile.

It was not long before the Medicis sent for Machiavelli, and had him tortured, seeking his confession that he had taken part in a conspiracy against them. No historical evidence exists to suggest that Machiavelli was involved in an anti-Medici plot, and, in the event, he managed to withstand six *strappados*, a form of torture in which a victim's wrists were tied behind their back, then used to hoist their body into the air before they were abruptly dropped, a process that causes intense pain and often lasting injury to shoulders and arms. Machiavelli was either wholly innocent, a man with an iron constitution, or both, for he did not confess to any transgressions after six such drops, and he was released after three weeks in custody.

After his ordeal, Machiavelli retired to his family farm outside the city, but he remained intellectually and socially active and, inasmuch as he was able, politically so too, albeit behind the scenes—reading, writing, corresponding with influential friends, and sniffing out his opportunities with the new rulers of Florence. A veritable one-man hive of energy, Machiavelli wrote several books, including one about war and another about the history of Florence, as well as poetry, plays, and even a bawdy comedy that was staged to great public success in Rome. But the work for which he earned his posterity is *The Prince*, which he dashed off in a flurry of intense activity following his arrest in 1513, some of it extrapolated from *The Discourses on Livy*, a much larger piece he was working on that was intended as a scholarly commentary on the first ten volumes of Livy's *History of Rome*. (Machiavelli eventually completed *The Discourses* in 1517, but it was only published posthumously, in 1531.) Whatever its inspiration, it has long been an article of faith to historians that *The Prince* amounts to a job application letter from Machiavelli to the Medicis, and it is hard to find fault with that analysis.

As a calling card, *The Prince* is nothing short of effusive, with Machiavelli dedicating it to none other than one of the dynasty's previous rulers, addressing him as "the Magnificent Lorenzo di Piero de' Medici," while describing his effort on the opening page as a "gift" to his son and heir, and Florence's new prince, Giuliano de' Medici. After outlining the pearls of wisdom gleaned from his readings of Livy and his own experiences as the Florentine Secretary, Machiavelli concluded his primer by beseeching the latest Medici prince to seek historic greatness by using his "illustrious house" to unite Italy. There are no signs that Giuliano de' Medici ever read the tract, however, nor did a job offer for Machiavelli ever arrive, and after another decade and a half of industrious hermitage, Machiavelli died of a sudden illness in 1527, at the age of fifty-eight—just as the Medicis were once again overthrown.

At the time of Machiavelli's death, *The Prince* remained unpublished, but had already begun to circulate privately in circles of power and to cause a stir among its readers. As the years went by and Machiavelli's writings became more widely disseminated—*The Discourses* was translated into English in 1536 and *The Prince* in 1640—his posthumous notoriety grew. Pope Paul IV banned *The Prince*, while in Tudor England, it was denounced as the work of Satan: "Old Nick" became a dual synonym for Machiavelli and the Devil. Over the ensuing centuries, not much has changed. Today, in spite of kinder treatment by modern historians ("Machiavelli no more invented political evil than Kinsey invented sex," wrote Claudia Roth Pierpont in the *New Yorker* in 2008), his name carries overwhelmingly negative connotations.

In his own 1950 introduction to *The Prince*, Max Lerner addressed the conundrum of Machiavelli's legacy. "Frederick, Richelieu, Napoleon, Bismarck, Clemenceau, Lenin, Mussolini, Hitler, Stalin, have gone to school to Machiavelli. But by bringing the work to this awareness Machiavelli did what every creative figure does. We might as well blame Shakespeare because, by creating *Hamlet*, he has intensified the agony of the indecisive and divided liberal."

Perhaps. But *Hamlet* was a play, while *The Prince* is a handbook for princes, and it is Machiavelli's clear-eyed cynicism in the way he set out the rules of power through a series of well-chiseled examples— much as Sun Tzu did in his *Art of War*—that will forever mark him as the man who came up with the phrase "the end justifies the means."

In today's world, power relationships are often costumed in less obvious ways than they were in the sixteenth century, but beneath the democratic trappings of many contemporary political regimes, violence remains an essential tool of power, just as the stratagems most commonly associated with Machiavelli, such as deceit or cunning— ruses deployed to avoid outright war while still gaining ground—are as useful and in use in our day as they were in his. While the rights of man have been institutionalized by modern states as a necessary legal concept, such rights coexist with the threat or the use of institutionalized violence by those same states. It is a duality that is as mutually exclusive, morally speaking, as it is ever-present, however dressed up by legal language or arguments made on behalf of humanity or the greater good of the community of nations.

It is in such murky waters that Machiavelli still swims, helping us out even now with the necessary language to rationalize the accidental civilian casualties caused when we use remote-controlled drones to assassinate suspected terrorists in foreign lands, not to mention the cumulative collateral damage of our recent wars in Iraq, Afghanistan, and Syria. How do we justify the sale of weapons to repressive regimes like Saudi Arabia? While previous American presidents may have felt personally discomfited by such relationships even as they authorized them on vague grounds of "national interest," Trump, a wannabee Machiavellian, took unabashed delight at the opportunity to express his support for Crown Prince Muhammad bin Salman following the gruesome murder of Jamal Khashoggi, explaining that the Saudis were about to spend billions of dollars on U.S. weapon systems, which was a good thing for the American economy. But Trump's support for the Saudi prince and his displays of friendship for other tyrants, including Vladimir Putin and Kim Jong Un, also belied his longing to possess their kind of absolute power himself.

The fact is that men (and it is almost always men) have a tendency to admire and emulate those who possess greater power or authority than they do—much as Machiavelli did with Borgia. Saddam Hussein modelled his own tyranny on that of Josef Stalin, whom he consciously sought to imitate, right down to his body language. A former friend and Ba'ath Party comrade of Saddam's once told me that as a young activist, Saddam had read Deutscher's biography of Stalin three times in a row. The Ba'athists had taken their early ideological inspiration from Mussolini's fascist state, but it was Stalin's personal style and brutally effective use of power that Saddam wanted for himself.

In the late nineties, in a series of encounters with the former Chilean dictator Augusto Pinochet, I learned that the old anticommunist despot was also an ardent admirer of the late Chairman Mao Tsetung. Pinochet acknowledged that he had visited Mao's mausoleum in Beijing not just once, but twice. When I asked him why, Pinochet expressed his awe for the power Mao had held "over the lives and deaths of millions."

It was clear from the way Pinochet spoke that he wished he had possessed similar powers himself, but destiny—or perhaps it was the Chilean desire for democracy—had thwarted those ambitions. A few years earlier, seventeen years after seizing power in a bloody 1973 coup against the elected Socialist president Salvador Allende, Pinochet had allowed a public referendum on his rule, and to his great surprise and chagrin, he had lost. Obliged to step down as president, he had nonetheless retained his military command for eight more years before relinquishing control to a loyalist a few months earlier. At the time we met, Pinochet enjoyed immunity from prosecution for his crimes as a Senator for Life, thanks to the terms of a new constitution he had pushed through during his time in office. Chile had technically returned its democracy but it remained a country held in his grip.

When I asked Pinochet whether he would define himself as having been a dictator, he chuckled, shook his head, and said: "I was only an *aspirant* dictator."

If he were alive, Machiavelli would surely have cracked a smile at Pinochet's false modesty and recalled his parable about how the success of princes depended on the ability to emulate foxes as well as lions. "He who has known best how to employ the fox has succeeded best," wrote Machiavelli. "But it is necessary to know well how to disguise this characteristic, and to be a great pretender and dissembler; and men are so simple, and so subject to present necessities, that he who seeks to deceive will always find someone who will allow himself to be deceived."

—JON LEE ANDERSON

Chronology

1469 Niccolò di Bernardo dei Machiavelli born May 3 in Florence, Italy to Bernardo di Niccolò Machiavelli and Bartolomea di Stefano Nelli, members of a prominent Florentine family.

1494 The Medici family are exiled from Florence and the state re-establishes a republic.

1498 Machiavelli instated at an office of the second chancery in Florence where he oversees the production of government documents.

1501–1502 Machiavelli undertakes diplomatic missions on behalf of Florence to quell riots in Pistoia.

1503 Machiavelli publishes *The Description*, a work about the ways that Cesare Borgia, the Duke of Valentinois, murdered and overpowered members of Rome's Orsini political family.

1502–1512 Machiavelli undertakes diplomatic missions to the Papal State, ruled by the Borgias, the court of Louis XII, and the Spanish court. Also spearheads the formation of a Florentine militia that he leads during a 1509 defeat of Pisa.

1512 The Medici re-establish power in Florence. Machiavelli is stripped of his government positions, and exiled.

1513 For three weeks, Machiavelli is detained and tortured, under the accusation of conspiracy against the Medici.

Upon his release, Machiavelli leaves to a small hamlet in Florence, where he takes to studying and writing political theory. Machiavelli also writes plays during this time, which are widely popular. *The Prince* is also published for the first time as a pamphlet this year, as an appeal to the Medici family. Machiavelli still fails to win their favor.

1517 Machiavelli completes *Discourses on the First Decade of Titus Livius*.

1520 Machiavelli publishes *The Life of Castruccio Castracani of Lucca*.

1521 Machiavelli publishes *The Art of War*.

1525 *Florentine Histories* published for the first time.

1526 Machiavelli's play *The Mandrake*, a political satire, premieres during Carnival season. The play has since been revived and reinterpreted many times for both stage and film.

1527 Florentine Republic re-established. Machiavelli dies at age fifty-eight.

1531 *Discourses on Livy* published for the first time.

1532 *The Prince* officially published for the first time.

1536 Cardinal Reginald Pole of England denounces *The Prince* as being harmful to justice and virtue.

1559 *The Prince* and *Discourses on Livy* are added to Pope Paul IV's Index of Prohibited Books. This leads to a ban on publication of the books in most of the Catholic world.

1576 Innocent Gentillet, a Huguenot, publishes *Discourse against Machiavelli*, a work that forms the basis of many subsequent criticisms of Machiavelli. Gentillet focuses on atheism and immorality as problems in Machiavelli's works.

1625 Sir Francis Bacon publishes *Essays or Councils, Both Civil and Moral.* "Of Truth," one of the essays from this collection, is thought to have been influenced by Machiavelli.

1640 Publication of the first English translation of *The Prince*, along with *The Life of Castruccio Castracani* and *The Description.*

1740 Frederick the Great of Prussia and Voltaire write the *Anti-Machiavel*, denouncing the precepts that Machiavelli espouses in *The Prince.*

1776 Edward Gibbon's *The Decline and Fall of the Roman Empire*, a book heavily influenced by Machiavelli's concept of *virtù*, is published. Machiavelli is thought to have had a significant influence on republican thought of the time, both in England and the newly forming free colonies in North America.

1862–1863 George Eliot publishes *Romola*, which features Machiavelli as a character.

1877–1882 Italian historian Pasquale de Villari writes *The Life and Times of Niccolò Machiavelli.* This biography is considered an authoritative work on Machiavelli's life and philosophy. De Villari also asserts that *The Prince* and *The Discourses on Livy* should be read together.

1883 Ninian Hill Thomson publishes his translation of *Discourses on the First Decade of Titus Livius*, excerpted in this edition.

1908 W. K. Marriott publishes his translation of *The Prince*, included in this edition.

1978 *The Mandrake* published by Dramatists Play Service for distribution to a U.S. audience.

1989 American political philosopher Harvey Mansfield publishes *Taming the Prince*, a book that argues that

Machiavelli's theories are the foundation of modern executive power.

2017   Catherine H. Zuckert publishes *Machiavelli's Politics*: a book that examines his oeuvre and attempts to find a unifying politics within his works.

Editor's Note

Niccolò Machiavelli's true views remain a topic of intense debate. Did he foresee the excesses of disdainful dictators like Hitler, Chávez, Erdoğan, Lukashenko, and Trump (the list is endless)? Did he admonish them *avant la lettre*? Was he a realist or a cynic? Or maybe a cynical realist? His writings, from the canonical *Il Principe* (1532) to *Discorsi sopra la prima deca di Tito Livio* (1531), are shrewdly enigmatic as to his own beliefs. They might be read as either a plan of action for the unscrupulous leader or a cautionary tale. His English-language translators, from Edward Dacres to W. K. Marriott, Ninian Hill Thomson, George Bull, and Tim Parks, have turned that enigma into a sport. This edition of Machiavelli's work, put together with the help of Annika Karody, doesn't purport to be complete. It includes *The Prince* in its entirety and crucial selections from Books I and III of *Discourses on Livy.* The objective is to give an accurate map of his political disquisitions, which, unhappily, seem as pertinent in the twenty-first century as they did in Cesare Borgia's Italy. That's because Machiavelli touched on a universal truth: everything we do is about power, but only the powerful matter. Yet how we approach power serves as a measure of who we are. In *The Republic,* Plato states that "the heaviest penalty for declining to rule is to be ruled by someone inferior to yourself." Machiavelli was less hesitant but apparently just as arrogant. He believed "there are three classes of intellect: one that comprehends by itself; another that appreciates what others comprehend; and a third that neither comprehends by itself nor by the showing of others; the first is the most excellent, the second is good, the third is useless." The vast majority of people, he believed (or wanted us to believe), fall into the last category. He was wrong: the best leaders are often the most useless because the best form of government is humble and self-effacing.

—ILAN STAVANS

The Prince

Translated from the Italian
by W. K. Marriott

Theseus could not have showed his abilities if he had not found the Athenians dispersed.

These opportunities, 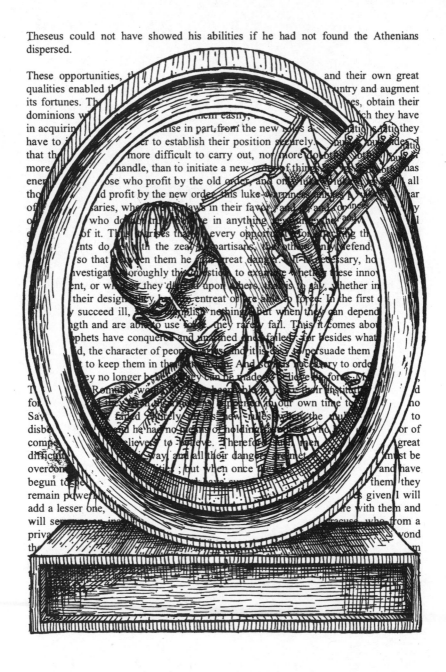 and their own great qualities enabled th... ...ntry and augment its fortunes. Th... ...es, obtain their dominions w... ...them easily; ...ch they have in acquirin... ...arise in part from the new r...es a... ...atio...atio they have to i... ...er to establish their position securely... ...de...d that th... ...more difficult to carry out, nor more do...o... ...on...o more... ...handle, than to initiate a new ord...r of thin... ...has ene... ...ose who profit by the old order, and on...lu...it... all tho... ...d profit by the new order; this luke-warm... ...ar off... ...aries, wh... ...laws in their favo... ...ni... ...y o... ...who do... ...e in anything... ...v... d... ...of it. Th...arises th...every opport...fo... ...g th ...nts do... ...th the zeal... partisans...th... ...efend so that... ...en them he... ...reat dan... ...ecessary, ho ...vestigat... ...oroughly thi...stion... to exa...whet...these inno ...ent, or wh... ...they d...upon... ...is to say, whether in ...their design... ...entreat or...s a... ...o force. In the first ...y succeed ill... ...plish nothing...ut when they can depend ...gth and are ab...to use for... ...they rar...fail. This it comes abo ...phets have conquered and...ed...fail...or besides what ...d, the character of peop... ...s and it is... ...persuade them ...t to keep them in th... ...And so...ry to orde ...ey no longer b... ...ey can be made...ieve...for... T... ...Roma... w... ...n...tit... ...d fo... ...ed in our own time t... ...no Sav... ...led...ly...s new...les...the mul... ...to disbe... ...d he had no means of holding... ...or of compe... ...ieve...lieve. Therefor... ...great difficult... ...way and all their dang... ...must be overco... ...; but when once... ...and have begun to... ...them they remain powe... ...s given I will add a lesser one, ...e with them and will se... ...in...use who from a priva... ...ond th...m

DEDICATION

To the Magnificent Lorenzo di Piero de' Medici:

Those who strive to obtain the good graces of a prince are accustomed to come before him with such things as they hold most precious, or in which they see him take most delight; whence one often sees horses, arms, cloth of gold, precious stones, and similar ornaments presented to princes, worthy of their greatness.

Desiring therefore to present myself to Your Magnificence with some testimony of my devotion toward you, I have not found among my possessions anything which I hold more dear than, or value so much as, the knowledge of the actions of great men, acquired by long experience in contemporary affairs, and a continual study of antiquity; which, having reflected upon it with great and prolonged diligence, I now send, digested into a little volume, to Your Magnificence.

And although I may consider this work unworthy of your countenance, nevertheless I trust much to your benignity that it may be acceptable, seeing that it is not possible for me to make a better gift than to offer you the opportunity of understanding in the shortest time all that I have learned in so many years, and with so many troubles and dangers; which work I have not embellished with swelling or magnificent words, nor stuffed with rounded periods, nor with any extrinsic allurements or adornments whatever, with which so many are accustomed to embellish their works; for I have wished either that no honour should be given it, or else that the truth of the matter and the weightiness of the theme shall make it acceptable.

Nor do I hold with those who regard it as a presumption if a man of low and humble condition dare to discuss and settle the concerns of princes; because, just as those who draw landscapes place themselves below in the plain to contemplate the nature of the mountains and of lofty places, and in order to contemplate the plains place themselves upon high mountains, even so to understand the nature of the people it needs to be a prince, and to understand that of princes it needs to be of the people.

Take then, Your Magnificence, this little gift in the spirit in which I send it; wherein, if it be diligently read and considered by you, you will learn my extreme desire that you should attain that greatness which fortune and your other attributes promise. And if Your Magnificence from the summit of your greatness will sometimes turn your eyes to these lower regions, you will see how unmeritedly I suffer a great and continued malignity of fortune.

I

How Many Kinds of Principalities There Are, and by What Means They Are Acquired

ALL STATES, all powers, that have held and hold rule over men have been and are either republics or principalities. Principalities are either hereditary, in which the family has been long established, or they are new.

The new are either entirely new, as was Milan to Francesco Sforza, or they are, as it were, members annexed to the hereditary state of the prince who has acquired them, as was the kingdom of Naples to that of the King of Spain.

Such dominions thus acquired are either accustomed to living under a prince, or to live in freedom, and are acquired either by the arms of the prince himself, or of others, or else by fortune or by ability.

II

Concerning Hereditary Principalities

I WILL LEAVE OUT all discussion on republics, inasmuch as in another place I have written of them at length, and will address myself only to principalities. In doing so I will keep to the order indicated above, and discuss how such principalities are to be ruled and preserved.

I say at once there are fewer difficulties in holding hereditary states, and those long accustomed to the family of their prince, than new ones, for it is sufficient only not to transgress the customs of his ancestors, and to deal prudently with circumstances as they arise, for a prince of average powers to maintain himself in his state, unless he be deprived of it by some extraordinary and excessive force; and if he should be so deprived of it, whenever anything sinister happens to the usurper, he will regain it.

We have in Italy, for example, the Duke of Ferrara, who could not have withstood the attacks of the Venetians in '84, nor those of Pope Julius in '10, unless he had been long established in his dominions. For the hereditary prince has less cause and less necessity to offend; hence it happens that he will be more loved; and unless extraordinary vices cause him to be hated, it is reasonable to expect that his subjects will be naturally well disposed toward him; and in the antiquity and duration of his rule the memories and motives that make for change are lost, for one change always leaves the toothing for another.

III

Concerning Mixed Principalities

B UT THE DIFFICULTIES occur in a new principality. And firstly, if it be not entirely new, but is, as it were, a member of a state which, taken collectively, may be called composite, the changes arise chiefly from an inherent difficulty that there is in all new principalities, for men change their rulers willingly, hoping to better themselves, and this hope induces them to take up arms against him who rules—wherein they are deceived, because they afterward find by experience they have gone from bad to worse. This follows also on another natural and common necessity, which always causes a new prince to burden those who have submitted to him with his soldiery and with infinite other hardships that he must put upon his new acquisition.

In this way you have enemies in all those whom you have injured in seizing that principality, and you are not able to keep those friends who put you there because of your not being able to satisfy them in the way they expected, and you cannot take strong measures against them, feeling bound to them. For, although one may be very strong in armed forces, yet in entering a province one always has need of the goodwill of the natives.

For these reasons Louis the Twelfth, King of France, quickly occupied Milan, and as quickly lost it; and to turn him out the first time it only needed Lodovico's own forces, because those who had

opened the gates to him, finding themselves deceived in their hopes of
future benefit, would not endure the ill-treatment of the new prince.
It is very true that, after acquiring rebellious provinces a second
time, they are not so lightly lost afterward, because the prince, with
little reluctance, takes the opportunity of the rebellion to punish the
delinquents, to clear out the suspects, and to strengthen himself in
the weakest places. Thus to cause France to lose Milan the first time
it was enough for the Duke Lodovico* to raise insurrections on the
borders, but to cause him to lose it a second time it was necessary
to bring the whole world against him, and that his armies should
be defeated and driven out of Italy, which followed from the causes
abovementioned.

Nevertheless Milan was taken from France both the first and the
second time. The general reasons for the first have been discussed; it
remains to name those for the second, and to see what resources he
had, and what anyone in his situation would have had for maintaining
himself more securely in his acquisition than did the King of France.

Now I say that those dominions that, when acquired, are added
to an ancient state by him who acquires them, are either of the same
country and language, or they are not. When they are, it is easier
to hold them, especially when they have not been accustomed to
self-government, and to hold them securely it is enough to have
destroyed the family of the prince who was ruling them, because
the two peoples, preserving in other things the old conditions, and
not being unlike in customs, will live quietly together, as one has
seen in Brittany, Burgundy, Gascony, and Normandy, which have
been bound to France for so long a time: and, although there may
be some difference in language, nevertheless the customs are alike,

---

* Duke Lodovico was Lodovico Moro, a son of Francesco Sforza, who married
Beatrice d'Este. He ruled over Milan from 1494 to 1500, and died in 1510.

and the people will easily be able to get on amongst themselves. He who has annexed them, if he wishes to hold them, has only to bear in mind two considerations: the one, that the family of their former lord is extinguished; the other, that neither their laws nor their taxes are altered, so that in a very short time they will become entirely one body with the old principality.

But when states are acquired in a country differing in language, customs, or laws, there are difficulties, and good fortune and great energy are needed to hold them, and one of the greatest and most real helps would be that he who has acquired them should go and reside there. This would make his position more secure and durable, as it has made that of the Turk in Greece, who, notwithstanding all the other measures taken by him for holding that state, if he had not settled there, would not have been able to keep it. Because, if one is on the spot, disorders are seen as they spring up, and one can quickly remedy them, but if one is not at hand, they are heard of only when they are great, and then one can no longer remedy them. Besides this, the country is not pillaged by your officials; the subjects are satisfied by prompt recourse to the prince; thus, wishing to be good, they have more cause to love him, and wishing to be otherwise, to fear him. He who would attack that state from the outside must have the utmost caution: as long as the prince resides there it can only be wrested from him with the greatest difficulty.

The other and better course is to send colonies to one or two places, which may be as keys to that state, for it is necessary either to do this or else to keep there a great number of cavalry and infantry. A prince does not spend much on colonies, for with little or no expense he can send them out and keep them there, and he offends a minority only of the citizens from whom he takes lands and houses to give them to the new inhabitants; and those whom he offends, remaining poor and scattered, are never able to injure him; while the rest being uninjured are easily kept quiet, and at the same time are anxious not to err for fear it should happen to them as it has to those who have been despoiled. In conclusion, I say that these colonies are not costly, they are more faithful, they injure less, and the injured, as has been said, being poor and scattered, cannot hurt. Upon this, one has to remark that men ought either to be well treated or crushed, because they can avenge themselves of lighter injuries, of more serious ones they cannot; therefore the injury that is to be done to a man ought to be of such a kind that one does not stand in fear of revenge.

But in maintaining armed men there in place of colonies one spends much more, having to consume on the garrison all the income from the state, so that the acquisition turns into a loss, and many more are exasperated, because the whole state is injured; through the shifting of the garrison up and down all become acquainted with hardship, and all become hostile, and they are enemies who, while beaten on their own ground, are yet able to do hurt. For every reason, therefore, such guards are as useless as a colony is useful.

Again, the prince who holds a country differing in the above respects ought to make himself the head and defender of his less powerful neighbors, and to weaken the more powerful amongst them, taking care that no foreigner as powerful as himself shall, by any accident, get a footing there, for it will always happen that such a one will be introduced by those who are discontented, either through excess of ambition or through fear, as one has seen already. The Romans were brought into Greece by the Aetolians, and in every other country where they obtained a footing they were brought in by the inhabitants. And the usual course of affairs is that, as soon as a powerful foreigner enters a country, all the subject states are drawn to him, moved by the hatred that they feel against the ruling power. So that in respect to those subject states he has not to take any trouble to gain them over to himself, for the whole of them quickly rally to the state that he has acquired there. He has only to take care that they do not get hold of too much power and too much authority, and then with his own forces, and with their goodwill, he can easily keep down the more powerful of them, so as to remain entirely master in the country. And he who does not properly manage this business will soon lose what he has acquired, and while he does hold it he will have endless difficulties and troubles.

The Romans, in the countries that they annexed, observed these measures closely: they sent colonies and maintained friendly relations with the minor powers, without increasing their strength; they kept down the greater, and did not allow any strong foreign powers to gain authority. Greece appears to me sufficient for an example. The Achaeans and Aetolians were kept friendly by them, the kingdom of Macedonia was humbled, Antiochus was driven out; yet the merits of the Achaeans and Aetolians never secured for them permission to increase their power, nor did the persuasions of Philip ever induce the Romans to be his friends without first humbling him, nor did the influence of Antiochus make them agree that he should retain any lordship over the country. Because the Romans did in these instances what all prudent princes ought to do, who have to regard not only present troubles, but also future ones, for which they must prepare with every energy, because, when foreseen, it is easy to remedy them; but if you wait until they approach, the medicine is no longer in time because the malady has become incurable; for it happens in this, as the physicians say it happens in hectic fever, that in the beginning of the malady it is easy to cure but difficult to detect, but in the course of time, not having been either detected or treated in the beginning, it becomes easy to detect but difficult to cure. Thus it happens in affairs of state, for when the evils that arise have been foreseen (which it is only given to a wise man to see), they can be quickly redressed, but when, through not having been foreseen, they have been permitted to grow in a way that everyone can see them, there is no longer a remedy. Therefore, the Romans, foreseeing troubles, dealt with them at once, and, even to avoid a war, would not let them come to a head, for they knew that war is not to be avoided, but is only to be put off to the advantage of others. Moreover they wished to fight with Philip and Antiochus in Greece so as not to have to do it in Italy; they could have avoided both, but this they did not wish; nor did that ever please them that is forever in the mouths of the wise ones of our time: "Let us enjoy the benefits of the time"; but rather the benefits of their own valor and prudence, for time drives everything before it, and is able to bring with it good as well as evil, and evil as well as good.

But let us turn to France and inquire whether she has done any of the things mentioned. I will speak of Louis* (and not of Charles)† as the one whose conduct is the better to be observed, he having held possession of Italy for the longest period, and you will see that he has done the opposite to those things that ought to be done to retain a state composed of divers elements.

King Louis was brought into Italy by the ambition of the Venetians, who desired to obtain half the state of Lombardy by his intervention. I will not blame the course taken by the king, because, wishing to get a foothold in Italy, and having no friends there—seeing rather that every door was shut to him owing to the conduct of Charles—he was forced to accept those friendships that he could get, and he would have succeeded very quickly in his design if in other matters he had not made some mistakes. The king, however, having acquired Lombardy, regained at once the authority that Charles had lost:

---

* Louis XII, King of France, "The Father of the People," born 1462, died 1515.

† Charles VIII, King of France, born 1470, died 1498.

Genoa yielded; the Florentines became his friends; the Marquess of Mantua, the Duke of Ferrara, the Bentivogli, my lady of Forli, the Lords of Faenza, of Pesaro, of Rimini, of Camerino, of Piombino, the Lucchese, the Pisans, the Sienese—everybody made advances to him to become his friend. Then could the Venetians realize the rashness of the course taken by them, which, in order that they might secure two towns in Lombardy, had made the king master of two-thirds of Italy.

Let anyone now consider with what little difficulty the king could have maintained his position in Italy had he observed the rules above laid down, and kept all his friends secure and protected; for although they were numerous they were both weak and timid, some afraid of the Church, some of the Venetians, and thus they would always have been forced to stand in with him, and by their means he could easily have made himself secure against those who remained powerful. But he was no sooner in Milan than he did the contrary by assisting Pope Alexander to occupy the Romagna. It never occurred to him that by this action he was weakening himself, depriving himself of friends and of those who had thrown themselves into his lap, while he aggrandized the Church by adding much temporal power to the spiritual, thus giving it greater authority. And having committed this prime error, he was obliged to follow it up, so much so that, to put an end to the ambition of Alexander, and to prevent his becoming the master of Tuscany, he was himself forced to come into Italy.

And as if it were not enough to have aggrandized the Church, and deprived himself of friends, he, wishing to have the kingdom of Naples, divided it with the King of Spain, and where he was the prime arbiter in Italy he takes an associate, so that the ambitious of that country and the malcontents of his own should have somewhere to shelter; and whereas he could have left in the kingdom his own pensioner as king, he drove him out, to put one there who was able to drive him, Louis, out in turn.

The wish to acquire is in truth very natural and common, and men always do so when they can, and for this they will be praised not blamed, but when they cannot do so, yet wish to do so by any means, then there is folly and blame. Therefore, if France could have attacked Naples with her own forces she ought to have done so; if she could not, then she ought not to have divided it. And if the partition that she made with the Venetians in Lombardy was justified by the excuse that by it she got a foothold in Italy, this other partition merited blame, for it had not the excuse of that necessity.

Therefore Louis made these five errors: he destroyed the minor powers, he increased the strength of one of the greater powers in Italy, he brought in a foreign power, he did not settle in the country, he did not send colonies. Which errors, had he lived, were not enough to injure him had he not made a sixth by taking away their dominions from the Venetians—because, had he not aggrandized the Church, nor brought Spain into Italy, it would have been very reasonable and necessary to humble them, but having first taken these steps, he ought never to have consented to their ruin, for they, being powerful, would always have kept off others from designs on Lombardy, to which the Venetians would never have consented except to become masters themselves there; also because the others would not wish to take Lombardy from France in order to give it to the Venetians, and to run counter to both they would not have had the courage.

And if anyone should say: "King Louis yielded the Romagna to Alexander and the kingdom to Spain to avoid war," I answer for the reasons given above that a blunder ought never to be perpetrated to avoid war, because it is not to be avoided, but is only deferred to your disadvantage. And if another should allege the pledge that the king had given to the pope that he would assist him in the enterprise, in exchange for the dissolution of his marriage* and for the cap to Rouen,† to that I reply what I shall write later on concerning the faith of princes, and how it ought to be kept.

Thus King Louis lost Lombardy by not having followed any of the conditions observed by those who have taken possession of countries and wished to retain them. Nor is there any miracle in this, but much that is reasonable and quite natural. And on these matters I spoke at Nantes with Rouen, when Valentino, as Cesare Borgia, the son of Pope Alexander, was usually called, occupied the Romagna, and on Cardinal Rouen observing to me that the Italians did not understand war, I replied to him that the French did not understand statecraft, meaning that otherwise they would not have allowed the Church to reach such greatness. And in fact it has been seen that the greatness of the Church and of Spain in Italy has been caused by France, and her ruin may be attributed to them. From this a general rule is drawn that never or rarely fails: that he who is the cause of another becoming powerful is ruined, because that predominance has been brought about either by astuteness or else by force, and both are distrusted by him who has been raised to power.

---

* Louis XII divorced his wife, Jeanne, daughter of Louis XI, and married in 1499 Anne of Brittany, widow of Charles VIII, in order to retain the Duchy of Brittany for the crown.

† The Archbishop of Rouen. He was Georges d'Amboise, created a cardinal by Alexander VI. Born 1460, died 1510.

IV

Why the Kingdom of Darius, Conquered by Alexander, Did Not Rebel against the Successors of Alexander at His Death

CONSIDERING THE DIFFICULTIES that men have had to hold to a newly acquired state, some might wonder how, seeing that Alexander the Great became the master of Asia in a few years, and died while it was scarcely settled (upon which it might have appeared reasonable that the whole empire would have rebelled), nevertheless his successors maintained themselves, and had to meet no other difficulty than those that arose among themselves from their own ambitions.

I answer that the principalities of which one has record are found to be governed in two different ways: either by a prince, with a body of servants, who assist him to govern the kingdom as ministers by his favor and permission; or by a prince and barons, who hold that dignity by antiquity of blood and not by the grace of the prince. Such barons have states and their own subjects, who recognize them as lords and hold them in natural affection. Those states that are governed by a prince and his servants hold their prince in more consideration, because in all the country there is no one who is recognized as superior to him, and if they yield obedience to another they do it as to a minister and official, and they do not bear him any particular affection.

The examples of these two governments in our time are the Turk and the King of France. The entire monarchy of the Turk is governed by one lord, the others are his servants; and, dividing his kingdom into *sanjaks*, he sends there different administrators, and shifts and changes them as he chooses. But the King of France is placed in the midst of an ancient body of lords, acknowledged by their own subjects, and beloved by them; they have their own prerogatives, nor can the king take these away except at his peril. Therefore, he who considers both of these states will recognize great difficulties in seizing the state of the Turk, but, once it is conquered, great ease in holding it. The causes of the difficulties in seizing the kingdom of the Turk are that the usurper cannot be called in by the princes of the kingdom, nor can he hope to be assisted in his designs by the revolt of those whom the lord has around him. This arises from the reasons given above, for his ministers, being all slaves and bondmen, can only be corrupted with great difficulty, and one can expect little advantage from them when they have been corrupted, as they cannot carry the people with them, for the reasons assigned. Hence, he who attacks the Turk must bear in mind that he will find him united, and he will have to rely more on his own strength than on the revolt of others; but, if once the Turk has been conquered, and routed in the field in such a way that he cannot replace his armies, there is nothing to fear but the family of this prince, and, this being exterminated, there remains no one to fear, the others having no credit with the people; and as the conqueror did not rely on them before his victory, so he ought not to fear them after it.

The contrary happens in kingdoms governed like that of France, because one can easily enter there by gaining over some baron of the kingdom, for one always finds malcontents and such who desire a change. Such men, for the reasons given, can open the way into the state and render the victory easy, but if you wish to hold it afterward, you meet with infinite difficulties, both from those who have assisted you and from those you have crushed. Nor is it enough for you to have exterminated the family of the prince, because the lords that remain make themselves the heads of fresh movements against you, and as you are unable either to satisfy or exterminate them, that state is lost whenever time brings the opportunity.

Now if you will consider what was the nature of the government of Darius, you will find it similar to the kingdom of the Turk, and therefore it was only necessary for Alexander first to overthrow him in the field, and then to take the country from him. After which victory, Darius being killed, the state remained secure to Alexander, for the above reasons. And if his successors had been united they would have enjoyed it securely and at their ease, for there were no tumults raised in the kingdom except those they provoked themselves.

But it is impossible to hold with such tranquility states constituted like that of France. Hence arose those frequent rebellions against the Romans in Spain, France, and Greece, owing to the many principalities there were in these states, of which, as long as the memory of them endured, the Romans always held an insecure possession; but with the power and long continuance of the empire the memory of them passed away, and the Romans then became secure possessors. And when fighting afterward amongst themselves, each one was able to attach to himself his own parts of the country, according to the authority he had assumed there, and the family of the former lord being exterminated, none other than the Romans were acknowledged.

When these things are remembered no one will marvel at the ease with which Alexander held the Empire of Asia, or at the difficulties that others have had to keep an acquisition, such as Pyrrhus and many more—this is not occasioned by the little or abundance of ability in the conqueror, but by the want of uniformity in the subject state.

V

*Concerning the Way to Govern
Cities or Principalities That
Lived under Their Own Laws
before They Were Annexed*

WHENEVER THOSE STATES that have been acquired as stated have been accustomed to live under their own laws and in freedom, there are three courses for those who wish to hold them: the first is to ruin them, the next is to reside there in person, the third is to permit them to live under their own laws, drawing a tribute, and establishing within it an oligarchy that will keep it friendly to you. Because such a government, being created by the prince, knows that it cannot stand without his friendship and interest, and does its utmost to support him, and therefore he who would keep a city accustomed to freedom will hold it more easily by the means of its own citizens than in any other way.

There are, for example, the Spartans and the Romans. The Spartans held Athens and Thebes, establishing an oligarchy there; nevertheless they lost them. The Romans, in order to hold Capua, Carthage, and Numantia, dismantled them, and did not lose them. They wished to hold Greece as the Spartans held it, making it free and permitting its laws, and did not succeed. So to hold it they were compelled to dismantle many cities in the country, for in truth there is no safe way to retain them otherwise than by ruining them. And he who becomes master of a city accustomed to freedom and does not destroy it may expect to be destroyed by it, for in rebellion it has always the watchword of liberty and its ancient privileges as a rallying point, which neither time nor benefits will ever cause it to forget. And whatever you may do or provide against, they never forget that name or their privileges unless they are disunited or dispersed, but at every chance they immediately rally to them, as Pisa after the hundred years she had been held in bondage by the Florentines.

But when cities or countries are accustomed to living under a prince, and his family is exterminated, they, being on the one hand accustomed to obeying and on the other hand not having the old prince, cannot agree in making one from amongst themselves, and they do not know how to govern themselves. For this reason they are very slow to take up arms, and a prince can gain them to himself and secure them much more easily. But in republics there is more vitality, greater hatred, and more desire for vengeance, which will never permit them to allow the memory of their former liberty to rest—so that the safest way is to destroy them or to reside there.

VI

Concerning New Principalities
That Are Acquired by One's
Own Arms and Ability

L ET NO ONE BE SURPRISED IF, in speaking of entirely new principalities as I shall do, I adduce the highest examples both of prince and of state; because men, walking almost always in paths beaten by others, and following by imitation their deeds, are yet unable to keep entirely to the ways of others or attain to the power of those they imitate. A wise man ought always to follow the paths beaten by great men, and to imitate those who have been supreme, so that if his ability does not equal theirs, at least it will savor of it. Let him act like the clever archers who, designing to hit the mark that yet appears too far distant, and knowing the limits to which the strength of their bow attains, take aim much higher than the mark, not to reach by their strength or arrow to so great a height, but to be able with the aid of so high an aim to hit the mark they wish to reach.

I say, therefore, that in entirely new principalities, where there is a new prince, more or less difficulty is found in keeping them, accordingly as there is more or less ability in him who has acquired the state. Now, as the fact of becoming a prince from a private station presupposes either ability or fortune, it is clear that one or other of these things will mitigate in some degree many difficulties. Nevertheless, he who has relied least on fortune is established the strongest. Further, it facilitates matters when the prince, having no other state, is compelled to reside there in person.

But to come to those who, by their own ability and not through fortune, have risen to be princes, I say that Moses, Cyrus, Romulus, Theseus, and such like are the most excellent examples. And although one may not discuss Moses, who was a mere executor of the will of God, he ought to be admired, if only for that favor that made him worthy to speak with God. But in considering Cyrus and others who have acquired or founded kingdoms, all will be found admirable; and if their particular deeds and conduct shall be considered, they will not be found inferior to those of Moses, although he had so great a preceptor. And in examining their actions and lives one cannot see that they owed anything to fortune beyond opportunity, which brought them the material to mold into the form that seemed best to them. Without that opportunity their powers of mind would have been extinguished, and without those powers the opportunity would have come in vain.

It was necessary, therefore, to Moses that he should find the people of Israel in Egypt enslaved and oppressed by the Egyptians, in order that they should be disposed to follow him so as to be delivered out of bondage. It was necessary that Romulus should not remain in Alba, and that he should be abandoned at his birth, in order that he should become King of Rome and founder of the fatherland. It was necessary that Cyrus should find the Persians discontented with the government of the Medes, and the Medes soft and effeminate through their long peace. Theseus could not have shown his ability had he not found the Athenians dispersed. These opportunities, therefore, made those men fortunate, and their high ability enabled them to recognize the opportunity whereby their country was ennobled and made famous.

Those who by valorous ways become princes, like these men, acquire a principality with difficulty, but they keep it with ease. The difficulties they have in acquiring it rise in part from the new rules and methods that they are forced to introduce to establish their government and its security. And it ought to be remembered that there is nothing more difficult to take in hand, more perilous to conduct, or more uncertain in its success, than to take the lead in the introduction of a new order of things, because the innovator has for enemies all those who have done well under the old conditions, and lukewarm defenders in those who may do well under the new. This coolness arises partly from fear of the opponents, who have the laws on their side, and partly from the incredulity of men, who do not readily believe in new things until they have had a long experience of them. Thus it happens that whenever those who are hostile have the opportunity to attack they do it like partisans, while the others defend lukewarmly, in such wise that the prince is endangered along with them.

It is necessary, therefore, if we desire to discuss this matter thoroughly, to inquire whether these innovators can rely on themselves or have to depend on others: that is to say, whether, to consummate their enterprise, have they to use prayers or can they use force? In the first instance they always succeed badly, and never compass anything, but when they can rely on themselves and use force, then they are rarely endangered. Hence it is that all armed prophets have conquered, and the unarmed ones have been destroyed. Besides the reasons mentioned, the nature of the people is variable, and while it is easy to persuade them, it is difficult to fix them in that persuasion. And thus it is necessary to take such measures that, when they believe no longer, it may be possible to make them believe by force.

If Moses, Cyrus, Theseus, and Romulus had been unarmed they could not have enforced their constitutions for long—as happened in our time to Fra Girolamo Savonarola, who was ruined with his new order of things immediately the multitude believed in him no longer, and he had no means of keeping steadfast those who believed or of making the unbelievers to believe. Therefore such as these have great difficulties in consummating their enterprise, for all their dangers are in the ascent, yet with ability they will overcome them; but when these are overcome, and those who envied them their success are exterminated, they will begin to be respected, and they will continue afterward powerful, secure, honored, and happy.

To these great examples I wish to add a lesser one. Still it bears some resemblance to them, and I wish it to suffice me for all of a like kind: it is Hiero the Syracusan.* This man rose from a private station to be Prince of Syracuse, nor did he, either, owe anything to fortune but opportunity, for the Syracusans, being oppressed, chose him for their captain; afterward he was rewarded by being made their prince. He was of so great ability, even as a private citizen, that one who writes of him says he wanted nothing but a kingdom to be a king. This man abolished the old soldiery, organized the new, gave up old alliances, made new ones; and as he had his own soldiers and allies, on such foundations he was able to build any edifice: thus, while he had endured much trouble in acquiring, he had but little in keeping.

---

* Hiero II, born about 307 B.C., died 216 B.C.

VII

Concerning New Principalities That Are Acquired Either by the Arms of Others or by Good Fortune

T HOSE WHO SOLELY by good fortune become princes from being private citizens have little trouble in rising, but much in keeping atop; they have not any difficulties on the way up, because they fly, but they have many when they reach the summit. Such are those to whom some state is given either for money or by the favor of him who bestows it; as happened to many in Greece, in the cities of Ionia and of the Hellespont, where princes were made by Darius, in order that they might hold the cities both for his security and his glory; as also were those emperors who, by the corruption of the soldiers, from being citizens came to empire. Such stand elevated simply upon the goodwill and the fortune of him who has elevated them—two most inconstant and unstable things. Neither have they the knowledge requisite for the position, because, unless they are men of great worth and ability, it is not reasonable to expect that they should know how to command, having always lived in a private condition. Besides, they cannot hold it because they have not forces that they can keep friendly and faithful.

States that rise unexpectedly, then, like all other things in nature that are born and grow rapidly, cannot leave their foundations and correspondencies* fixed in such a way that the first storm will not overthrow them; unless, as is said, those who unexpectedly become princes are men of so much ability that they know they have to be prepared at once to hold that which fortune has thrown into their laps, and that those foundations, which others have laid BEFORE they became princes, they must lay AFTERWARD.

Concerning these two methods of rising to be a prince by ability or fortune, I wish to adduce two examples within our own recollection, and these are Francesco Sforza† and Cesare Borgia. Francesco, by proper means and with great ability, from being a private person rose to be Duke of Milan, and that which he had acquired with a thousand anxieties he kept with little trouble. On the other hand, Cesare Borgia, called by the people Duke Valentino, acquired his state during the ascendancy of his father, and on its decline he lost it, notwithstanding that he had taken every measure and done all that ought to be done by a wise and able man to fix firmly his roots in the states that the arms and fortunes of others had bestowed on him.

Because, as is stated above, he who has not first laid his foundations may be able with great ability to lay them afterward, but they will be laid with trouble to the architect and danger to the building.

---

* "*Le radici e corrispondenze*," their roots (i.e. foundations) and correspondencies or relations with other states—a common meaning of "correspondence" and "correspondency" in the sixteenth and seventeenth centuries.

† Francesco Sforza, born 1401, died 1466. He married Bianca Maria Visconti, a natural daughter of Filippo Visconti, the Duke of Milan, on whose death he procured his own elevation to the duchy. Machiavelli was the accredited agent of the Florentine Republic to Cesare Borgia (1478–1507) during the transactions that led up to the assassinations of the Orsini and Vitelli at Sinigallia, and along with his letters to his chiefs in Florence he has left an account, written ten years before *The Prince*, of the proceedings of the duke in his *Descritione del modo tenuto dal duca Valentino nello ammazzare Vitellozzo Vitelli*, etc., a translation of which is appended to the present work.

If, therefore, all the steps taken by the duke be considered, it will be seen that he laid solid foundations for his future power, and I do not consider it superfluous to discuss them, because I do not know what better precepts to give a new prince than the example of his actions; and if his dispositions were of no avail, that was not his fault, but the extraordinary and extreme malignity of fortune.

Alexander the Sixth, in wishing to aggrandize the duke, his son, had many immediate and prospective difficulties. Firstly, he did not see his way to make him master of any state that was not a state of the Church; and if he was willing to rob the Church he knew that the Duke of Milan and the Venetians would not consent, because Faenza and Rimini were already under the protection of the Venetians. Besides this, he saw the arms of Italy, especially those by which he might have been assisted, in hands that would fear the aggrandizement of the pope, namely, the Orsini and the Colonnesi and their following. It behooved him, therefore, to upset this state of affairs and embroil the powers, so as to make himself securely master of part of their states. This was easy for him to do, because he found the Venetians, moved by other reasons, inclined to bring back the French into Italy; he would not only not oppose this, but he would render it more easy by dissolving the former marriage of King Louis. Therefore the king came into Italy with the assistance of the Venetians and the consent of Alexander. He was no sooner in Milan than the pope had soldiers from him for the attempt on the Romagna, which yielded to him on the reputation of the king. The duke, therefore, having acquired the Romagna and beaten the Colonnesi, while wishing to hold that and to advance further, was hindered by two things: the one, his forces did not appear loyal to him, the other, the goodwill of France: that is to say, he feared that the forces of the Orsini, which he was using, would not stand to him, that not only might they hinder him from winning more, but might themselves seize what he had won, and that the king might also do the same. Of the Orsini he had a warning when, after taking Faenza and attacking Bologna, he saw them go very unwillingly to that attack. And as to the king, he learned his mind when he himself, after taking the Duchy of Urbino, attacked Tuscany, and the king made him desist from that undertaking; hence the duke decided to depend no more upon the arms and the luck of others.

For the first thing he weakened the Orsini and Colonnesi parties in Rome, by gaining to himself all their adherents who were gentlemen, making them his gentlemen, giving them good pay, and, according to their rank, honoring them with office and command in such a way that in a few months all attachment to the factions was destroyed and turned entirely to the duke. After this he awaited an opportunity to crush the Orsini, having scattered the adherents of the Colonna house. This came to him soon and he used it well; for the Orsini, perceiving at length that the aggrandizement of the duke and the Church was ruin to them, called a meeting of the Magione in Perugia. From this sprung the rebellion at Urbino and the tumults in the Romagna, with endless dangers to the duke, all of which he overcame with the help of the French. Having restored his authority, not to leave it at risk by trusting either to the French or other outside forces, he had recourse to his wiles, and he knew so well how to conceal his mind that, by the mediation of Signor Pagolo—whom the duke did not fail to secure with all kinds of attention, giving him money, apparel, and horses—the Orsini were reconciled, so that their simplicity brought them into his power at Sinigallia.* Having exterminated the leaders, and turned their partisans into his friends, the duke laid sufficiently good foundations to his power, having all the Romagna and the Duchy of Urbino; and the people now beginning to appreciate their prosperity, he gained them all over to himself. And as this point is

---

* Sinigallia, December 31, 1502.

worthy of notice, and to be imitated by others, I am not willing to leave it out.

When the duke occupied the Romagna he found it under the rule of weak masters, who rather plundered their subjects than ruled them, and gave them more cause for disunion than for union, so that the country was full of robbery, quarrels, and every kind of violence; and so, wishing to bring back peace and obedience to authority, he considered it necessary to give it a good governor. Thereupon he promoted Messer Ramiro d'Orco,* a swift and cruel man, to whom he gave the fullest power. This man in a short time restored peace and unity with the greatest success. Afterward the duke considered that it was not advisable to confer such excessive authority, for he had no doubt but that he would become odious, so he set up a court of judgment in the country, under a most excellent president, wherein all cities had their advocates. And because he knew that the past severity had caused some hatred against himself, so, to clear himself in the minds of the people, and gain them entirely to himself, he desired to show that, if any cruelty had been practiced, it had not originated with him, but in the natural sternness of the minister. Under this pretense he took Ramiro, and one morning caused him to be executed and left on the piazza at Cesena with the block and a bloody knife at his side. The barbarity of this spectacle caused the people to be at once satisfied and dismayed.

But let us return to where we started. I say that the duke, finding himself now sufficiently powerful and partly secured from immediate dangers by having armed himself in his own way, and having in a great measure crushed those forces in his vicinity that could injure him if he wished to proceed with his conquest, had next to consider France, for he knew that the king, who too late was aware of his mistake,

---

* Ramiro de Lorqua.

would not support him. And from this time he began to seek new alliances and to temporize with France in the expedition that she was making toward the kingdom of Naples against the Spaniards who were besieging Gaeta. It was his intention to secure himself against them, and this he would have quickly accomplished had Alexander lived.

Such was his line of action as to present affairs. But as to the future he had to fear, in the first place, that a new successor to the Church might not be friendly to him and might seek to take from him that which Alexander had given him, so he decided to act in four ways. Firstly, by exterminating the families of those lords whom he had despoiled, so as to take away that pretext from the pope. Secondly, by winning to himself all the gentlemen of Rome, so as to be able to curb the pope with their aid, as has been observed. Thirdly, by converting the college more to himself. Fourthly, by acquiring so much power before the pope should die that he could by his own measures resist the first shock. Of these four things, at the death of Alexander, he had accomplished three. For he had killed as many of the dispossessed lords as he could lay hands on, and few had escaped; he had won over the Roman gentlemen, and he had the most numerous party in the college. And as to any fresh acquisition, he intended to become master of Tuscany, for he already possessed Perugia and Piombino, and Pisa was under his protection. And as he no longer had to study France (for the French were already driven out of the kingdom of Naples by the Spaniards, and in this way both were compelled to buy his goodwill), he pounced down upon Pisa. After this, Lucca and Siena yielded at once, partly through hatred and partly through fear of the Florentines; and the Florentines would have had no remedy had he continued to prosper, as he was prospering the year that Alexander died, for he had acquired so much power and reputation that he would have stood by himself, and no longer have depended on the luck and the forces of others, but solely on his own power and ability.

But Alexander died five years after he had first drawn the sword. He left the duke with the state of Romagna alone consolidated, with the rest in the air, between two most powerful hostile armies, and sick unto death. Yet there were in the duke such boldness and ability, and he knew so well how men are to be won or lost, and so firm were the foundations that in so short a time he had laid, that if he had not had those armies on his back, or if he had been in good health, he would have overcome all difficulties. And it is seen that his foundations were good, for the Romagna awaited him for more than a month. In Rome, although he was but half alive, he remained secure, and while the Baglioni, the Vitelli, and the Orsini might come to Rome, they could not effect anything against him. If he could not have made pope him whom he wished, at least the one whom he did not wish would not have been elected. But if he had been in sound health at the death of Alexander,* everything would have been different to him. On the day that Julius the Second† was elected, he told me that he had thought of everything that might occur at the death of his father, and had provided a remedy for all, except that he had never anticipated that, when the death did happen, he himself would be on the point to die.

When all the actions of the duke are recalled, I do not know how to blame him, but rather it appears to be, as I have said, that I ought to offer him for imitation to all those who, by the fortune or the arms of others, are raised to government. Because he, having a lofty spirit and far-reaching aims, could not have regulated his conduct otherwise, and only the shortness of the life of Alexander and his own sickness frustrated his designs. Therefore, he who considers it

---

* Alexander VI died of fever, August 18, 1503.

† Julius II was Giuliano della Rovere, Cardinal of San Pietro ad Vincula, born 1443, died 1513.

necessary to secure himself in his new principality, to win friends, to overcome either by force or fraud, to make himself beloved and feared by the people, to be followed and revered by the soldiers, to exterminate those who have power or reason to hurt him, to change the old order of things for new, to be severe and gracious, magnanimous and liberal, to destroy a disloyal soldiery and to create new, to maintain friendship with kings and princes in such a way that they must help him with zeal and offend with caution, cannot find a more lively example than the actions of this man.

Only can he be blamed for the election of Julius the Second, in whom he made a bad choice, because, as is said, not being able to elect a pope to his own mind, he could have hindered any other from being elected pope; and he ought never to have consented to the election of any cardinal whom he had injured or who had cause to fear him if they became pontiffs. For men injure from either fear or hatred. Those whom he had injured, amongst others, were San Pietro ad Vincula, Colonna, San Giorgio, and Ascanio.* The rest, in becoming pope, had to fear him, Rouen and the Spaniards excepted, the latter from their relationship and obligations, the former from his influence, the kingdom of France having relations with him. Therefore, above everything, the duke ought to have created a Spaniard pope, and, failing him, he ought to have consented to Rouen and not San Pietro ad Vincula. He who believes that new benefits will cause great personages to forget old injuries is deceived. Therefore, the duke erred in his choice, and it was the cause of his ultimate ruin.

---

* San Giorgio is Raffaello Riario. Ascanio is Ascanio Sforza.

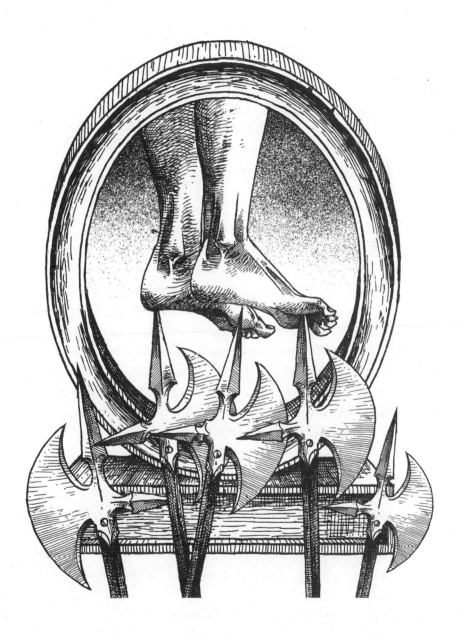

VIII

Concerning Those Who Have Obtained a Principality by Wickedness

ALTHOUGH A PRINCE may rise from a private station in two ways, neither of which can be entirely attributed to fortune or genius, yet it is manifest to me that I must not be silent on them, although one could be more copiously treated when I discuss republics. These methods are when, either by some wicked or nefarious ways, one ascends to the principality, or when by the favor of his fellow citizens a private person becomes the prince of his country. And speaking of the first method, it will be illustrated by two examples—one ancient, the other modern—and without entering further into the subject, I consider these two examples will suffice those who may be compelled to follow them.

Agathocles, the Sicilian,* became King of Syracuse not only from a private but from a low and abject position. This man, the son of a potter, through all the changes in his fortunes always led an infamous life. Nevertheless, he accompanied his infamies with so much ability of mind and body that, having devoted himself to the military profession, he rose through its ranks to be Praetor of Syracuse. Being established in that position, and having deliberately resolved to make

---

* Agathocles the Sicilian, born 361 B.C., died 289 B.C.

himself prince and to seize by violence, without obligation to others, that which had been conceded to him by assent, he came to an understanding for this purpose with Amilcar, the Carthaginian, who, with his army, was fighting in Sicily. One morning he assembled the people and the senate of Syracuse, as if he had to discuss with them things relating to the Republic, and at a given signal the soldiers killed all the senators and the richest of the people; these dead, he seized and held the princedom of that city without any civil commotion. And although he was twice routed by the Carthaginians, and ultimately besieged, yet not only was he able to defend his city, but leaving part of his men for its defense, with the others he attacked Africa, and in a short time raised the siege of Syracuse. The Carthaginians, reduced to extreme necessity, were compelled to come to terms with Agathocles, and, leaving Sicily to him, had to be content with the possession of Africa.

Therefore, he who considers the actions and the genius of this man will see nothing, or little, which can be attributed to fortune, inasmuch as he attained preeminence, as is shown above, not by the favor of anyone, but step by step in the military profession, which steps were gained with a thousand troubles and perils, and were afterward boldly held by him with many hazardous dangers. Yet it cannot be called talent to slay fellow citizens, to deceive friends, to be without faith, without mercy, without religion; such methods may gain empire, but not glory. Still, if the courage of Agathocles in entering into and extricating himself from dangers be considered, together with his greatness of mind in enduring and overcoming hardships, it cannot be seen why he should be esteemed less than the most notable captain. Nevertheless, his barbarous cruelty and inhumanity with infinite wickedness do not permit him to be celebrated among the most excellent men. What he achieved cannot be attributed either to fortune or genius.

In our times, during the rule of Alexander the Sixth, Oliverotto da Fermo, having been left an orphan many years before, was brought up by his maternal uncle, Giovanni Fogliani, and in the early days of his youth sent to fight under Pagolo Vitelli, that, being trained under his discipline, he might attain some high position in the military profession. After Pagolo died, he fought under his brother Vitellozzo, and in a very short time, being endowed with wit and a vigorous body and mind, he became the first man in his profession. But it appearing a paltry thing to serve under others, he resolved, with the aid of some citizens of Fermo, to whom the slavery of their country was dearer than its liberty, and with the help of the Vitelleschi, to seize Fermo. So he wrote to Giovanni Fogliani that, having been away from home for many years, he wished to visit him and his city, and in some measure to look upon his patrimony; and although he had not labored to acquire anything except honor, yet, in order that the citizens should see he had not spent his time in vain, he desired to come honorably, so would be accompanied by one hundred horsemen, his friends and retainers; and he entreated Giovanni to arrange that he should be received honorably by the Fermians, all of which would be not only to his honor, but also to that of Giovanni himself, who had brought him up.

Giovanni, therefore, did not fail in any attentions due to his nephew, and he caused him to be honorably received by the Fermians, and he lodged him in his own house, where, having passed some days, and having arranged what was necessary for his wicked designs, Oliverotto gave a solemn banquet to which he invited Giovanni Fogliani and the chiefs of Fermo. When the viands and all the other entertainments that are usual in such banquets were finished, Oliverotto artfully began certain grave discourses, speaking of the greatness of Pope Alexander and his son Cesare, and of their enterprises, to which discourse Giovanni and others answered; but he rose at once, saying that such matters ought to be discussed in a more private place, and he betook himself to a chamber, whither Giovanni and the rest of the citizens went in after him. No sooner were they seated than soldiers issued from secret places and slaughtered Giovanni and the rest. After these murders Oliverotto, mounted on horseback, rode up and down the town and besieged the chief magistrate in the palace, so that in fear the people were forced to obey him, and to form a government, of which he made himself the prince. He killed all the malcontents who were able to injure him, and strengthened himself with new civil and military ordinances, in such a way that, in the year during which he held the principality, not only was he secure in the city of Fermo, but he had become formidable to all his neighbors. And his destruction would have been as difficult as that of Agathocles if he had not allowed himself to be overreached by Cesare Borgia, who took him with the Orsini and Vitelli at Sinigallia, as was stated above. Thus one year after he had committed this parricide, he was strangled, together with Vitellozzo, whom he had made his leader in valor and wickedness.

Some may wonder how it can happen that Agathocles, and his like, after infinite treacheries and cruelties, should live for long secure in his country, and defend himself from external enemies, and never be conspired against by his own citizens, seeing that many others, by means of cruelty, have never been able even in peaceful times to hold the state, still less in the doubtful times of war. I believe that this follows from severities* being badly or properly used. Those may be called properly used, if of evil it is possible to speak well, that are applied at one blow and are necessary to one's security, and

---

* Lawrence Burd suggests that this word probably comes near the modern equivalent of Machiavelli's thought when he speaks of *crudeltà* than the more obvious "cruelties."

that are not persisted in afterward unless they can be turned to the advantage of the subjects. The badly employed are those which, notwithstanding they may be few in the commencement, multiply with time rather than decrease. Those who practice the first system are able, by aid of God or man, to mitigate in some degree their rule, as Agathocles did. It is impossible for those who follow the other to maintain themselves.

Hence it is to be remarked that, in seizing a state, the usurper ought to examine closely into all those injuries that it is necessary for him to inflict, and to do them all at one stroke so as not to have to repeat them daily, and thus by not unsettling men he will be able to reassure them, and win them to himself by benefits. He who does otherwise, either from timidity or evil advice, is always compelled to keep the knife in his hand; neither can he rely on his subjects, nor can they attach themselves to him, owing to their continued and repeated wrongs. For injuries ought to be done all at one time, so that, being tasted less, they offend less; benefits ought to be given little by little, so that the flavor of them may last longer.

And above all things, a prince ought to live amongst his people in such a way that no unexpected circumstances, whether of good or evil, shall make him change, because if the necessity for this comes in troubled times, you are too late for harsh measures; and mild ones will not help you, for they will be considered as forced from you, and no one will be under any obligation to you for them.

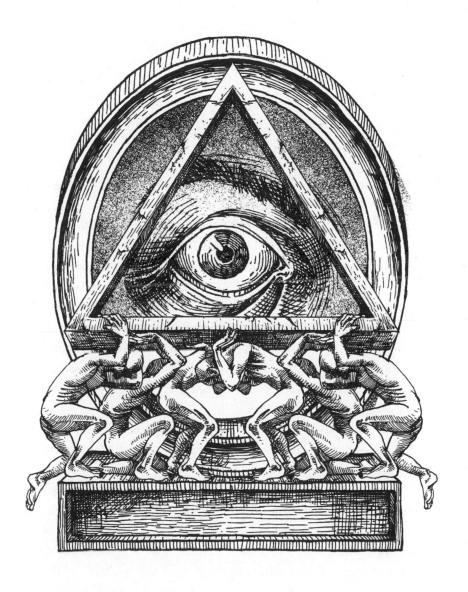

IX

Concerning a Civil Principality

B
UT COMING to the other point—where a leading citizen becomes the prince of his country, not by wickedness or any intolerable violence, but by the favor of his fellow citizens—this may be called a civil principality: nor is genius or fortune altogether necessary to attain to it, but rather a happy shrewdness. I say then that such a principality is obtained either by the favor of the people or by the favor of the nobles. Because in all cities these two distinct parties are found, and from this it arises that the people do not wish to be ruled nor oppressed by the nobles, and the nobles wish to rule and oppress the people; and from these two opposite desires there arises in cities one of three results, either a principality, self-government, or anarchy.

A principality is created either by the people or by the nobles, accordingly as one or other of them has the opportunity, for the nobles, seeing they cannot withstand the people, begin to cry up the reputation of one of themselves, and they make him a prince, so that under his shadow they can give vent to their ambitions. The people, finding they cannot resist the nobles, also cry up the reputation of one of themselves, and make him a prince so as to be defended by his authority. He who obtains sovereignty by the assistance of the nobles maintains himself with more difficulty than he who comes to it by the aid of the people, because the former finds himself with many around him who consider themselves his equals, and because of this he can neither rule nor manage them to his liking. But he who reaches sovereignty by popular favor finds himself alone, and has none around him, or few, who are not prepared to obey him.

Besides this, one cannot by fair dealing, and without injury to others, satisfy the nobles, but you can satisfy the people, for their object is more righteous than that of the nobles, the latter wishing to oppress, while the former only desire not to be oppressed. It is to be added also that a prince can never secure himself against a hostile people, because of there being too many, while from the nobles he can secure himself, as they are few in number. The worst that a prince may expect from a hostile people is to be abandoned by them—but from hostile nobles he has not only to fear abandonment, but also that they will rise against him, for they, being in these affairs more far-seeing and astute, always come forward in time to save themselves, and to obtain favors from him whom they expect to prevail. Further, the prince is compelled to live always with the same people, but he can do well without the same nobles, being able to make and unmake them daily, and to give or take away authority when it pleases him.

Therefore, to make this point clearer, I say that the nobles ought to be looked at mainly in two ways: that is to say, they either shape their course in such a way as binds them entirely to your fortune, or they do not. Those who so bind themselves, and are not rapacious, ought to be honored and loved; those who do not bind themselves may be dealt with in two ways. They may fail to do this through pusillanimity and a natural want of courage, in which case you ought to make use of them, especially of those who are of good counsel; and thus, while in prosperity you honor them, in adversity you do not have to fear them. But when for their own ambitious ends they shun binding themselves, it is a token that they are giving more thought to themselves than to you, and a prince ought to guard against such, and to fear them as if they were open enemies, because in adversity they always help to ruin him.

Therefore, one who becomes a prince through the favor of the people ought to keep them friendly, and this he can easily do seeing they only ask not to be oppressed by him. But one who, in opposition to the people, becomes a prince by the favor of the nobles, ought, above everything, to seek to win the people over to himself, and this he may easily do if he takes them under his protection. Because men, when they receive good from him of whom they were expecting evil, are bound more closely to their benefactor; thus the people quickly become more devoted to him than if he had been raised to the principality by their favors, and the prince can win their affections in many ways, but as these vary according to the circumstances one cannot give fixed rules, so I omit them—but, I repeat, it is necessary for a prince to have the people friendly, otherwise he has no security in adversity.

Nabis,* Prince of the Spartans, sustained the attack of all Greece, and of a victorious Roman army, and against them he defended his country and his government; and for the overcoming of this peril it was only necessary for him to make himself secure against a few, but this would not have been sufficient had the people been hostile. And do not let anyone impugn this statement with the trite proverb that "He who builds on the people, builds on the mud," for this is true when a private citizen makes a foundation there, and persuades himself that the people will free him when he is oppressed by his enemies or by the magistrates; wherein he would find himself very often deceived, as happened to the Gracchi in Rome and to Messer

---

* Nabis, tyrant of Sparta, conquered by the Romans under Flamininus in 195 B.C.; killed 192 B.C.

Giorgio Scali* in Florence. But granted a prince who has established himself as above, who can command, and is a man of courage, undismayed in adversity, who does not fail in other qualifications, and who, by his resolution and energy, keeps the whole people encouraged—such a one will never find himself deceived in them, and it will be shown that he has laid his foundations well.

These principalities are liable to danger when they are passing from the civil to the absolute order of government, for such princes either rule personally or through magistrates. In the latter case their government is weaker and more insecure, because it rests entirely on the goodwill of those citizens who are raised to the magistracy, and who, especially in troubled times, can destroy the government with great ease, either by intrigue or open defiance; and the prince has not the chance amid tumults to exercise absolute authority, because the citizens and subjects, accustomed to receive orders from magistrates, are not of a mind to obey him amid these confusions, and there will always be in doubtful times a scarcity of men whom he can trust. For such a prince cannot rely upon what he observes in quiet times, when citizens have need of the state, because then everyone agrees with him: they all promise, and when death is far distant they all wish to die for him. But in troubled times, when the state has need of its citizens, then he finds but few. And so much the more is this experiment dangerous, inasmuch as it can only be tried once. Therefore a wise prince ought to adopt such a course that his citizens will always in every sort and kind of circumstance have need of the state and of him, and then he will always find them faithful.

---

* This event is to be found in Machiavelli's *Florentine History*, Book III.

X

Concerning the Way in Which the Strength of All Principalities Ought to Be Measured

I T IS NECESSARY to consider another point in examining the character of these principalities: that is, whether a prince has such power that, in case of need, he can support himself with his own resources, or whether he always has need of the assistance of others. And to make this quite clear I say that I consider those who are able to support themselves by their own resources who can, either by abundance of men or money, raise a sufficient army to join battle against anyone who comes to attack them; and I consider those always to have need of others who cannot show themselves against the enemy in the field, but are forced to defend themselves by sheltering behind walls. The first case has been discussed, but we will speak of it again should it recur. In the second case one can say nothing except to encourage such princes to provision and fortify their towns, and not on any account to defend the country. And whoever shall fortify his town well, and shall have managed the other concerns of his subjects in the way stated above, and to be often repeated, will never be attacked without great caution, for men are always averse to enterprises where difficulties can be seen, and it will be seen not to be an easy thing to attack one who has his town well fortified, and is not hated by his people.

The cities of Germany are absolutely free, they own but little country around them, and they yield obedience to the emperor when it suits them, nor do they fear this or any other power they may have near them, because they are fortified in such a way that everyone thinks taking of them by assault would be tedious and difficult, seeing they have proper ditches and walls, they have sufficient artillery, and they always keep in public depots enough for one year's eating, drinking, and firing. And beyond this, to keep the people quiet and without loss to the state, they always have the means of giving work to the community in those labors that are the life and strength of the city, and on the pursuit of which the people are supported; they also hold military exercises in repute, and moreover have many ordinances to uphold them.

Therefore, a prince who has a strong city, and had not made himself odious, will not be attacked, or if anyone should attack he will only be driven off with disgrace; again, because that the affairs of this world are so changeable, it is almost impossible to keep an army a whole year in the field without being interfered with. And whoever should reply: "If the people have property outside the city, and see it burned, they will not remain patient, and the long siege and self-interest will make them forget their prince"—to this I answer that a powerful and courageous prince will overcome all such difficulties by giving at one time hope to his subjects that the evil will not be for long, at another time fear of the cruelty of the enemy, then preserving himself adroitly from those subjects who seem to him to be too bold.

Further, the enemy would naturally on his arrival at once burn and ruin the country at the time when the spirits of the people are still hot and ready for the defense—and, therefore, so much the less ought the prince to hesitate, because after a time, when spirits have cooled, the damage is already done, the ills are incurred, and there is no longer any remedy, and therefore they are so much the more ready to unite with their prince, he appearing to be under obligations to them now that their houses have been burned and their possessions ruined in his defense. For it is the nature of men to be bound by the benefits they confer as much as by those they receive. Therefore, if everything is well considered, it will not be difficult for a wise prince to keep the minds of his citizens steadfast from first to last, when he does not fail to support and defend them.

XI

Concerning Ecclesiastical
Principalities

I T ONLY REMAINS NOW TO SPEAK of ecclesiastical principalities, touching which all difficulties are prior to getting
possession, because they are acquired either by capacity or good
fortune, and they can be held without either, for they are sustained
by the ancient ordinances of religion, which are so all-powerful, and
of such a character, that the principalities may be held no matter how
their princes behave and live. These princes alone have states and
do not defend them; and they have subjects and do not rule them;
and the states, although unguarded, are not taken from them, and
the subjects, although not ruled, do not care, and they have neither
the desire nor the ability to alienate themselves. Such principalities
only are secure and happy. But being upheld by powers, to which the
human mind cannot reach, I shall speak no more of them, because,
being exalted and maintained by God, it would be the act of a presumptuous and rash man to discuss them.

Nevertheless, if anyone should ask of me how comes it that the
Church has attained such greatness in temporal power, seeing that
from Alexander backward the Italian potentates (not only those who
have been called potentates, but every baron and lord, though the
smallest) have valued the temporal power very slightly—yet now a
king of France trembles before it, and it has been able to drive him

from Italy, and to ruin the Venetians—although this may be very manifest, it does not appear to me superfluous to recall it in some measure to memory.

Before Charles, King of France, passed into Italy,* this country was under the dominion of the pope, the Venetians, the King of Naples, the Duke of Milan, and the Florentines. These potentates had two principal anxieties: the one, that no foreigner should enter Italy under arms; the other, that none of themselves should seize more territory. Those about whom there was the most anxiety were the pope and the Venetians. To restrain the Venetians the union of all the others was necessary, as it was for the defense of Ferrara; and to keep down the pope they made use of the barons of Rome, who, being divided into two factions, Orsini and Colonnesi, had always a pretext for disorder, and, standing with arms in their hands under the eyes of the pontiff, kept the pontificate weak and powerless. And although there might arise sometimes a courageous pope, such as Sixtus, yet neither fortune nor wisdom could rid him of these annoyances. And the short life of a pope is also a cause of weakness; for in the ten years, which is the average life of a pope, he can with difficulty lower one of the factions, and if, so to speak, one people should almost destroy the Colonnesi, another would arise hostile to the Orsini, who would support their opponents, and yet would not have time to ruin the Orsini. This was the reason why the temporal powers of the pope were little esteemed in Italy.

Alexander the Sixth arose afterward, who of all the pontiffs that have ever been showed how a pope with both money and arms was able to prevail, and through the instrumentality of the Duke Valentino, and by reason of the entry of the French, he brought about all those things that I have discussed above in the actions of the duke. And

---

* Charles VIII invaded Italy in 1494.

although his intention was not to aggrandize the Church, but the duke, nevertheless, what he did contributed to the greatness of the Church, which, after his death and the ruin of the duke, became the heir to all his labors.

Pope Julius came afterward and found the Church strong, possessing all the Romagna, the barons of Rome reduced to impotence, and, through the chastisements of Alexander, the factions wiped out; he also found the way open to accumulate money in a manner such as had never been practiced before Alexander's time. Such things Julius not only followed, but improved upon, and he intended to gain Bologna, to ruin the Venetians, and to drive the French out of Italy. All of these enterprises prospered with him, and so much the more to his credit, inasmuch as he did everything to strengthen the Church and not any private person. He kept also the Orsini and Colonnesi factions within the bounds in which he found them; and although there was among them some mind to make disturbance, nevertheless he held two things firm: the one, the greatness of the Church, with which he terrified them; and the other, not allowing them to have their own cardinals, who caused the disorders among them. For whenever these factions have their cardinals they do not remain quiet for long, because cardinals foster the factions in Rome and out of it, and the barons are compelled to support them, and thus from the ambitions of prelates arise disorders and tumults among the barons. For these reasons His Holiness Pope Leo* found the pontificate most powerful, and it is to be hoped that, if others made it great in arms, he will make it still greater and more venerated by his goodness and infinite other virtues.

---

* Pope Leo X was the Cardinal de' Medici.

XII

How Many Kinds of Soldiery There Are, and Concerning Mercenaries

HAVING DISCOURSED particularly on the characteristics of such principalities as in the beginning I proposed to discuss, and having considered in some degree the causes of there being good or bad, and having shown the methods by which many have sought to acquire them and to hold them, it now remains for me to discuss generally the means of offense and defense that belong to each of them.

We have seen above how necessary it is for a prince to have his foundations well laid, otherwise it follows that he will go to ruin. The chief foundations of all states, new as well as old or composite, are good laws and good arms; and as there cannot be good laws where the state is not well armed, it follows that where they are well armed they have good laws. I shall leave the laws out of the discussion and shall speak of the arms.

I say, therefore, that the arms with which a prince defends his state are either his own, or they are mercenaries, auxiliaries, or mixed. Mercenaries and auxiliaries are useless and dangerous, and if one holds his state based on these arms, he will stand neither firm nor safe; for they are disunited, ambitious, and without discipline, unfaithful, valiant before friends, cowardly before enemies. They have neither the fear of God nor fidelity to men, and destruction is deferred only so long as the attack is, for in peace one is robbed by them, and in war by the enemy. The fact is, they have no other attraction or reason for keeping the field than a trifle of stipend, which is not sufficient to make them willing to die for you. They are ready enough to be your soldiers while you do not make war, but if war comes they take themselves off or run from the foe; which I should have little trouble to prove, for the ruin of Italy has been caused by nothing else than by resting all her hopes for many years on mercenaries, and although they formerly made some display and appeared valiant amongst themselves, yet when the foreigners came they showed what they were. Thus it was that Charles, King of France, was allowed to seize Italy with chalk in hand,* and he who told us that our sins were the cause of it told the truth, but they were not the sins he imagined, but those that I have related. And as they were the sins of princes, it is the princes who have also suffered the penalty.

I wish to demonstrate further the infelicity of these arms. The mercenary captains are either capable men or they are not; if they are, you cannot trust them, because they always aspire to their own greatness, either by oppressing you, who are their master, or others contrary to your intentions; but if the captain is not skillful, you are ruined in the usual way.

And if it be urged that whoever is armed will act in the same way, whether mercenary or not, I reply that when arms have to be resorted

---

* "With chalk in hand," "*col gesso*." This is one of the bons mots of Alexander VI, and refers to the ease with which Charles VIII seized Italy, implying that it was only necessary for him to send his quartermasters to chalk up the billets for his soldiers to conquer the country. Cf. *The History of Henry VII*, by Lord Bacon: "King Charles had conquered the realm of Naples, and lost it again, in a kind of a felicity of a dream. He passed the whole length of Italy without resistance: so that it was true what Pope Alexander was wont to say: That the Frenchmen came into Italy with chalk in their hands, to mark up their lodgings, rather than with swords to fight."

to, either by a prince or a republic, then the prince ought to go in person and perform the duty of a captain; the republic has to send its citizens, and when one is sent who does not turn out satisfactorily, it ought to recall him, and when one is worthy, to hold him by the laws so that he does not leave the command. And experience has shown princes and republics, single-handed, making the greatest progress, and mercenaries doing nothing except damage; and it is more difficult to bring a republic, armed with its own arms, under the sway of one of its citizens than it is to bring one armed with foreign arms. Rome and Sparta stood for many ages armed and free. The Switzers are completely armed and quite free.

Of ancient mercenaries, for example, there are the Carthaginians, who were oppressed by their mercenary soldiers after the first war with the Romans, although the Carthaginians had their own citizens for captains. After the death of Epaminondas, Philip of Macedon was made captain of their soldiers by the Thebans, and after victory he took away their liberty.

Duke Filippo being dead, the Milanese enlisted Francesco Sforza against the Venetians, and he, having overcome the enemy at Caravaggio,* allied himself with them to crush the Milanese, his masters. His father, Sforza, having been engaged by Queen Johanna† of Naples, left her unprotected, so that she was forced to throw herself into the arms of the King of Aragon, in order to save her kingdom. And if the Venetians and Florentines formerly extended their dominions by these arms, and yet their captains did not make themselves princes, but have defended them, I reply that the Florentines in this case have been favored by chance, for of the able captains, of whom they might have stood in fear, some have not conquered, some have been

---

* Battle of Caravaggio, September 15, 1448.
† Johanna II of Naples, the widow of Ladislao, King of Naples.

opposed, and others have turned their ambitions elsewhere. One who did not conquer was Giovanni Acuto,* and since he did not conquer his fidelity cannot be proved, but everyone will acknowledge that, had he conquered, the Florentines would have stood at his discretion. Sforza had the Bracceschi always against him, so they watched each other. Francesco turned his ambition to Lombardy, Braccio against the Church and the kingdom of Naples. But let us come to that which happened a short while ago. The Florentines appointed as their captain Pagolo Vitelli, a most prudent man, who from a private position had risen to the greatest renown. If this man had taken Pisa, nobody can deny that it would have been proper for the Florentines to keep in with him, for if he became the soldier of their enemies they had no means of resisting, and if they held to him they must obey him. The Venetians, if their achievements are considered, will be seen to have acted safely and gloriously so long as they sent to war their own men, when with armed gentlemen and plebeians they did valiantly. This was before they turned to enterprises on land, but when they began to fight on land they forsook this virtue and followed the custom of Italy. And in the beginning of their expansion on land, through not having much territory, and because of their great reputation, they had not much to fear from their captains, but when they expanded, as under Carmignuola,† they had a taste of this mistake—for, having found him a most valiant man (they beat the Duke of Milan under

---

* An English knight whose name was Sir John Hawkwood. He fought in the English wars in France, and was knighted by Edward III; afterward he collected a body of troops and went into Italy. These became the famous "White Company." He took part in many wars, and died in Florence in 1394. He was born about 1320 at Sible Hedingham, a village in Essex. He married Domnia, a daughter of Bernabò Visconti.

† Francesco Bussone, born at Carmagnola about 1390, executed at Venice, May 5, 1432.

his leadership), and, on the other hand, knowing how lukewarm he was in the war, they feared they would no longer conquer under him, and for this reason they were not willing, nor were they able, to let him go; and so, not to lose again that which they had acquired, they were compelled, in order to secure themselves, to murder him. They had afterward for their captains Bartolomeo da Bergamo, Roberto da San Severino, the count of Pitigliano,* and the like, under whom they had to dread loss and not gain, as happened afterward at Vailà,† where in one battle they lost that which in eight hundred years they had acquired with so much trouble. Because from such arms conquests come but slowly, long delayed and inconsiderable, but the losses sudden and portentous.

And as with these examples I have reached Italy, which has been ruled for many years by mercenaries, I wish to discuss them more seriously, in order that, having seen their rise and progress, one may be better prepared to counteract them. You must understand that the empire has recently come to be repudiated in Italy, that the pope has acquired more temporal power, and that Italy has been divided up into more states, for the reason that many of the great cities took up arms against their nobles, who, formerly favored by the emperor, were oppressing them, while the Church was favoring them so as to gain authority in temporal power: in many others their citizens became princes. From this it came to pass that Italy fell partly into the hands of the Church and of republics, and, the Church consisting of priests and the republic of citizens unaccustomed to arms, both commenced to enlist foreigners.

---

* Bartolomeo Colleoni of Bergamo, died 1457. Roberto of San Severino, died fighting for Venice against Sigismund, Duke of Austria, in 1487; *"primo capitano in Italia"*—Machiavelli. "Count of Pitigliano": Nicolo Orsini, born 1442, died 1510.
† Battle of Vailà in 1509.

The first who gave renown to this soldiery was Alberigo da Conio,[*] the Romagnian. From the school of this man sprang, among others, Braccio and Sforza, who in their time were the arbiters of Italy. After these came all the other captains who till now have directed the arms of Italy, and the end of all their valor has been that she has been over-run by Charles, robbed by Louis, ravaged by Ferdinand, and insulted by the Switzers. The principle that has guided them has been, first, to lower the credit of infantry so that they might increase their own. They did this because, subsisting on their pay and without territory, they were unable to support many soldiers, and a few infantry did not give them any authority; so they were led to employ cavalry, with a moderate force of which they were maintained and honored; and affairs were brought to such a pass that, in an army of twenty thousand soldiers, there were not to be found two thousand foot soldiers. They had, besides this, used every art to lessen fatigue and danger to themselves and their soldiers, not killing in the fray, but taking prisoners and liberating without ransom. They did not attack towns at night, nor did the garrisons of the towns attack encampments at night; they did not surround the camp either with stockade or ditch, nor did they campaign in the winter. All these things were permitted by their military rules, and devised by them to avoid, as I have said, both fatigue and dangers; thus they have brought Italy to slavery and contempt.

---

[*]   Alberico da Barbiano, Count of Cunio in Romagna. He was the leader of the famous "Company of St George," composed entirely of Italian soldiers. He died in 1409.

XIII

Concerning Auxiliaries, Mixed Soldiery, and One's Own

A UXILIARIES, which are the other useless arm, are employed when a prince is called in with his forces to aid and defend, as was done by Pope Julius in the most recent times; for he, having, in the enterprise against Ferrara, had poor proof of his mercenaries, turned to auxiliaries, and stipulated with Ferdinand, King of Spain,* for his assistance with men and arms. These arms may be useful and good in themselves, but for him who calls them in they are always disadvantageous, for losing, one is undone, and winning, one is their captive.

And although ancient histories may be full of examples, I do not wish to leave this recent one of Pope Julius the Second, the peril of which cannot fail to be perceived; for he, wishing to get Ferrara, threw himself entirely into the hands of the foreigner. But his good fortune brought about a third event, so that he did not reap the fruit of his rash choice—because, having his auxiliaries routed at Ravenna, and the Switzers having risen and driven out the conquerors (against all expectation, both his and others), it so came to pass that he did not become prisoner to his enemies, they

---

* Ferdinand V (F. II of Aragon and Sicily, F. III of Naples), surnamed "The Catholic," born 1452, died 1516.

having fled, nor to his auxiliaries, he having conquered by other arms than theirs.

The Florentines, being entirely without arms, sent ten thousand Frenchmen to take Pisa, whereby they ran more danger than at any other time of their troubles.

The Emperor of Constantinople,* to oppose his neighbors, sent ten thousand Turks into Greece, who, on the war being finished, were not willing to quit; this was the beginning of the servitude of Greece to the infidels.

Therefore, let him who has no desire to conquer make use of these arms, for they are much more hazardous than mercenaries, because with them the ruin is ready made; they are all united, all yield obedience to others; but with mercenaries, when they have conquered, more time and better opportunities are needed to injure you; they are not all of one community, they are found and paid by you, and a third party, which you have made their head, is not able all at once to assume enough authority to injure you. In conclusion, in mercenaries dastardliness is most dangerous; in auxiliaries, valor. The wise prince, therefore, has always avoided these arms and turned to his own; and has been willing rather to lose with them than to conquer with the others, not deeming that a real victory that is gained with the arms of others.

I shall never hesitate to cite Cesare Borgia and his actions. This duke entered the Romagna with auxiliaries, taking there only French soldiers, and with them he captured Imola and Forli; but afterward, such forces not appearing to him reliable, he turned to mercenaries, discerning less danger in them, and enlisted the Orsini and Vitelli, whom presently, on handling and finding them doubtful, unfaithful, and dangerous, he destroyed and turned to his own men. And the difference between one and the other of these forces can easily be seen

---

* Joannes Cantacuzenus, born 1300, died 1383.

when one considers the difference there was in the reputation of the duke, when he had the French, when he had the Orsini and Vitelli, and when he relied on his own soldiers, on whose fidelity he could always count and found it ever increasing; he was never esteemed more highly than when everyone saw that he was complete master of his own forces.

I was not intending to go beyond Italian and recent examples, but I am unwilling to leave out Hiero, the Syracusan, he being one of those I have named above. This man, as I have said, made head of the army by the Syracusans, soon found out that a mercenary soldiery, constituted like our Italian *condottieri*, was of no use; and it appearing to him that he could neither keep them not let them go, he had them all cut to pieces, and afterward made war with his own forces and not with aliens.

I wish also to recall to memory an instance from the Old Testament applicable to this subject. David offered himself to Saul to fight with Goliath, the Philistine champion, and, to give him courage, Saul armed him with his own weapons, which David rejected as soon as he had them on his back, saying he could make no use of them, and that he wished to meet the enemy with his sling and his knife. In conclusion, the arms of others either fall from your back, or they weigh you down, or they bind you fast.

Charles the Seventh,[*] the father of King Louis the Eleventh,[†] having by good fortune and valor liberated France from the English, recognized the necessity of being armed with forces of his own, and he established in his kingdom ordinances concerning men-at-arms and infantry.

Afterward his son, King Louis, abolished the infantry and began to enlist the Switzers, which mistake, followed by others, is, as is

---

[*]   Charles VII of France, surnamed "The Victorious," born 1403, died 1461.
[†]   Louis XI, son of the above, born 1423, died 1483.

now seen, a source of peril to that kingdom; because, having raised the reputation of the Switzers, he has entirely diminished the value of his own arms, for he has destroyed the infantry altogether; and his men-at-arms he has subordinated to others, for, being as they are so accustomed to fight along with Switzers, it does not appear that they can now conquer without them. Hence it arises that the French cannot stand against the Switzers, and without the Switzers they do not come off well against others. The armies of the French have thus become mixed, partly mercenary and partly national, both of which arms together are much better than mercenaries alone or auxiliaries alone, but much inferior to one's own forces. And this example proves it, for the kingdom of France would be unconquerable if the ordinance of Charles had been enlarged or maintained.

But the scanty wisdom of man, on entering into an affair that looks well at first, cannot discern the poison that is hidden in it, as I have said above of hectic fevers. Therefore, if he who rules a principality cannot recognize evils until they are upon him, he is not truly wise, and this insight is given to few. And if the first disaster to the Roman Empire* should be examined, it will be found to have commenced only with the enlisting of the Goths, because from that time the vigor of the Roman Empire began to decline, and all that valor that had raised it passed away to others.

---

* "Many speakers to the House the other night in the debate on the reduction of armaments seemed to show a most lamentable ignorance of the conditions under which the British Empire maintains its existence. When Mr. Balfour replied to the allegations that the Roman Empire sank under the weight of its military obligations, he said that this was 'wholly unhistorical.' He might well have added that the Roman power was at its zenith when every citizen acknowledged his liability to fight for the state, but that it began to decline as soon as this obligation was no longer recognized."—*Pall Mall Gazette*, May 15, 1906.

I conclude, therefore, that no principality is secure without having its own forces; on the contrary, it is entirely dependent on good fortune, not having the valor that in adversity would defend it. And it has always been the opinion and judgment of wise men that nothing can be so uncertain or unstable as fame or power not founded on its own strength. And one's own forces are those that are composed either of subjects, citizens, or dependants; all others are mercenaries or auxiliaries. And the way to make ready one's own forces will be easily found if the rules suggested by me shall be reflected upon, and if one will consider how Philip, the father of Alexander the Great, and many republics and princes have armed and organized themselves, to which rules I entirely commit myself.

XIV

That Which Concerns a Prince on the Subject of the Art of War

A PRINCE OUGHT TO HAVE NO OTHER aim or thought, nor select anything else for his study, than war and its rules and discipline; for this is the sole art that belongs to him who rules, and it is of such force that it not only upholds those who are born princes, but it often enables men to rise from a private station to that rank. And, on the contrary, it is seen that when princes have thought more of ease than of arms they have lost their states. And the first cause of your losing it is to neglect this art, and what enables you to acquire a state is to be master of the art. Francesco Sforza, through being martial, from a private person became Duke of Milan, and the sons, through avoiding the hardships and troubles of arms, from dukes became private persons. For among other evils that being unarmed brings you, it causes you to be despised, and this is one of those ignominies against which a prince ought to guard himself, as is shown later on. Because there is nothing proportionate between the armed and the unarmed, and it is not reasonable that he who is armed should yield obedience willingly to him who is unarmed, or that the unarmed man should be secure among armed servants. Because, there being in one disdain and in the other suspicion, it is not possible for them to work well together. And therefore a prince who does not understand the art of war, over and above the other misfortunes already mentioned, cannot be respected by his soldiers, nor can he rely on them. He ought never, therefore, to have out of his thoughts this subject of war, and in peace he should addict himself more to its exercise than in war. This he can do in two ways, the one by action, the other by study.

As regards action, he ought above all things to keep his men well organized and drilled, to follow incessantly the chase, by which he accustoms his body to hardships, and learns something of the nature of localities, and gets to find out how the mountains rise, how the valleys open out, how the plains lie, and to understand the nature of rivers and marshes, and in all this to take the greatest care. Which knowledge is useful in two ways. Firstly, he learns to know his country, and is better able to undertake its defense; afterward, by means of the knowledge and observation of that locality, he understands with ease any other that it may be necessary for him to study hereafter, because the hills, valleys, and plains, and rivers and marshes that are, for instance, in Tuscany, have a certain resemblance to those of other countries, so that with a knowledge of the aspect of one country one can easily arrive at a knowledge of others. And the prince that lacks this skill lacks the essential that it is desirable that a captain should possess, for it teaches him to surprise his enemy, to select quarters, to lead armies, to array the battle, to besiege towns to advantage.

Philopoemen,* Prince of the Achaeans, among other praises that writers have bestowed on him, is commended because in time of peace he never had anything in his mind but the rules of war, and when he was in the country with friends, he often stopped and reasoned with them: "If the enemy should be upon that hill, and we should find ourselves here with our army, with whom would be the advantage? How should one best advance to meet him, keeping the ranks? If we

---

* Philopoemen, "the last of the Greeks," born 252 B.C., died 183 B.C.

should wish to retreat, how ought we to pursue?" And he would set forth to them, as he went, all the chances that could befall an army; he would listen to their opinion and state his, confirming it with reasons, so that by these continual discussions there could never arise, in time of war, any unexpected circumstances that he could not deal with.

But to exercise the intellect the prince should read histories, and study there the actions of illustrious men, to see how they have borne themselves in war, to examine the causes of their victories and defeat, so as to avoid the latter and imitate the former; and above all do as an illustrious man did, who took as an exemplar one who had been praised and famous before him, and whose achievements and deeds he always kept in his mind, as it is said Alexander the Great imitated Achilles, Caesar Alexander, Scipio Cyrus. And whoever reads the life of Cyrus, written by Xenophon, will recognize afterward in the life of Scipio how that imitation was his glory, and how in chastity, affability, humanity, and liberality Scipio conformed to those things that have been written of Cyrus by Xenophon. A wise prince ought to observe some such rules, and never in peaceful times stand idle, but increase his resources with industry in such a way that they may be available to him in adversity, so that if fortune chances it may find him prepared to resist her blows.

XV

Concerning Things for Which Men, and Especially Princes, Are Praised or Blamed

IT REMAINS NOW TO SEE WHAT ought to be the rules of conduct for a prince toward subject and friends. And as I know that many have written on this point, I expect I shall be considered presumptuous in mentioning it again, especially as in discussing it I shall depart from the methods of other people. But, it being my intention to write a thing that shall be useful to him who apprehends it, it appears to me more appropriate to follow up the real truth of the matter than the imagination of it; for many have pictured republics and principalities that in fact have never been known or seen, because how one lives is so far distant from how one ought to live that he who neglects what is done for what ought to be done sooner effects his ruin than his preservation; for a man who wishes to act entirely up to his professions of virtue soon meets with what destroys him among so much that is evil.

Hence it is necessary for a prince wishing to hold his own to know how to do wrong, and to make use of it or not according to necessity. Therefore, putting on one side imaginary things concerning a prince, and discussing those that are real, I say that all men when they are spoken of, and chiefly princes for being more highly placed, are remarkable for some of those qualities that bring them either blame or praise, and thus it is that one is reputed liberal, another miserly, using a Tuscan term (because an avaricious person in our language is still he who desires to possess by robbery, while we call one miserly who deprives himself too much of the use of his own); one is reputed generous, one rapacious; one cruel, one compassionate; one faithless, another faithful; one effeminate and cowardly, another bold and brave; one affable, another haughty; one lascivious, another chaste; one sincere, another cunning; one hard, another easy; one grave, another frivolous; one religious, another unbelieving, and the like. And I know that everyone will confess that it would be most praiseworthy in a prince to exhibit all the above qualities that are considered good, but because they can be neither entirely possessed nor observed, for human conditions do not permit it, it is necessary for him to be sufficiently prudent that he may know how to avoid the reproach of those vices that would lose him his state, and also to keep himself, if it be possible, from those that would not lose him it—but this not being possible, he may with less hesitation abandon himself to them. And again, he need not make himself uneasy at incurring a reproach for those vices without which the state can only be saved with difficulty, for if everything is considered carefully, it will be found that something that looks like virtue, if followed, would be his ruin, while something else, which looks like vice, yet followed brings him security and prosperity.

XVI

Concerning Liberality and Meanness

COMMENCING THEN with the first of the abovenamed characteristics, I say that it would be well to be reputed liberal. Nevertheless, liberality exercised in a way that does not bring you the reputation for it injures you, for if one exercises it honestly and as it should be exercised, it may not become known, and you will not avoid the reproach of its opposite. Therefore, anyone wishing to maintain among men the name of liberal is obliged to avoid no attribute of magnificence; so that a prince thus inclined will consume in such acts all his property, and will be compelled in the end, if he wish to maintain the name of liberal, to unduly weigh down his people, and tax them, and do everything he can to get money. This will soon make him odious to his subjects, and becoming poor he will be little valued by anyone—thus, with his liberality, having offended many and rewarded few, he is affected by the very first trouble and imperiled by whatever may be the first danger. Recognizing this himself, and wishing to draw back from it, he runs at once into the reproach of being miserly.

Therefore, a prince, not being able to exercise this virtue of liberality in such a way that it is recognized, except to his cost, if he is wise he ought not to fear the reputation of being mean, for in time he will come to be more considered than if liberal, seeing that with his economy his revenues are enough, that he can defend himself against all attacks, and is able to engage in enterprises without burdening his people; thus it comes to pass that he exercises liberality toward all from whom he does not take, who are numberless, and meanness toward those to whom he does not give, who are few.

We have not seen great things done in our time except by those who have been considered mean; the rest have failed. Pope Julius the Second was assisted in reaching the papacy by a reputation for liberality, yet he did not strive afterward to keep it up, when he made war on the King of France, and he made many wars without imposing any extraordinary tax on his subjects, for he supplied his additional expenses out of his long thriftiness. The present King of Spain would not have undertaken or conquered in so many enterprises if he had been reputed liberal. A prince, therefore, provided that he has not to rob his subjects, that he can defend himself, that he does not become poor and abject, that he is not forced to become rapacious, ought to hold of little account a reputation for being mean, for it is one of those vices that will enable him to govern.

And if anyone should say: Caesar obtained empire by liberality, and many others have reached the highest positions by having been liberal, and by being considered so, I answer: Either you are a prince in fact, or in a way to become one. In the first case this liberality is dangerous, in the second it is very necessary to be considered liberal; and Caesar was one of those who wished to become preeminent in Rome; but if he had survived after becoming so, and had not moderated his expenses, he would have destroyed his government. And if anyone should reply: Many have been princes, and have done great things with armies, who have been considered very liberal, I reply: A prince spends either that which is his own or his subjects' or else that of others. In the first case he ought to be sparing, in the second he ought not to neglect any opportunity for liberality. And to the prince who goes forth with his army, supporting it by pillage, sack, and extortion, handling that which belongs to others, this liberality is necessary, otherwise he would not be followed by soldiers. And of that which is neither yours nor your subjects' you can be a ready giver, as were Cyrus, Caesar, and Alexander, because it does not take away your reputation if you squander that of others, but adds to it—it is only squandering your own that injures you.

And there is nothing that wastes so rapidly as liberality, for even while you exercise it you lose the power to do so, and so become either poor or despised, or else, in avoiding poverty, rapacious and hated. And a prince should guard himself, above all things, against being despised and hated—and liberality leads you to both. Therefore it is wiser to have a reputation for meanness that brings reproach without hatred, than to be compelled through seeking a reputation for liberality to incur a name for rapacity that begets reproach with hatred.

XVII

Concerning Cruelty and Clemency, and Whether It Is Better to Be Loved than Feared

C OMING NOW to the other qualities mentioned above, I say that every prince ought to desire to be considered clement and not cruel. Nevertheless he ought to take care not to misuse this clemency. Cesare Borgia was considered cruel; notwithstanding, his cruelty reconciled the Romagna, unified it, and restored it to peace and loyalty. And if this be rightly considered, he will be seen to have been much more merciful than the Florentine people, who, to avoid a reputation for cruelty, permitted Pistoia to be destroyed.* Therefore a prince, so long as he keeps his subjects united and loyal, ought not to mind the reproach of cruelty; because with a few examples he will be more merciful than those who, through too much mercy, allow disorders to arise, from which follow murders or robberies; for these are wont to injure the whole people, while those executions that originate with a prince offend the individual only.

And of all princes, it is impossible for the new prince to avoid the imputation of cruelty, owing to new states being full of dangers.

---

* During the rioting between the Cancellieri and Panciatichi factions in 1502 and 1503.

Hence Virgil, through the mouth of Dido, excuses the inhumanity of her reign owing to its being new, saying:

> *Res dura, et regni novitas me talia cogunt*
> *Moliri, et late fines custode tueri.*

Nevertheless he ought to be slow to believe and to act, nor should he himself show fear, but proceed in a temperate manner with prudence and humanity, so that too much confidence may not make him incautious and too much distrust render him intolerable.

Upon this a question arises: whether it be better to be loved than feared or feared than loved? It may be answered that one should wish to be both, but, because it is difficult to unite them in one person, it is much safer to be feared than loved, when, of the two, either must be dispensed with. Because this is to be asserted in general of men, that they are ungrateful, fickle, false, cowardly, covetous, and as long as you succeed they are yours entirely; they will offer you their blood, property, life, and children, as is said above, when the need is far distant, but when it approaches they turn against you. And that prince who, relying entirely on their promises, has neglected other precautions, is ruined, because friendships that are obtained by payments, and not by greatness or nobility of mind, may indeed be earned, but they are not secured, and in time of need cannot be relied upon; and men have less scruple in offending one who is beloved than one who is feared, for love is preserved by the link of obligation that, owing to the baseness of men, is broken at every opportunity for their advantage; but fear preserves you by a dread of punishment that never fails.

---

* . . . against my will, my fate / A throne unsettled, and an infant state, / Bid me defend my realms with all my pow'rs, / And guard with these severities my shores. —Christopher Pitt.

Nevertheless a prince ought to inspire fear in such a way that, if he does not win love, he avoids hatred, because he can endure very well being feared while he is not hated, which will always be as long as he abstains from the property of his citizens and subjects and from their women. But when it is necessary for him to proceed against the life of someone, he must do it on proper justification and for manifest cause, but above all things he must keep his hands off the property of others, because men more quickly forget the death of their father than the loss of their patrimony. Besides, pretexts for taking away the property are never wanting, for he who has once begun to live by robbery will always find pretexts for seizing what belongs to others—but reasons for taking life, on the contrary, are more difficult to find and sooner lapse. But when a prince is with his army, and has under control a multitude of soldiers, then it is quite necessary for him to disregard the reputation of cruelty, for without it he would never hold his army united or disposed to its duties.

Among the wonderful deeds of Hannibal this one is enumerated: that having led an enormous army, composed of many various races of men, to fight in foreign lands, no dissensions arose either among them or against the prince, whether in his bad or in his good fortune. This arose from nothing else than his inhuman cruelty, which, with his boundless valor, made him revered and terrible in the sight of his soldiers, but without that cruelty, his other virtues were not sufficient to produce this effect. And short-sighted writers admire his deeds from one point of view and from another condemn the principal cause of them. That it is true his other virtues would not have been sufficient for him may be proved by the case of Scipio, that most excellent man, not only of his own times but within the memory of man, against whom, nevertheless, his army rebelled in Spain; this arose from nothing but his too great forbearance, which gave his soldiers more license than is consistent with military discipline. For this he was upbraided in the Senate by Fabius Maximus, and called the corrupter of the Roman soldiery. The Locrians were laid waste by a legate of Scipio, yet they were not avenged by him, nor was the insolence of the legate punished, owing entirely to his easy nature. Insomuch that someone in the Senate, wishing to excuse him, said there were many men who knew much better how not to err than to correct the errors of others. This disposition, if he had been continued in the command, would have destroyed in time the fame and glory of Scipio; but, he being under the control of the Senate, this injurious characteristic not only concealed itself, but contributed to his glory.

Returning to the question of being feared or loved, I come to the conclusion that, men loving according to their own will and fearing according to that of the prince, a wise prince should establish himself on that which is in his own control and not in that of others; he must endeavor only to avoid hatred, as is noted.

•

XVIII*

Concerning the Way in Which Princes Should Keep Faith

E VERYONE ADMITS how praiseworthy it is in a prince
to keep faith, and to live with integrity and not with craft.
Nevertheless our experience has been that those princes
who have done great things have held good faith of little account,
and have known how to circumvent the intellect of men by craft,
and in the end have overcome those who have relied on their word.
You must know there are two ways of contesting,† the one by the law,
the other by force; the first method is proper to men, the second to
beasts; but because the first is frequently not sufficient, it is necessary
to have recourse to the second. Therefore it is necessary for a prince
to understand how to avail himself of the beast and the man. This has
been figuratively taught to princes by ancient writers, who describe
how Achilles and many other princes of old were given to the Centaur
Chiron to nurse, who brought them up in his discipline; which means
solely that, as they had for a teacher one who was half beast and half

---

* "The present chapter has given greater offense than any other portion of
Machiavelli's writings." Burd, *Il Principe.*

† "Contesting," i.e. "striving for mastery." Mr. Burd points out that this passage
is imitated directly from Cicero's *De Officiis*: "*Nam cum sint duo genera decertandi,
unum per disceptationem, alterum per vim; cumque illud proprium sit hominis, hoc
beluarum; confugiendum est ad posterius, si uti non licet superiore.*"

man, so it is necessary for a prince to know how to make use of both natures, and that one without the other is not durable. A prince, therefore, being compelled knowingly to adopt the beast, ought to choose the fox and the lion; because the lion cannot defend himself against snares and the fox cannot defend himself against wolves. Therefore, it is necessary to be a fox to discover the snares and a lion to terrify the wolves. Those who rely simply on the lion do not understand what they are about. Therefore a wise lord cannot, nor ought he to, keep faith when such observance may be turned against him, and when the reasons that caused him to pledge it exist no longer. If men were entirely good this precept would not hold, but because they are bad, and will not keep faith with you, you too are not bound to observe it with them. Nor will there ever be wanting to a prince legitimate reasons to excuse this non-observance. Of these endless modern examples could be given, showing how many treaties and engagements have been made void and of no effect through the faithlessness of princes, and he who has known best how to employ the fox has succeeded best.

But it is necessary to know well how to disguise this characteristic, and to be a great pretender and dissembler; and men are so simple, and so subject to present necessities, that he who seeks to deceive will always find someone who will allow himself to be deceived. One recent example I cannot pass over in silence. Alexander the Sixth did nothing else but deceive men, nor ever thought of doing otherwise, and he always found victims, for there never was a man who had greater power in asserting, or who with greater oaths would affirm a thing, yet would observe it less. Nevertheless his deceits always succeeded according to his wishes,* because he well understood this side of mankind.

---

* "*Nondimanco sempre gli succederono gli inganni (ad votum).*" The words "*ad votum*" are omitted in the Testina addition, 1550. "Alexander never did what he said, Cesare never said what he did." — Italian Proverb.

Therefore it is unnecessary for a prince to have all the good qualities I have enumerated, but it is very necessary to appear to have them. And I shall dare to say this also, that to have them and always to observe them is injurious, and that to appear to have them is useful; to appear merciful, faithful, humane, religious, upright, and to be so, but with a mind so framed that should you require not to be so, you may be able and know how to change to the opposite.

And you have to understand this, that a prince, especially a new one, cannot observe all those things for which men are esteemed, being often forced, in order to maintain the state, to act contrary to fidelity,* friendship, humanity, and religion. Therefore it is necessary for him to have a mind ready to turn itself accordingly as the winds and variations of fortune force it, yet, as I have said above, not to diverge from the good if he can avoid doing so, but, if compelled, then to know how to set about it.

For this reason a prince ought to take care that he never lets anything slip from his lips that is not replete with the abovenamed five qualities, that he may appear to him who sees and hears him altogether merciful, faithful, humane, upright, and religious. There is nothing more necessary to appear to have than this last quality,

---

* "Contrary to fidelity" or "faith," "*contro alla fede*," and "*tutto fede*," "altogether faithful," in the next paragraph. It is noteworthy that these two phrases, "*contro alla fede*" and "*tutto fede*," were omitted in the Testina edition, which was published with the sanction of the papal authorities. It may be that the meaning attached to the word "*fede*" was "the faith," i.e. the Catholic creed, and not as rendered here "fidelity" and "faithful." Observe that the word "*religione*" was suffered to stand in the text of the Testina, being used to signify indifferently every shade of belief, as witness "the religion," a phrase inevitably employed to designate the Huguenot heresy. Robert South in his Sermon IX, p. 69, ed. 1843, comments on this passage as follows: "That great patron and Coryphaeus of this tribe, Nicolo Machiavel, laid down this for a master rule in his political scheme: 'That the show of religion was helpful to the politician, but the reality of it hurtful and pernicious.'"

inasmuch as men judge generally more by the eye than by the hand, because it belongs to everybody to see you, to few to come in touch with you. Everyone sees what you appear to be, few really know what you are, and those few dare not oppose themselves to the opinion of the many, who have the majesty of the state to defend them; and in the actions of all men, and especially of princes, which it is not prudent to challenge, one judges by the result.

For that reason, let a prince have the credit of conquering and holding his state, the means will always be considered honest, and he will be praised by everybody, because the vulgar are always taken by what a thing seems to be and by what comes of it, and in the world there are only the vulgar, for the few find a place there only when the many have no ground to rest on.

One prince* of the present time, whom it is not well to name, never preaches anything else but peace and good faith, and to both he is most hostile, and either, if he had kept it, would have deprived him of reputation and kingdom many a time.

---

*   Ferdinand of Aragon. "When Machiavelli was writing *The Prince* it would have been clearly impossible to mention Ferdinand's name here without giving offense." Burd's *Il Principe*.

XIX

*That One Should Avoid Being
Despised and Hated*

NOW, CONCERNING the characteristics of which mention is made above, I have spoken of the more important ones, the others I wish to discuss briefly under this generality, that the prince must consider, as has been in part said before, how to avoid those things that will make him hated or contemptible; and as often as he shall have succeeded he will have fulfilled his part, and he need not fear any danger in other reproaches.

It makes him hated above all things, as I have said, to be rapacious, and to be a violator of the property and women of his subjects, from both of which he must abstain. And when neither their property nor their honor is touched, the majority of men live content, and he has only to contend with the ambition of a few, whom he can curb with ease in many ways.

It makes him contemptible to be considered fickle, frivolous, effeminate, mean-spirited, irresolute, from all of which a prince should guard himself as from a rock, and he should endeavor to show in his actions greatness, courage, gravity, and fortitude, and in his private dealings with his subjects let him show that his judgments are irrevocable, and maintain himself in such reputation that no one can hope either to deceive him or to get round him.

That prince is highly esteemed who conveys this impression of himself, and he who is highly esteemed is not easily conspired against—for, provided it is well known that he is an excellent man and revered by his people, he can only be attacked with difficulty. For this reason a prince ought to have two fears, one from within, on account of his subjects, the other from without, on account of external powers. From the latter he is defended by being well armed and having good allies, and if he is well armed he will have good friends, and affairs will always remain quiet within when they are quiet without, unless they should have been already disturbed by conspiracy; and even should affairs outside be disturbed, if he has carried out his preparations and has lived as I have said, as long as he does not despair, he will resist every attack, as I said Nabis the Spartan did.

But concerning his subjects, when affairs outside are disturbed he has only to fear that they will conspire secretly, from which a prince can easily secure himself by avoiding being hated and despised, and by keeping the people satisfied with him, which it is most necessary for him to accomplish, as I said above at length. And one of the most efficacious remedies that a prince can have against conspiracies is not to be hated and despised by the people, for he who conspires against a prince always expects to please them by his removal, but when the conspirator can only look forward to offending them, he will not have the courage to take such a course, for the difficulties that confront a conspirator are infinite. And as experience shows, many have been the conspiracies, but few have been successful, because he who conspires cannot act alone, nor can he take a companion except from those whom he believes to be malcontents, and as soon as you have opened your mind to a malcontent you have given him the material with which to content himself, for by denouncing you he can look for every advantage—so that, seeing the gain from this course to be assured, and seeing the other to be doubtful and full of dangers, he must be a very rare friend, or a thoroughly obstinate enemy of the prince, to keep faith with you.

And, to reduce the matter into a small compass, I say that, on the side of the conspirator, there is nothing but fear, jealousy, prospect of punishment to terrify him. But on the side of the prince there is the majesty of the principality, the laws, the protection of friends and the state to defend him, so that, adding to all these things the popular goodwill, it is impossible that anyone should be so rash as to conspire. For whereas in general the conspirator has to fear before the execution of his plot, in this case he has also to fear the sequel to the crime, because on account of it he has the people for an enemy, and thus cannot hope for any escape.

Endless examples could be given on this subject, but I will be content with one, brought to pass within the memory of our fathers: Messer Annibale Bentivogli, who was prince in Bologna (grandfather of the present Annibale), and murdered by the Canneschi, who had conspired against him. Not one of his family survived but Messer Giovanni,* who was in childhood; immediately after his assassination the people rose and murdered all the Canneschi. This sprung from the popular goodwill that the house of Bentivogli enjoyed in those days in Bologna, which was so great that, although none remained there after the death of Annibale who was able to rule the state, the Bolognese, having information that there was one of the Bentivogli family in Florence, who up to that time had been considered the son of a blacksmith, sent to Florence for him and gave him the government

---

* Giovanni Bentivogli, born in Bologna 1438, died at Milan 1508. He ruled Bologna from 1462 to 1506. Machiavelli's strong condemnation of conspiracies may get its edge from his own very recent experience (February 1513), when he had been arrested and tortured for his alleged complicity in the Boscoli conspiracy.

of their city, and it was ruled by him until Messer Giovanni came in due course to the government.

For this reason I consider that a prince ought to reckon conspiracies of little account when his people hold him in esteem, but when it is hostile to him, and bears hatred toward him, he ought to fear everything and everybody. And well-ordered states and wise princes have taken every care not to drive the nobles to desperation, and to keep the people satisfied and contented, for this is one of the most important objects a prince can have.

Among the best-ordered and -governed kingdoms of our times is France, and in it are found many good institutions on which depend the liberty and security of the king. Of these the first is the parliament and its authority, because he who founded the kingdom, knowing the ambition of the nobility and their boldness, considered that a bit to their mouths would be necessary to hold them in; and, on the other side, knowing the hatred of the people, founded in fear, against the nobles, he wished to protect them, yet he was not anxious for this to be the particular care of the king. Therefore, to take away the reproach that he would be liable to from the nobles for favoring the people, and from the people for favoring the nobles, he set up an arbiter, who should be one who could beat down the great and favor the lesser without reproach to the king. Neither could you have a better or a more prudent arrangement, or a greater source of security to the king and kingdom. From this one can draw another important conclusion, that princes ought to leave affairs of reproach to the management of others, and keep those of grace in their own hands. And further, I consider that a prince ought to cherish the nobles, but not so as to make himself hated by the people.

It may appear, perhaps, to some who have examined the lives and deaths of the Roman emperors that many of them would be an example contrary to my opinion, seeing that some of them lived nobly and showed great qualities of soul, nevertheless they have lost their empire or have been killed by subjects who have conspired against them. Wishing, therefore, to answer these objections, I will recall the characters of some of the emperors, and will show that the causes of their ruin were not different to those alleged by me; at the same time I will only submit for consideration those things that are noteworthy to him who studies the affairs of those times.

It seems to me sufficient to take all those emperors who succeeded to the empire from Marcus the philosopher down to Maximinus; they were Marcus and his son Commodus, Pertinax, Julian, Severus and his son Antoninus Caracalla, Macrinus, Heliogabalus, Alexander, and Maximinus.

There is first to note that, whereas in other principalities the ambition of the nobles and the insolence of the people only have to be contended with, the Roman emperors had a third difficulty in having to put up with the cruelty and avarice of their soldiers, a matter so beset with difficulties that it was the ruin of many; for it was a hard thing to give satisfaction to both soldiers and people, because the people loved peace, and for this reason they loved the unaspiring prince, while the soldiers loved the warlike prince who was bold, cruel, and rapacious, which qualities they were quite willing he should exercise upon the people, so that they could get double pay and give vent to their own greed and cruelty. Hence it arose that those emperors were always overthrown who, either by birth or training, had no great authority, and most of them, especially those who came new to the principality, recognizing the difficulty of these two opposing humors, were inclined to give satisfaction to the soldiers, caring little about injuring the people. Which course was necessary, because, as princes cannot help being hated by someone, they ought, in the first place, to avoid being hated by everyone, and when they cannot compass this, they ought to endeavor with the utmost diligence to avoid the hatred of the most powerful. Therefore, those emperors who through inexperience had need of special favor adhered more readily to the soldiers than to the people, a course that turned out advantageous to them or not, accordingly as the prince knew how to maintain authority over them.

From these causes it arose that Marcus, Pertinax, and Alexander, being all men of modest life, lovers of justice, enemies to cruelty, humane, and benignant, came to a sad end except Marcus—he alone lived and died honored, because he had succeeded to the throne by hereditary title, and owed nothing either to the soldiers or to the people; and afterward, being possessed of many virtues that made him respected, he always kept both orders in their places while he lived, and was neither hated nor despised.

But Pertinax was created emperor against the wishes of the soldiers, who, being accustomed to living licentiously under Commodus, could not endure the honest life to which Pertinax wished to reduce them; thus, having given cause for hatred, to which hatred there was added contempt for his old age, he was overthrown at the very beginning of his administration. And here it should be noted that hatred is acquired as much by good works as by bad ones; therefore, as I said before, a prince wishing to keep his state is very often forced to do evil, for when that body is corrupt whom you think you have need of to maintain yourself—it may be either the people or the soldiers or the nobles—you have to submit to its humors and to gratify them, and then good works will do you harm.

But let us come to Alexander, who was a man of such great goodness that among the other praises that are accorded him is this, that in the fourteen years he held the empire no one was ever put to death by him unjudged. Nevertheless, being considered effeminate and a man who allowed himself to be governed by his mother, he became despised, the army conspired against him, and murdered him.

Turning now to the opposite characters of Commodus, Severus, Antoninus Caracalla, and Maximinus, you will find them all cruel and rapacious—men who, to satisfy their soldiers, did not hesitate to commit every kind of iniquity against the people; and all, except Severus, came to a bad end; but in Severus there was so much valor that, keeping the soldiers friendly, although the people were oppressed by him, he reigned successfully, for his valor made him so much admired in the sight of the soldiers and people that the latter were kept in a way astonished and awed and the former respectful and satisfied. And because the actions of this man, as a new prince, were great, I wish to show briefly that he knew well how to counterfeit the fox and the lion, which natures, as I said above, it is necessary for a prince to imitate.

Knowing the sloth of the Emperor Julian, he persuaded the army in Sclavonia, of which he was captain, that it would be right to go to Rome and avenge the death of Pertinax, who had been killed by the praetorian soldiers, and under this pretext, without appearing to aspire to the throne, he moved the army on Rome, and reached Italy before it was known that he had started. On his arrival at Rome, the Senate, through fear, elected him emperor and killed Julian. After this there remained for Severus, who wished to make himself master of the whole empire, two difficulties: one in Asia, where Niger, head of the Asiatic army, had caused himself to be proclaimed emperor; the other in the west where Albinus was, who also aspired to the throne. And as he considered it dangerous to declare himself hostile to both, he decided to attack Niger and to deceive Albinus. To the latter he wrote that, being elected emperor by the Senate, he was willing to share that dignity with him and sent him the title of Caesar, and, moreover, that the Senate had made Albinus his colleague, which things were accepted by Albinus as true. But after Severus had conquered and killed Niger, and settled oriental affairs, he returned to

Rome and complained to the Senate that Albinus, little recognizing the benefits that he had received from him, had by treachery sought to murder him, and for this ingratitude he was compelled to punish him. Afterward he sought him out in France, and took from him his government and life. He who will, therefore, carefully examine the actions of this man will find him a most valiant lion and a most cunning fox; he will find him feared and respected by everyone, and not hated by the army; and it need not be wondered at that he, a new man, was able to hold the empire so well, because his supreme renown always protected him from that hatred that the people might have conceived against him for his violence.

But his son Antoninus was a most eminent man, and had very excellent qualities, which made him admirable in the sight of the people and acceptable to the soldiers, for he was a warlike man, most enduring of fatigue, a despiser of all delicate food and other luxuries, which caused him to be beloved by the armies. Nevertheless, his ferocity and cruelties were so great and so unheard of that, after endless single murders, he killed a large number of the people of Rome and all those of Alexandria. He became hated by the whole world, and also feared by those he had around him, to such an extent that he was murdered in the midst of his army by a centurion. And here it must be noted that suchlike deaths, which are deliberately inflicted with a resolved and desperate courage, cannot be avoided by princes, because anyone who does not fear to die can inflict them; but a prince may fear them the less because they are very rare; he has only to be careful not to do any grave injury to those whom he employs or has around him in the service of the state. Antoninus had not taken this care, but had disgracefully killed a brother of that centurion, whom also he daily threatened, yet retained in his bodyguard—which, as it turned out, was a rash thing to do, and proved the emperor's ruin.

But let us come to Commodus, to whom it should have been very easy to hold the empire, for, being the son of Marcus, he had inherited it, and he had only to follow in the footsteps of his father to please his people and soldiers, but, being by nature cruel and brutal, he gave himself up to amusing the soldiers and corrupting them, so that he might indulge his rapacity upon the people. On the other hand, not maintaining his dignity, often descending to the theater to compete with gladiators, and doing other vile things little worthy of the imperial majesty, he fell into contempt with the soldiers, and being hated by one party and despised by the other, he was conspired against and was killed.

It remains to discuss the character of Maximinus. He was a very warlike man, and the armies, being disgusted with the effeminacy of Alexander, of whom I have already spoken, killed him and elected Maximinus to the throne. This he did not possess for long, for two things made him hated and despised: the one, his having kept sheep in Thrace, which brought him into contempt (it being well known to all, and considered a great indignity by everyone), and the other, his having at the accession to his dominions deferred going to Rome and taking possession of the imperial seat. He had also gained a reputation for the utmost ferocity by having, through his prefects in Rome and elsewhere in the empire, practiced many cruelties, so that the whole world was moved to anger at the meanness of his birth and to fear at his barbarity. First Africa rebelled, then the Senate with all the people of Rome, and all Italy conspired against him, to which may be added his own army; this latter, besieging Aquileia and meeting with difficulties in taking it, were disgusted with his cruelties, and fearing him less when they found so many against him, murdered him.

I do not wish to discuss Heliogabalus, Macrinus, or Julian, who, being thoroughly contemptible, were quickly wiped out, but I will bring this discourse to a conclusion by saying that princes in our times have this difficulty of giving inordinate satisfaction to their soldiers in a far less degree, because, notwithstanding one has to give them some indulgence, that is soon done; none of these princes have armies that are veterans in the governance and administration of provinces, as were the armies of the Roman Empire, and whereas it was then more necessary to give satisfaction to the soldiers than to the people, it is now more necessary to all princes, except the Turk and the Soldan, to satisfy the people rather the soldiers, because the people are the more powerful.

From the above I have excepted the Turk, who always keeps round him twelve thousand infantry and fifteen thousand cavalry on which depend the security and strength of the kingdom, and it is necessary that, putting aside every consideration for the people, he should keep them his friends. The kingdom of the Soldan is similar: being entirely in the hands of soldiers, it follows again that, without regard to the people, he must keep them his friends. But you must note that the state of the Soldan is unlike all other principalities, for the reason that it is like the Christian pontificate, which cannot be called either a hereditary or a newly formed principality, because the sons of the old prince are not the heirs, but he who is elected to that position by those who have authority, and the sons remain only noblemen. And this being an ancient custom, it cannot be called a new principality, because there are none of those difficulties in it that are met with in new ones, for although the prince is new, the constitution of the state is old, and it is framed so as to receive him as if he were its hereditary lord.

But returning to the subject of our discourse, I say that whoever will consider it will acknowledge that either hatred or contempt has been fatal to the abovenamed emperors, and it will be recognized also how it happened that, a number of them acting in one way and a number in another, only one in each way came to a happy end and the rest to unhappy ones. Because it would have been useless and dangerous for Pertinax and Alexander, being new princes, to imitate Marcus, who was heir to the principality, and likewise it would have been utterly destructive to Caracalla, Commodus, and Maximinus to have imitated Severus, they not having sufficient valor to enable them to tread in his footsteps. Therefore a prince, new to the principality, cannot imitate the actions of Marcus, nor, again, is it necessary to follow those of Severus, but he ought to take from Severus those parts that are necessary to found his state, and from Marcus those that are proper and glorious to keep a state that may already be stable and firm.

XX

Are Fortresses, and Many Other Things to Which Princes Often Resort, Advantageous or Hurtful?

1. Some princes, so as to hold securely the state, have disarmed their subjects; others have kept their subject towns distracted by factions; others have fostered enmities against themselves; others have laid themselves out to gain over those whom they distrusted in the beginning of their governments; some have built fortresses; some have overthrown and destroyed them. And although one cannot give a final judgment on all of these things unless one possesses the particulars of those states in which a decision has to be made, nevertheless I will speak as comprehensively as the matter of itself will admit.

2. There never was a new prince who has disarmed his subjects; rather when he has found them disarmed he has always armed them, because, by arming them, those arms become yours, those men who were distrusted become faithful, and those who were faithful are kept so, and your subjects become your adherents. And whereas all subjects cannot be armed, yet when those whom you do arm are benefited, the others can be handled more freely, and this difference in their treatment, which they quite understand, makes the former your dependants, and the latter, considering it

to be necessary that those who have the most danger and service should have the most reward, excuse you. But when you disarm them, you at once offend them by showing that you distrust them, either for cowardice or for want of loyalty, and either of these opinions breeds hatred against you. And because you cannot remain unarmed, it follows that you turn to mercenaries, which are of the character already shown; even if they should be good they would not be sufficient to defend you against powerful enemies and distrusted subjects. Therefore, as I have said, a new prince in a new principality has always distributed arms. Histories are full of examples. But when a prince acquires a new state, which he adds as a province to his old one, then it is necessary to disarm the men of that state, except those who have been his adherents in acquiring it; and these again, with time and opportunity, should be rendered soft and effeminate; and matters should be managed in such a way that all the armed men in the state shall be your own soldiers who in your old state were living near you.

3. Our forefathers, and those who were reckoned wise, were accustomed to say that it was necessary to hold Pistoia by factions and Pisa by fortresses, and with this idea they fostered quarrels in some of their tributary towns so as to keep possession of them the more easily. This may have been well enough in those times when Italy was in a way balanced, but I do not believe that it can be accepted as a precept for today, because I do not believe that factions can ever be of use; rather it is certain that when the enemy comes upon you in divided cities you are quickly lost, because the weakest party will always assist the outside forces and the other will not be able to resist. The Venetians, moved, as I believe, by the above reasons, fostered the Guelph and Ghibelline factions in their tributary cities, and although they never allowed them

to come to bloodshed, yet they nursed these disputes amongst them, so that the citizens, distracted by their differences, should not unite against them. Which, as we saw, did not afterward turn out as expected, because, after the rout at Vailà, one party at once took courage and seized the state. Such methods argue, therefore, weakness in the prince, because these factions will never be permitted in a vigorous principality; such methods for enabling one the more easily to manage subjects are only useful in times of peace, but if war comes this policy proves fallacious.

4. Without doubt princes become great when they overcome the difficulties and obstacles by which they are confronted, and therefore fortune, especially when she desires to make a new prince great, who has a greater necessity to earn renown than an hereditary one, causes enemies to arise and form designs against him, in order that he may have the opportunity of overcoming them, and by them to mount higher, as by a ladder that his enemies have raised. For this reason many consider that a wise prince, when he has the opportunity, ought with craft to foster some animosity against himself, so that, having crushed it, his renown may rise higher.

5. Princes, especially new ones, have found more fidelity and assistance in those men who in the beginning of their rule were distrusted than among those who in the beginning were trusted. Pandolfo Petrucci, Prince of Siena, ruled his state more by those who had been distrusted than by others. But on this question one cannot speak generally, for it varies so much with the individual; I will only say this, that those men who at the commencement of a princedom have been hostile, if they are of a description to need assistance to support themselves, can always be gained over with the greatest ease, and they will be tightly held to serve the prince

with fidelity, inasmuch as they know it to be very necessary for them to cancel by deeds the bad impression that he had formed of them; and thus the prince always extracts more profit from them than from those who, serving him in too much security, may neglect his affairs. And since the matter demands it, I must not fail to warn a prince who, by means of secret favors, has acquired a new state, that he must well consider the reasons that induced those to favor him who did so; and if it be not a natural affection toward him, but only discontent with their government, then he will only keep them friendly with great trouble and difficulty, for it will be impossible to satisfy them. And weighing well the reasons for this in those examples that can be taken from ancient and modern affairs, we shall find that it is easier for the prince to make friends of those men who were contented under the former government, and are therefore his enemies, than of those who, being discontented with it, were favorable to him and encouraged him to seize it.

6. It has been a custom with princes, in order to hold their states more securely, to build fortresses that may serve as a bridle and bit to those who might design to work against them, and as a place of refuge from a first attack. I praise this system because it has been made use of. Notwithstanding that, Messer Nicolo Vitelli in our times has been seen to demolish two fortresses in Citta di Castello so that he might keep that state; Guido Ubaldo, Duke of Urbino, on returning to his dominion, where he had been driven by Cesare Borgia, razed to the foundations all the fortresses in that province, and considered that without them it would be more difficult to lose it; the Bentivogli returning to Bologna came to a similar decision. Fortresses, therefore, are useful or not according to circumstances: if they do you good in one way they injure you in

another. And this question can be reasoned thus: the prince who has more to fear from the people than from foreigners ought to build fortresses, but he who has more to fear from foreigners than from the people ought to leave them alone. The castle of Milan, built by Francesco Sforza, has made, and will make, more trouble for the house of Sforza than any other disorder in the state. For this reason the best possible fortress is not to be hated by the people, because, although you may hold the fortresses, yet they will not save you if the people hate you, for there will never be wanting foreigners to assist a people who have taken arms against you. It has not been seen in our times that such fortresses have been of use to any prince, unless to the Countess of Forli,* when the Count Girolamo, her consort, was killed, for by that means she was able to withstand the popular attack and wait for assistance from Milan, and thus recover her state; and the posture of affairs was such at that time that the foreigners could not assist the people. But fortresses were of little value to her afterward when Cesare Borgia attacked her, and when the people, her enemy, were allied with foreigners. Therefore, it would have been safer for her, both then and before, not to have been hated by the people than to have had the fortresses. All these things considered then, I shall praise him who builds fortresses as well as him who does not, and I shall blame whoever, trusting in them, cares little about being hated by the people.

---

* Catherine Sforza, a daughter of Galeazzo Sforza and Lucrezia Landriani, born 1463, died 1509. It was to the Countess of Forli that Machiavelli was sent as envoy on 1499. A letter from Fortunati to the countess announces the appointment: "I have been with the signori," wrote Fortunati, "to learn whom they would send and when. They tell me that Niccolò Machiavelli, a learned young Florentine noble, secretary to my Lords of the Ten, is to leave with me at once." Cf. *Catherine Sforza*, by Count Pasolini, translated by P. Sylvester, 1898.

XXI

*How a Prince Should Conduct
Himself so as to Gain Renown*

NOTHING MAKES A PRINCE so much esteemed as great enterprises and setting a fine example. We have in our time Ferdinand of Aragon, the present King of Spain. He can almost be called a new prince, because he has risen, by fame and glory, from being an insignificant king to be the foremost king in Christendom; and if you will consider his deeds you will find them all great and some of them extraordinary. In the beginning of his reign he attacked Granada, and this enterprise was the foundation of his dominions. He did this quietly at first and without any fear of hindrance, for he held the minds of the barons of Castile occupied in thinking of the war and not anticipating any innovations; thus they did not perceive that by these means he was acquiring power and authority over them. He was able with the money of the Church and of the people to sustain his armies, and by that long war to lay the foundation for the military skill that has since distinguished him. Further, always using religion as a plea, so as to undertake greater schemes, he devoted himself with pious cruelty to driving out and clearing his kingdom of the Moors; nor could there be a more admirable example, nor one more rare. Under this same cloak he assailed Africa, he came down on Italy, he has finally attacked France; and thus his achievements and designs have always been great, and have kept the minds of his people in suspense and admiration and occupied with the issue of them. And his actions have arisen in such a way, one out of the other, that men have never been given time to work steadily against him.

Again, it much assists a prince to set unusual examples in internal affairs, similar to those that are related of Messer Bernabò da Milano, who, when he had the opportunity, by anyone in civil life doing some extraordinary thing, either good or bad, would take some method of rewarding or punishing him, which would be much spoken about. And a prince ought, above all things, always to endeavor in every action to gain for himself the reputation of being a great and remarkable man.

A prince is also respected when he is either a true friend or a downright enemy, that is to say, when, without any reservation, he declares himself in favor of one party against the other, which course will always be more advantageous than standing neutral, because if two of your powerful neighbors come to blows, they are of such a character that, if one of them conquers, you have either to fear him or not. In either case it will always be more advantageous for you to declare yourself and to make war strenuously, because, in the first case, if you do not declare yourself, you will invariably fall a prey to the conqueror, to the pleasure and satisfaction of him who has been conquered, and you will have no reasons to offer, nor anything to protect or to shelter you. Because he who conquers does not want doubtful friends who will not aid him in the time of trial, and he who loses will not harbor you because you did not willingly, sword in hand, court his fate.

Antiochus went into Greece, being sent for by the Aetolians to drive out the Romans. He sent envoys to the Achaeans, who were friends of the Romans, exhorting them to remain neutral, and on the other hand the Romans urged them to take up arms. This question came to be discussed in the council of the Achaeans, where the legate of Antiochus urged them to stand neutral. To this the Roman legate answered: "As for that which has been said, that it is better and more advantageous for your state not to interfere in our war, nothing can be more erroneous because by not interfering you will be left, without favor or consideration, the prize of the conqueror." Thus it will always happen that he who is not your friend will demand your neutrality, while he who is your friend will entreat you to declare yourself with arms. And irresolute princes, to avoid present dangers, generally follow the neutral path, and are generally ruined. But when a prince declares himself gallantly in favor of one side, if the party with whom he allies himself conquers, although the victor may be powerful and may have him at his mercy, yet he is indebted to him, and there is established a bond of amity, and men are never so shameless as to become a monument of ingratitude by oppressing you. Victories after all are never so complete that the victor must not show some regard, especially to justice. But if he with whom you ally yourself loses, you may be sheltered by him, and while he is able he may aid you, and you become companions on a fortune that may rise again.

In the second case, when those who fight are of such a character that you have no anxiety as to who may conquer, so much the more is it greater prudence to be allied, because you assist at the destruction of one by the aid of another who, if he had been wise, would have saved him; and conquering, as it is impossible that he should not do with your assistance, he remains at your discretion. And here it is to be noted that a prince ought to take care never to make an alliance with one more powerful than himself for the purposes of attacking others, unless necessity compels him, as is said above, because if he conquers you are at his discretion, and princes ought to avoid as much as possible being at the discretion of anyone. The Venetians joined with France against the Duke of Milan, and this alliance, which caused their ruin, could have been avoided. But when it cannot be avoided, as happened to the Florentines when the pope and Spain sent armies to attack Lombardy, then in such a case, for the above reasons, the prince ought to favor one of the parties.

Never let any government imagine that it can choose perfectly safe courses; rather let it expect to have to take very doubtful ones, because it is found in ordinary affairs that one never seeks to avoid one trouble without running into another; but prudence consists in knowing how to distinguish the character of troubles, and for choice to take the lesser evil.

A prince ought also to show himself a patron of ability, and to honor the proficient in every art. At the same time he should encourage his citizens to practice their callings peaceably, both in commerce and agriculture, and in every other following, so that the one should not be deterred from improving his possessions for fear lest they be taken away from him or another from opening up trade for fear of taxes; but the prince ought to offer rewards to whoever wishes to do these things and designs in any way to honor his city or state.

Further, he ought to entertain the people with festivals and spectacles at convenient seasons of the year, and as every city is divided into guilds or into societies,* he ought to hold such bodies

---

* "Guilds or societies," "*in arti o in tribu.*" "*Arti*" were craft or trade guilds, cf. Florio: "Arte . . . a whole company of any trade in any city or corporation town." The guilds of Florence are most admirably described by Mr. Edgcumbe Staley in his work on the subject (Methuen, 1906). Institutions of a somewhat similar character, called "*artel*," exist in Russia today, cf. Sir Mackenzie Wallace's *Russia*, ed. 1905: "The sons . . . were always during the working season members of an artel. In some of the larger towns there are artels of a much more complex kind— permanent associations, possessing large capital, and pecuniarily responsible

in esteem, and associate with them sometimes, and show himself an example of courtesy and liberality—nevertheless, always maintaining the majesty of his rank, for this he must never consent to abate in anything.

---

for the acts of the individual members." The word *"artel,"* despite its apparent similarity, has, Mr. Aylmer Maude assures me, no connection with *"ars"* or *"arte."* Its root is that of the verb *"rotisya,"* to bind oneself by an oath; and it is generally admitted to be only another form of *"rota,"* which now signifies a "regimental company." In both words the underlying idea is that of a body of men united by an oath. *"Tribu"* were possibly gentile groups, united by common descent, and included individuals connected by marriage. Perhaps our words "sects" or "clans" would be most appropriate.

XXII

Concerning the Secretaries of Princes

T HE CHOICE OF SERVANTS is of no little importance to a prince, and they are good or not according to the discrimination of the prince. And the first opinion that one forms of a prince, and of his understanding, is by observing the men he has around him; and when they are capable and faithful he may always be considered wise, because he has known how to recognize the capable and to keep them faithful. But when they are otherwise one cannot form a good opinion of him, for the prime error that he made was in choosing them.

There were none who knew Messer Antonio da Venafro as the servant of Pandolfo Petrucci, Prince of Siena, who would not consider Pandolfo to be a very clever man in having Venafro as his servant. Because there are three classes of intellect: one that comprehends by itself; another that appreciates what others comprehended; and a third that neither comprehends by itself nor by the showing of others; the first is the most excellent, the second is good, the third is useless. Therefore, it follows necessarily that, if Pandolfo was not in the first rank, he was in the second, for whenever one has judgment to know good and bad when it is said and done, although he himself may not have the initiative, yet he can recognize the good and the bad in his servant, and the one he can praise and the other correct; thus the servant cannot hope to deceive him, and is kept honest.

But to enable a prince to form an opinion of his servant there is one test that never fails: when you see the servant thinking more of his own interests than of yours, and seeking inwardly his own profit in everything, such a man will never make a good servant, nor will you ever be able to trust him, because he who has the state of another in his hands ought never to think of himself, but always of his prince, and never pay any attention to matters in which the prince is not concerned.

On the other hand, to keep his servant honest the prince ought to study him, honoring him, enriching him, doing him kindnesses, sharing with him the honors and cares, and at the same time let him see that he cannot stand alone, so that many honors may not make him desire more, many riches make him wish for more, and that many cares may make him dread chances. When, therefore, servants, and princes toward servants, are thus disposed, they can trust each other, but when it is otherwise, the end will always be disastrous for either one or the other.

XXIII

How Flatterers Should Be Avoided

I DO NOT WISH to leave out an important branch of this subject, for it is a danger from which princes are with difficulty preserved, unless they are very careful and discriminating. It is that of flatterers, of whom courts are full, because men are so self-complacent in their own affairs, and in a way so deceived in them that they are preserved with difficulty from this pest, and if they wish to defend themselves they run the danger of falling into contempt. Because there is no other way of guarding oneself from flatterers except letting men understand that to tell you the truth does not offend you; but when everyone may tell you the truth, respect for you abates.

Therefore a wise prince ought to hold a third course by choosing the wise men in his state, and giving to them only the liberty of speaking the truth to him, and then only of those things of which he inquires, and of none others; but he ought to question them upon everything, and listen to their opinions, and afterward form his own conclusions. With these counsellors, separately and collectively, he ought to carry himself in such a way that each of them should know that, the more freely he shall speak, the more he shall be preferred; outside of these, he should listen to no one, pursue the thing resolved on, and be steadfast in his resolutions. He who does otherwise is either overthrown by flatterers, or so often changed by varying opinions that he falls into contempt.

I wish on this subject to adduce a modern example. Fra Luca, the man of affairs to Maximilian,* the present emperor, speaking of His Majesty, said that he consulted with no one, yet never got his own way in anything. This arose because of his following a practice the opposite to the above, for the emperor is a secretive man—he does not communicate his designs to anyone, nor does he receive opinions on them. But as in carrying them into effect they become revealed and known, they are at once obstructed by those men whom he has around him, and he, being pliant, is diverted from them. Hence it follows that those things he does one day he undoes the next, and no one ever understands what he wishes or intends to do, and no one can rely on his resolutions.

A prince, therefore, ought always to take counsel, but only when he wishes and not when others wish; he ought rather to discourage everyone from offering advice unless he asks it; however, he ought to be a constant inquirer, and afterward a patient listener concerning the things of which he inquired; also, on learning that anyone, on any consideration, has not told him the truth, he should let his anger be felt.

And if there are some who think that a prince who conveys an impression of his wisdom is not so through his own ability, but through the good advisers that he has around him, beyond doubt they are deceived, because this is an axiom that never fails: that a prince who is not wise himself will never take good advice, unless by chance he has yielded his affairs entirely to one person who happens to be a very prudent man. In this case indeed he may be well governed, but it would not be for long, because such a governor would in a short time take away his state from him.

---

* Maximilian I, born in 1459, died 1519, Emperor of the Holy Roman Empire. He married, first, Mary, daughter of Charles the Bold; after her death, Bianca Sforza; and thus became involved in Italian politics.

But if a prince who is not inexperienced should take counsel from more than one he will never get united counsels, nor will he know how to unite them. Each of the counsellors will think of his own interests, and the prince will not know how to control them or to see through them. And they are not to be found otherwise, because men will always prove untrue to you unless they are kept honest by constraint. Therefore it must be inferred that good counsels, however they come, are born of the wisdom of the prince, and not the wisdom of the prince from good counsels.

XXIV

Why the Princes of Italy
Have Lost Their States

THE PREVIOUS SUGGESTIONS, carefully observed, will enable a new prince to appear well established, and render him at once more secure and fixed in the state than if he had been long seated there. For the actions of a new prince are more narrowly observed than those of an hereditary one, and when they are seen to be able they gain more men and bind far tighter than ancient blood, because men are attracted more by the present than by the past, and when they find the present good they enjoy it and seek no further. They will also make the utmost defense of a prince if he fails them not in other things. Thus it will be a double glory for him to have established a new principality, and adorned and strengthened it with good laws, good arms, good allies, and with a good example; so will it be a double disgrace to him who, born a prince, shall lose his state by want of wisdom.

And if those seigniors are considered who have lost their states in Italy in our times, such as the King of Naples, the Duke of Milan, and others, there will be found in them, firstly, one common defect in regard to arms from the causes that have been discussed at length; in the next place, some one of them will be seen either to have had the people hostile or, if he has had the people friendly, he has not known how to secure the nobles. In the absence of these defects states that have power enough to keep an army in the field cannot be lost.

Philip of Macedon, not the father of Alexander the Great, but he who was conquered by Titus Quintius, had not much territory compared to the greatness of the Romans and of Greece who attacked him, yet being a warlike man who knew how to attract the people and secure the nobles, he sustained the war against his enemies for many years, and if in the end he lost the dominion of some cities, nevertheless he retained the kingdom.

Therefore, do not let our princes accuse fortune for the loss of their principalities after so many years' possession, but rather their own sloth, because in quiet times they never thought there could be a change (it is a common defect in man not to make any provision in the calm against the tempest), and when afterward the bad times came they thought of flight and not of defending themselves, and they hoped that the people, disgusted with the insolence of the conquerors, would recall them. This course, when others fail, may be good, but it is very bad to have neglected all other expedients for that, since you would never wish to fall because you trusted to be able to find someone later on to restore you. This again either does not happen, or, if it does, it will not be for your security, because that deliverance is of no avail that does not depend upon yourself; those only are reliable, certain, and durable that depend on yourself and your valor.

XXV

What Fortune Can Effect in Human Affairs and How to Withstand Her

I T IS NOT UNKNOWN to me how many men have had, and still have, the opinion that the affairs of the world are in such wise governed by Fortune and by God that men with their wisdom cannot direct them and that no one can even help them; and because of this they would have us believe that it is not necessary to labor much in affairs, but to let chance govern them. This opinion has been more credited in our times because of the great changes in affairs that have been seen, and may still be seen, every day, beyond all human conjecture. Sometimes pondering over this, I am in some degree inclined to their opinion. Nevertheless, not to extinguish our free will, I hold it to be true that Fortune is the arbiter of one-half of our actions,* but that she still leaves us to direct the other half, or perhaps a little less.

I compare her to one of those raging rivers that, when in flood, overflows the plains, sweeping away trees and buildings, bearing away the soil from place to place—everything flies before it, all yield to its violence, without being able in any way to withstand it, and yet,

---

* Frederick the Great was accustomed to say: "The older one gets the more convinced one becomes that His Majesty King Chance does three-quarters of the business of this miserable universe." Albert Sorel's *Eastern Question.*

though its nature be such, it does not follow therefore that men, when the weather becomes fair, shall not make provision, both with defenses and barriers, in such a manner that, rising again, the waters may pass away by canal, and their force be neither so unrestrained nor so dangerous. So it happens with Fortune, who shows her power where valor has not prepared to resist her, and thither she turns her forces where she knows that barriers and defenses have not been raised to constrain her.

And if you will consider Italy, which is the seat of these changes, and which has given to them their impulse, you will see it to be an open country without barriers and without any defense. For if it had been defended by proper valor, as are Germany, Spain, and France, either this invasion would not have made the great changes it has made or it would not have come at all. And this I consider enough to say concerning resistance to Fortune in general.

But confining myself more to the particular, I say that a prince may be seen happy today and ruined tomorrow without having shown any change of disposition or character. This, I believe, arises firstly from causes that have already been discussed at length, namely, that the prince who relies entirely on fortune is lost when it changes. I believe also that he will be successful who directs his actions according to the spirit of the times, and that he whose actions do not accord with the times will not be successful. Because men are seen, in affairs that lead to the end that every man has before him, namely, glory and riches, to get there by various methods: one with caution, another with haste; one by force, another by skill; one by patience, another by its opposite; and each one succeeds in reaching the goal by a different method. One can also see of two cautious men the one attain his end, the other fail, and similarly, two men by different observances are equally successful, the one being cautious, the other impetuous. All this arises from nothing else than whether or not they conform in their methods to the spirit of the times. This follows from what I have said, that two men working differently bring about the same effect, and of two working similarly, one attains his object and the other does not.

Changes in estate also issue from this, for if, to one who governs himself with caution and patience, times and affairs converge in such a way that his administration is successful, his fortune is made; but if times and affairs change, he is ruined if he does not change his course of action. But a man is not often found sufficiently circumspect to know how to accommodate himself to the change, both because he cannot deviate from what nature inclines him to do, and also because, having always prospered by acting in one way, he cannot be persuaded that it is well to leave it; and, therefore, the cautious man, when it is time to turn adventurous, does not know how to do it, hence he is ruined—but had he changed his conduct with the times fortune would not have changed.

Pope Julius the Second went to work impetuously in all his affairs, and found the times and circumstances conform so well to that line of action that he always met with success. Consider his first enterprise against Bologna, Messer Giovanni Bentivogli being still alive. The Venetians were not agreeable to it, nor was the King of Spain, and he had the enterprise still under discussion with the King of France; nevertheless he personally entered upon the expedition with his accustomed boldness and energy, a move that made Spain and the Venetians stand irresolute and passive, the latter from fear, the former from desire to recover the kingdom of Naples. On the other hand, he drew after him the King of France, because that king, having observed the movement, and desiring to make the pope his friend so as to humble the Venetians, found it impossible to refuse him. Therefore Julius with his impetuous action accomplished what no other pontiff with simple human wisdom could have done, for if he had waited in Rome until he could get away, with his plans arranged and everything fixed, as any other pontiff would have done, he would never have succeeded. Because the King of France would have made a thousand excuses, and the others would have raised a thousand fears.

I will leave his other actions alone, as they were all alike, and they all succeeded, for the shortness of his life did not let him experience the contrary; but if circumstances had arisen that required him to go cautiously, his ruin would have followed, because he would never have deviated from those ways to which nature inclined him.

I conclude that, Fortune being changeful and mankind steadfast in their ways, so long as the two are in agreement, men are successful, but unsuccessful when they fall out. For my part I consider that it is better to be adventurous than cautious, because Fortune is a woman, and if you wish to keep her under it is necessary to beat and ill-use her; and it is seen that she allows herself to be mastered by the adventurous rather than by those who go to work more coldly. She is, therefore, always, woman-like, a lover of young men, because they are less cautious, more violent, and with more audacity command her.

XXVI

An Exhortation to Liberate Italy from the Barbarians

H AVING CAREFULLY considered the subject of the above discourses, and wondering within myself whether the present times were propitious to a new prince, and whether there were elements that would give an opportunity to a wise and virtuous one to introduce a new order of things that would do honor to him and good to the people of this country, it appears to me that so many things concur to favor a new prince that I never knew a time more fit than the present.

And if, as I said, it was necessary that the people of Israel should be captive so as to make manifest the ability of Moses; that the Persians should be oppressed by the Medes so as to discover the greatness of the soul of Cyrus; and that the Athenians should be dispersed to illustrate the capabilities of Theseus—then at the present time, in order to discover the virtue of an Italian spirit, it was necessary that Italy should be reduced to the extremity that she is now in, that she should be more enslaved than the Hebrews, more oppressed than the Persians, more scattered than the Athenians; without head, without order, beaten, despoiled, torn, overrun; and to have endured every kind of desolation.

Although lately some spark may have been shown by one which made us think he was ordained by God for our redemption, nevertheless it was afterward seen, in the height of his career, that fortune rejected him; so that Italy, left as without life, waits for him who shall yet heal her wounds and put an end to the ravaging and plundering of Lombardy, to the swindling and taxing of the kingdom and of Tuscany, and cleanse those sores that for long have festered. It is seen how she entreats God to send someone who shall deliver her from these wrongs and barbarous insolencies. It is seen also that she is ready and willing to follow a banner if only someone will raise it.

Nor is there to be seen at present one in whom she can place more hope than in your illustrious house,* with its valor and fortune, favored by God and by the Church of which it is now the chief, and that could be made the head of this redemption. This will not be difficult if you will recall to yourself the actions and lives of the men I have named. And although they were great and wonderful men, yet they were men, and each one of them had no more opportunity than the present offers, for their enterprises were neither more just nor easier than this, nor was God more their friend than He is yours.

With us there is great justice, because that war is just that is necessary, and arms are hallowed when there is no other hope but in them. Here there is the greatest willingness, and where the willingness is great the difficulties cannot be great if you will only follow those men to whom I have directed your attention. Further than this, how extraordinarily the ways of God have been manifested beyond example: the sea is divided, a cloud has led the way, the rock has poured forth water, it has rained manna, everything has contributed to your greatness; you ought to do the rest. God is not willing to do everything, and thus take away our free will and that share of glory that belongs to us.

---

* Giuliano de Medici. He had just been created a cardinal by Leo X. In 1523 Giuliano was elected pope, and took the title of Clement VII.

And it is not to be wondered at if none of the abovenamed Italians have been able to accomplish all that is expected from your illustrious house; and if in so many revolutions in Italy, and in so many campaigns, it has always appeared as if military virtue were exhausted, this has happened because the old order of things was not good, and none of us have known how to find a new one. And nothing honors a man more than to establish new laws and new ordinances when he himself was newly risen. Such things when they are well founded and dignified will make him revered and admired, and in Italy there are not wanting opportunities to bring such into use in every form.

Here there is great valor in the limbs while it fails in the head. Look attentively at the duels and the hand-to-hand combats, how superior the Italians are in strength, dexterity, and subtlety. But when it comes to armies they do not bear comparison, and this springs entirely from the insufficiency of the leaders, since those who are capable are not obedient, and each one seems to himself to know, there having never been anyone so distinguished above the rest, either by valor or fortune, that others would yield to him. Hence it is that for so long a time, and during so much fighting in the past twenty years, whenever there has been an army wholly Italian, it has always given a poor account of itself; the first witness to this is Il Taro, afterward Alessandria, Capua, Genoa, Vailà, Bologna, Mestri.[*]

If, therefore, your illustrious house wishes to follow these remarkable men who have redeemed their country, it is necessary before all things, as a true foundation for every enterprise, to be provided with your own forces, because there can be no more faithful, truer, or better soldiers. And although singly they are good, altogether they will be much better when they find themselves commanded by their

---

[*]   The battles of Il Taro, 1495; Alessandria, 1499; Capua, 1501; Genoa, 1507; Vailà, 1509; Bologna, 1511; Mestri, 1513.

prince, honored by him, and maintained at his expense. Therefore it is necessary to be prepared with such arms, so that you can be defended against foreigners by Italian valor.

And although Swiss and Spanish infantry may be considered very formidable, nevertheless there is a defect in both, by reason of which a third order would not only be able to oppose them, but might be relied upon to overthrow them. For the Spaniards cannot resist cavalry, and the Switzers are afraid of infantry whenever they encounter them in close combat. Owing to this, as has been and may again be seen, the Spaniards are unable to resist French cavalry, and the Switzers are overthrown by Spanish infantry. And although a complete proof of this latter cannot be shown, nevertheless there was some evidence of it at the battle of Ravenna, when the Spanish infantry were confronted by German battalions, who follow the same tactics as the Swiss; when the Spaniards, by agility of body and with the aid of their shields, got in under the pikes of the Germans and stood out of danger, able to attack, while the Germans stood helpless, and, if the cavalry had not dashed up, all would have been over with them. It is possible, therefore, knowing the defects of both these infantries, to invent a new one, which will resist cavalry and not be afraid of infantry. This need not create a new order of arms, but a variation upon the old. And these are the kind of improvements that confer reputation and power upon a new prince.

This opportunity, therefore, ought not to be allowed to pass for letting Italy at last see her liberator appear. Nor can one express the love with which he would be received in all those provinces that have suffered so much from these foreign scourings, with what thirst for revenge, with what stubborn faith, with what devotion, with what tears. What door would be closed to him? Who would refuse obedience to him? What envy would hinder him? What Italian would refuse him homage? To all of us this barbarous dominion stinks. Let, therefore, your illustrious house take up this charge with that courage and hope with which all just enterprises are undertaken, so that under its standard our native country may be ennobled, and under its auspices may be verified that saying of Petrarch:

> *Virtù contro al Furore*
> *Prenderà l'arme, e fia il combatter corto:*
> *Chè l'antico valore*
> *Negli italici cuor non è ancor morto.*

> Virtue against fury shall advance the fight,
> And it i' th' combat soon shall put to flight:
> For the old Roman valor is not dead,
> Nor in th' Italians' breasts extinguished.

—EDWARD DACRES, 1640.

Description

of the Methods Adopted by the Duke Valentino When Murdering Vitellozzo Vitelli, Oliverotto Da Fermo, the Signor Pagolo, and the Duke di Gravina Orsini

---

Translated from the Italian
by W. K. Marriott

T HE DUKE VALENTINO had returned from Lombardy, where he had been to clear himself with the King of France from the calumnies that had been raised against him by the Florentines concerning the rebellion of Arezzo and other towns in the Val di Chiana, and had arrived at Imola, where he intended with his army to enter upon the campaign against Giovanni Bentivogli, the tyrant of Bologna: for he intended to bring that city under his domination, and to make it the head of his Romagnian duchy.

These matters coming to the knowledge of the Vitelli and Orsini and their following, it appeared to them that the duke would become too powerful, and it was feared that, having seized Bologna, he would seek to destroy them in order that he might become supreme in Italy. Upon this a meeting was called at Magione in the district of Perugia, to which came the cardinal, Pagolo, and the Duke di Gravina Orsini, Vitellozzo Vitelli, Oliverotto da Fermo, Gianpagolo Baglioni, the tyrant of Perugia, and Messer Antonio da Venafro, sent by Pandolfo Petrucci, the Prince of Siena. Here were discussed the power and courage of the duke and the necessity of curbing his ambitions, which might otherwise bring danger to the rest of being ruined. And they decided not to abandon the Bentivogli, but to strive to win over the Florentines; and they sent their men to one place and another, promising to one party assistance and to another encouragement to unite with them against the common enemy. This meeting was at once reported throughout all Italy, and those who were discontented under the duke, among whom were the people of Urbino, took hope of effecting a revolution.

Thus it arose that, men's minds being thus unsettled, it was decided by certain men of Urbino to seize the fortress of San Leo, which was held for the duke, and which they captured by the following means. The castellan was fortifying the rock and causing timber to be taken there; so the conspirators watched, and when certain beams that were being carried to the rock were upon the bridge, so that it was prevented from being drawn up by those inside, they took the opportunity of leaping upon the bridge and from there into the fortress. Upon this capture being effected, the whole state rebelled and recalled the old duke, being encouraged in this, not so much by the capture of the fort, as by the Diet at Magione, from whom they expected to get assistance.

Those who heard of the rebellion at Urbino thought they would not lose the opportunity, and at once assembled their men so as to take any town, should any remain in the hands of the duke in that state; and they sent again to Florence to beg that republic to join with them in destroying the common firebrand, showing that the risk was lessened and that they ought not to wait for another opportunity.

But the Florentines, from hatred, for sundry reasons, of the Vitelli and Orsini, not only would not ally themselves, but sent Niccolò Machiavelli, their secretary, to offer shelter and assistance to the duke against his enemies. The duke was found full of fear at Imola, because, against everybody's expectation, his soldiers had at once gone over to the enemy and he found himself disarmed and war at his door. But recovering courage from the offers of the Florentines, he decided to temporize before fighting with the few soldiers that remained to him, and to negotiate for a reconciliation, and also to get assistance. This latter he obtained in two ways: by sending to the King of France for men and by enlisting men-at-arms and others whom he turned into cavalry of a sort; to all he gave money.

Notwithstanding this, his enemies drew near to him, and approached Fossombrone, where they encountered some men of the duke and, with the aid of the Orsini and Vitelli, routed them. When this happened, the duke resolved at once to see if he could not close the trouble with offers of reconciliation, and being a most perfect dissembler he did not fail in any practices to make the insurgents understand that he wished every man who had acquired anything to keep it, as it was enough for him to have the title of prince, while others might have the principality.

And the duke succeeded so well in this that they sent Signor Pagolo to him to negotiate for a reconciliation, and they brought their army to a standstill. But the duke did not stop his preparations, and took every care to provide himself with cavalry and infantry, and that such preparations might not be apparent to the others, he sent his troops in separate parties to every part of the Romagna. In the meanwhile there came also to him five hundred French lancers, and although he found himself sufficiently strong to take vengeance on his enemies in open war, he considered that it would be safer and more advantageous to outwit them, and for this reason he did not stop the work of reconciliation.

And that this might be effected the duke concluded a peace with them in which he confirmed their former covenants; he gave them four thousand ducats at once; he promised not to injure the Bentivogli; and he formed an alliance with Giovanni; and moreover he would not force them to come personally into his presence unless it pleased them to do so. On the other hand, they promised to restore to him the duchy of Urbino and other places seized by them, to serve him in all his expeditions, and not to make war against or ally themselves with anyone without his permission.

This reconciliation being completed, Guido Ubaldo, the Duke of Urbino, again fled to Venice, having first destroyed all the fortresses in his state—because, trusting in the people, he did not wish that the fortresses, which he did not think he could defend, should be held by the enemy, since by these means a check would be kept upon his friends. But the Duke Valentino, having completed this convention, and dispersed his men throughout the Romagna, set out for Imola at the end of November together with his French men-at-arms: from there he went to Cesena, where he stayed some time to negotiate with the envoys of the Vitelli and Orsini, who had assembled with their men in the duchy of Urbino, as to the enterprise in which they should now take part; but nothing being concluded, Oliverotto da Fermo was sent to propose that if the duke wished to undertake an expedition against Tuscany they were ready; if he did not wish it, then they would besiege Sinigallia. To this the duke replied that he did not wish to enter into war with Tuscany, and thus become hostile to the Florentines, but that he was very willing to proceed against Sinigallia.

It happened that not long afterward the town surrendered, but the fortress would not yield to them because the castellan would not give it up to anyone but the duke in person; therefore they exhorted him to come there. This appeared a good opportunity to the duke, as, being invited by them, and not going of his own will, he would awaken no suspicions. And the more to reassure them, he allowed all the French men-at-arms who were with him in Lombardy to depart, except the hundred lancers under Mons. di Candales, his brother-in-law. He left Cesena about the middle of December, and went to Fano, and with the utmost cunning and cleverness he persuaded the Vitelli and Orsini to wait for him at Sinigallia, pointing out to them that any lack of compliance would cast a doubt upon the sincerity and permanency of the reconciliation, and that he was a man who wished to make use of the arms and councils of his friends. But Vitellozzo remained very stubborn, for the death of his brother warned him that he should not offend a prince and afterward trust him; nevertheless, persuaded by Pagolo Orsini, whom the duke had corrupted with gifts and promises, he agreed to wait.

Upon this the duke, before his departure from Fano, which was to be on December 30, 1502, communicated his designs to eight of his most trusted followers, among whom were Don Michele and the Monsignor d'Euna, who was afterward cardinal; and he ordered that, as soon as Vitellozzo, Pagolo Orsini, the Duke di Gravina, and Oliverotto should arrive, his followers in pairs should take them one by one, entrusting certain men to certain pairs, who should entertain them until they reached Sinigallia; nor should they be permitted to leave until they came to the duke's quarters, where they should be seized.

The duke afterward ordered all his horsemen and infantry, of which there were more than two thousand cavalry and ten thousand footmen, to assemble by daybreak at the Metauro, a river five miles distant from Fano, and await him there. He found himself, therefore, on the last day of December at the Metauro with his men, and having sent a cavalcade of about two hundred horsemen before him, he then moved forward the infantry, whom he accompanied with the rest of the men-at-arms.

Fano and Sinigallia are two cities of La Marca situated on the shore of the Adriatic Sea, fifteen miles distant from each other, so that he who goes toward Sinigallia has the mountains on his right hand, the bases of which are touched by the sea in some places. The city of Sinigallia is distant from the foot of the mountains a little more than a bowshot and from the shore about a mile. On the side opposite to the city runs a little river that bathes that part of the walls looking toward Fano, facing the high road. Thus he who draws near to Sinigallia comes for a good space by road along the mountains, and reaches the river that passes by Sinigallia. If he turns to his left hand along the bank of it, and goes for the distance of a bowshot, he arrives at a bridge that crosses the river; he is then almost abreast of the gate that leads into Sinigallia, not by a straight line, but transversely. Before this gate there stands a collection of houses with a square to which the bank of the river forms one side.

The Vitelli and Orsini, having received orders to wait for the duke, and to honor him in person, sent away their men to several castles distant from Sinigallia about six miles, so that room could be made for the men of the duke; and they left in Sinigallia only Oliverotto and his band, which consisted of one thousand infantry and one hundred and fifty horsemen, who were quartered in the suburb mentioned above. Matters having been thus arranged, the Duke Valentino left for Sinigallia, and when the leaders of the cavalry reached the bridge they did not pass over, but having opened it, one portion wheeled toward the river and the other toward the country, and a way was left in the middle through which the infantry passed, without stopping, into the town.

Vitellozzo, Pagolo, and the Duke di Gravina on mules, accompanied by a few horsemen, went toward the duke; Vitellozzo, unarmed and wearing a cape lined with green, appeared very dejected, as if conscious of his approaching death—a circumstance that, in view of the ability of the man and his former fortune, caused some amazement. And it is said that when he parted from his men before setting out for Sinigallia to meet the duke he acted as if it were his last parting from them. He recommended his house and its fortunes to his captains, and advised his nephews that it was not the fortune of their house, but the virtues of their fathers that should be kept in mind. These three, therefore, came before the duke and saluted him respectfully, and were received by him with goodwill; they were at once placed between those who were commissioned to look after them.

But the duke, noticing that Oliverotto, who had remained with his band in Sinigallia, was missing—for Oliverotto was waiting in the square before his quarters near the river, keeping his men in order and drilling them—signaled with his eye to Don Michelle, to whom the care of Oliverotto had been committed, that he should take measures that Oliverotto should not escape. Therefore Don Michele rode off and joined Oliverotto, telling him that it was not right to keep his men out of their quarters, because these might be taken up by the men of the duke; and he advised him to send them at once to their quarters and to come himself to meet the duke. And Oliverotto, having taken this advice, came before the duke, who, when he saw him, called to him; and Oliverotto, having made his obeisance, joined the others.

So the whole party entered Sinigallia, dismounted at the duke's quarters, and went with him into a secret chamber, where the duke made them prisoners; he then mounted on horseback, and issued orders that the men of Oliverotto and the Orsini should be stripped of their arms. Those of Oliverotto, being at hand, were quickly settled, but those of the Orsini and Vitelli, being at a distance, and having a presentiment of the destruction of their masters, had time to prepare themselves, and bearing in mind the valor and discipline of the Orsinian and Vitellian houses, they stood together against the hostile forces of the country and saved themselves.

But the duke's soldiers, not being content with having pillaged the men of Oliverotto, began to sack Sinigallia, and if the duke had not repressed this outrage by killing some of them they would have completely sacked it. Night having come and the tumult being silenced, the duke prepared to kill Vitellozzo and Oliverotto; he led them into a room and caused them to be strangled. Neither of them used words in keeping with their past lives: Vitellozzo prayed that he might ask of the pope full pardon for his sins; Oliverotto cringed and laid the blame for all injuries against the duke on Vitellozzo. Pagolo and the

Duke di Gravina Orsini were kept alive until the duke heard from Rome that the pope had taken the Cardinal Orsino, the Archbishop of Florence, and Messer Jacopo da Santa Croce. After which news, on January 18, 1502, in the castle of Pieve, they also were strangled in the same way.

The Life of Castruccio
Castracani of Lucca

Written by Niccolò Machiavelli
and Sent to His Friends Zanobi
Buondelmonti and Luigi Alamanni

CASTRUCCIO CASTRACANI
1284–1328

Translated from the Italian
by W. K. Marriott

I T APPEARS, dearest Zanobi and Luigi, a wonderful thing to
those who have considered the matter, that all men, or the larger
number of them, who have performed great deeds in the world,
and excelled all others in their day, have had their birth and beginning in baseness and obscurity, or have been aggrieved by Fortune
in some outrageous way. Either they have been exposed to the mercy
of wild beasts, or they have had so mean a parentage that in shame
they have given themselves out to be sons of Jove or of some other
deity. It would be wearisome to relate who these persons may have
been because they are well known to everybody, and, as such tales
would not be particularly edifying to those who read them, they are
omitted. I believe that these lowly beginnings of great men occur
because Fortune is desirous of showing to the world that such men
owe much to her and little to wisdom, because she begins to show
her hand when wisdom can really take no part in their career: thus
all success must be attributed to her. Castruccio Castracani of Lucca
was one of those men who did great deeds, if he is measured by the
times in which he lived and the city in which he was born; but, like
many others, he was neither fortunate nor distinguished in his birth,
as the course of this history will show. It appeared to be desirable to
recall his memory, because I have discerned in him such indications
of valor and fortune as should make him a great exemplar to men.
I think also that I ought to call your attention to his actions, because
you of all men I know delight most in noble deeds.

The family of Castracani was formerly numbered among the noble families of Lucca, but in the days of which I speak it had somewhat fallen in estate, as so often happens in this world. To this family was born a son, Antonio, who became a priest of the order of San Michele of Lucca, and for this reason was honored with the title of Messer Antonio. He had an only sister, who had been married to Buonaccorso Cenami, but Buonaccorso dying she became a widow, and not wishing to marry again went to live with her brother. Messer Antonio had a vineyard behind the house where he resided, and as it was bounded on all sides by gardens, any person could have access to it without difficulty. One morning, shortly after sunrise, Madonna Dianora, as the sister of Messer Antonio was called, had occasion to go into the vineyard as usual to gather herbs for seasoning the dinner, and hearing a slight rustling among the leaves of a vine she turned her eyes in that direction, and heard something resembling the cry of an infant. Whereupon she went toward it, and saw the hands and face of a baby who was lying enveloped in the leaves and who seemed to be crying for its mother. Partly wondering and partly fearing, yet full of compassion, she lifted it up and carried it to the house, where she washed it and clothed it with clean linen as is customary, and showed it to Messer Antonio when he returned home. When he heard what had happened and saw the child he was not less surprised or compassionate than his sister. They discussed between themselves what should be done, and seeing that he was a priest and that she had no children, they finally determined to bring it up. They had a nurse for it, and it was reared and loved as if it were their own child. They baptized it, and gave it the name of Castruccio after their father. As the years passed Castruccio grew very handsome, and gave evidence of wit and discretion, and learned with a quickness beyond his years those lessons that Messer Antonio imparted to him. Messer Antonio intended to make a priest of him, and in time would have inducted him into his canonry and other benefices, and all his instruction was given with this object; but Antonio discovered that the character of Castruccio was quite unfitted for the priesthood. As soon as Castruccio reached the age of fourteen he began to take less notice of the chiding of Messer Antonio and Madonna Dianora and no longer to fear them; he left off reading ecclesiastical books, and turned to playing with arms, delighting in nothing so much as in learning their uses, and in running, leaping, and wrestling with other boys. In all exercises he far excelled his companions in courage and bodily strength, and if at any time he did turn to books, only those pleased him that told of wars and the mighty deeds of men. Messer Antonio beheld all this with vexation and sorrow.

There lived in the city of Lucca a gentleman of the Guinigi family, named Messer Francesco, whose profession was arms and who in riches, bodily strength, and valor excelled all other men in Lucca. He had often fought under the command of the Visconti of Milan, and as a Ghibelline was the valued leader of that party in Lucca. This gentleman resided in Lucca and was accustomed to assembling with others most mornings and evenings under the balcony of the Podesta, which is at the top of the square of San Michele, the finest square in Lucca, and he had often seen Castruccio taking part with other children of the street in those games of which I have spoken. Noticing that Castruccio far excelled the other boys, and that he appeared to exercise a royal authority over them, and that they loved and obeyed him, Messer Francesco became greatly desirous of learning who he was. Being informed of the circumstances of the bringing up of Castruccio he felt a greater desire to have him near to him. Therefore he called him one day and asked him whether he would more willingly live in the house of a gentleman, where he would learn to ride horses and use arms, or in the house of a priest, where he would learn nothing but masses and the services of the Church.

Messer Francesco could see that it pleased Castruccio greatly to hear horses and arms spoken of, even though he stood silent, blushing modestly; but being encouraged by Messer Francesco to speak, he answered that if his master were agreeable, nothing would please him more than to give up his priestly studies and take up those of a soldier. This reply delighted Messer Francesco, and in a very short time he obtained the consent of Messer Antonio, who was driven to yield by his knowledge of the nature of the lad, and the fear that he would not be able to hold him much longer.

Thus Castruccio passed from the house of Messer Antonio the priest to the house of Messer Francesco Guinigi the soldier, and it was astonishing to find that in a very short time he manifested all that virtue and bearing that we are accustomed to associate with a true gentleman. In the first place he became an accomplished horseman, and could manage with ease the most fiery charger, and in all jousts and tournaments, although still a youth, he was observed beyond all others, and he excelled in all exercises of strength and dexterity. But what enhanced so much the charm of these accomplishments was the delightful modesty that enabled him to avoid offense in either act or word to others, for he was deferential to the great men, modest with his equals, and courteous to his inferiors. These gifts made him beloved, not only by all the Guinigi family, but by all Lucca. When Castruccio had reached his eighteenth year, the Ghibellines were driven from Pavia by the Guelphs, and Messer Francesco was sent by the Visconti to assist the Ghibellines, and with him went Castruccio, in charge of his forces. Castruccio gave ample proof of his prudence and courage in this expedition, acquiring greater reputation than any other captain, and his name and fame were known, not only in Pavia, but throughout all Lombardy.

Castruccio, having returned to Lucca in far higher estimation than he left it, did not omit to use all the means in his power to gain as many friends as he could, neglecting none of those arts that are necessary for that purpose. About this time Messer Francesco died, leaving a son thirteen years of age named Pagolo, and having appointed Castruccio to be his son's tutor and administrator of his estate. Before he died Francesco called Castruccio to him, and prayed him to show Pagolo that goodwill that he (Francesco) had always shown to *him*, and to render to the son the gratitude that he had not been able to repay to the father. Upon the death of Francesco, Castruccio became the governor and tutor of Pagolo, which increased enormously his power and position, and created a certain amount of envy against him in Lucca in place of the former universal goodwill, for many men suspected him of harboring tyrannical intentions. Among these the leading man was Giorgio degli Opizi, the head of the Guelph party. This man hoped after the death of Messer Francesco to become the chief man in Lucca, but it seemed to him that Castruccio, with the great abilities that he already showed, and holding the position of governor, deprived him of his opportunity; therefore he began to sow those seeds that should rob Castruccio of his eminence. Castruccio at first treated this with scorn, but afterward he grew alarmed, thinking that Messer Giorgio might be able to bring him into disgrace with the deputy of King Ruberto of Naples and have him driven out of Lucca.

The Lord of Pisa at that time was Uguccione of the Faggiuola of Arezzo, who being in the first place elected their captain afterward became their lord. There resided in Paris some exiled Ghibellines from Lucca, with whom Castruccio held communications with the object of effecting their restoration by the help of Uguccione. Castruccio also brought into his plans friends from Lucca who would not endure the authority of the Opizi. Having fixed upon a plan to be followed, Castruccio cautiously fortified the tower of the Onesti, filling it with supplies and munitions of war, in order that it might stand a siege for a few days in case of need. When the night came that had been agreed upon with Uguccione, who had occupied the plain between the mountains and Pisa with many men, the signal was given, and without being observed Uguccione approached the gate of San Piero and set fire to the portcullis. Castruccio raised a great uproar within the city, calling the people to arms and forcing open the gate from his side. Uguccione entered with his men, poured through the town, and killed Messer Giorgio with all his family and many of his friends and supporters. The governor was driven out, and the government reformed according to the wishes of Uguccione, to the detriment of the city, because it was found that more than one hundred families were exiled at that time. Of those who fled, part went to Florence and part to Pistoia, which city was the headquarters of the Guelph party, and for this reason it became most hostile to Uguccione and the Lucchese.

As it now appeared to the Florentines and others of the Guelph party that the Ghibellines absorbed too much power in Tuscany, they determined to restore the exiled Guelphs to Lucca. They assembled a large army in the Val di Nievole, and seized Montecatini; from there they marched to Montecarlo, in order to secure the free passage into Lucca. Upon this Uguccione assembled his Pisan and Lucchese forces, and with a number of German cavalry that he drew out of Lombardy, he moved against the quarters of the Florentines, who upon the appearance of the enemy withdrew from Montecarlo, and posted themselves between Montecatini and Pescia. Uguccione now took up a position near to Montecarlo, and within about two miles of the enemy, and slight skirmishes between the horses of both parties occurred daily. Owing to the illness of Uguccione, the Pisans and Lucchese delayed coming to battle with the enemy. Uguccione, finding himself growing worse, went to Montecarlo to be cured, and left the command of the army in the hands of Castruccio. This change brought about the ruin of the Guelphs, who, thinking that the hostile army having lost its captain had lost its head, grew over-confident. Castruccio observed this, and allowed some days to pass in order to encourage this belief; he also showed signs of fear, and did not allow any of the munitions of the camp to be used. On the other side, the Guelphs grew more insolent the more they saw these evidences of fear, and every day they drew out in the order of battle in front of the army of Castruccio. Presently, deeming that the enemy was sufficiently emboldened, and having mastered their tactics, he decided to join battle with them. First he spoke a few words of encouragement to his soldiers, and pointed out to them the certainty of victory if they would but obey his commands. Castruccio had noticed how the enemy had placed all his best troops in the center of the line of battle, and his less reliable men on the wings of the army; whereupon he did exactly the opposite, putting his most valiant men on the flanks, while those on whom he could not so strongly rely he moved to the center. Observing this order of battle, he drew out of his lines and quickly came in sight of the hostile army, who, as usual, had come in their insolence to defy him. He then commanded his center squadrons to march slowly, while he moved rapidly forward those on the wings. Thus, when they came into contact with the enemy, only the wings of the two armies became engaged, while the center battalions remained out of action, for these two portions of the line of battle were separated from each other by a long interval and thus unable to reach each other. By this expedient the more valiant part of Castruccio's men were opposed to the weaker part of the enemy's troops, and the most efficient men of the enemy were disengaged; and thus the Florentines were unable to fight with those who were arrayed opposite to them, or to give any assistance to their own flanks. So, without much difficulty, Castruccio put the enemy to flight on both flanks, and the center battalions took to flight when they found themselves exposed to attack, without having a chance of displaying their valor. The defeat was complete, and the loss in men very heavy, there being more than ten thousand men killed with many officers and knights of the Guelph party in Tuscany, and also many princes who had come to help them, among whom were Piero, the brother of King Ruberto, and Carlo, his nephew, and Filippo, the lord of Taranto. On the part of Castruccio the loss did not amount to more than three hundred men, among whom was Francesco, the son of Uguccione, who, being young and rash, was killed in the first onset.

This victory so greatly increased the reputation of Castruccio that Uguccione conceived some jealousy and suspicion of him, because it appeared to Uguccione that this victory had given him no increase of power, but rather had diminished it. Being of this mind, he only waited for an opportunity to give effect to it. This occurred on the death of Pier Agnolo Micheli, a man of great repute and abilities in Lucca, the murderer of whom fled to the house of Castruccio for refuge. On the sergeants of the captain going to arrest the murderer, they were driven off by Castruccio, and the murderer escaped. This affair came to the knowledge of Uguccione, who was then at Pisa, and it appeared to him a proper opportunity to punish Castruccio. He therefore sent for his son Neri, who was the governor of Lucca, and commissioned him to take Castruccio prisoner at a banquet and put him to death. Castruccio, fearing no evil, went to the governor in a friendly way, was entertained at supper, and then thrown into prison. But Neri, fearing to put him to death lest the people should be incensed, kept him alive, in order to hear further from his father concerning his intentions. Uguccione cursed the hesitation and cowardice of his son, and at once set out from Pisa to Lucca with four hundred horsemen to finish the business in his own way; but he had not yet reached the baths when the Pisans rebelled and put his deputy to death and created Count Gaddo della Gherardesca their lord. Before Uguccione reached Lucca he heard of the occurrences at

Pisa, but it did not appear wise to him to turn back, lest the Lucchese with the example of Pisa before them should close their gates against him. But the Lucchese, having heard of what had happened at Pisa, availed themselves of this opportunity to demand the liberation of Castruccio, notwithstanding that Uguccione had arrived in their city. They first began to speak of it in private circles, afterward openly in the squares and streets; then they raised a tumult, and with arms in their hands went to Uguccione and demanded that Castruccio should be set at liberty. Uguccione, fearing that worse might happen, released him from prison. Whereupon Castruccio gathered his friends around him, and with the help of the people attacked Uguccione; who, finding he had no resource but in flight, rode away with his friends to Lombardy, to the lords of Scale, where he died in poverty.

But Castruccio from being a prisoner became almost a prince in Lucca, and he carried himself so discreetly with his friends and the people that they appointed him captain of their army for one year. Having obtained this, and wishing to gain renown in war, he planned the recovery of the many towns that had rebelled after the departure of Uguccione, and with the help of the Pisans, with whom he had concluded a treaty, he marched to Serezzana. To capture this place he constructed a fort against it, which is called today Zerezzanello; in the course of two months Castruccio captured the town. With the reputation gained at that siege, he rapidly seized Massa, Carrara, and Lavenza, and in a short time had overrun the whole of Lunigiana. In order to close the pass that leads from Lombardy to Lunigiana, he besieged Pontremoli and wrested it from the hands of Messer Anastagio Palavicini, who was the lord of it. After this victory he returned to Lucca, and was welcomed by the whole people. And now Castruccio, deeming it imprudent any longer to defer making himself a prince, got himself created the lord of Lucca by the help of Pazzino del Poggio, Puccinello dal Portico, Francesco Boccansacchi, and Cecco Guinigi, all of whom he had corrupted; and he was afterward solemnly and deliberately elected prince by the people. At this time Frederick of Bavaria, the King of the Romans, came into Italy to assume the Imperial crown, and Castruccio, in order that he might make friends with him, met him at the head of five hundred horsemen. Castruccio had left as his deputy in Lucca Pagolo Guinigi, who was held in high esteem, because of the people's love for the memory of his father. Castruccio was received in great honor by Frederick, and many privileges were conferred upon him, and he was appointed the emperor's lieutenant in Tuscany. At this time the Pisans were in great fear of Gaddo della Gherardesca, whom they had driven out of Pisa, and they had recourse for assistance to Frederick. Frederick created Castruccio the lord of Pisa, and the Pisans, in dread of the Guelph party, and particularly of the Florentines, were constrained to accept him as their lord.

Frederick, having appointed a governor in Rome to watch his Italian affairs, returned to Germany. All the Tuscan and Lombardian Ghibellines, who followed the imperial lead, had recourse to Castruccio for help and counsel, and all promised him the governorship of his country, if enabled to recover it with his assistance. Among these exiles were Matteo Guidi, Nardo Scolari, Lapo Uberti, Gerozzo Nardi, and Piero Buonaccorsi, all exiled Florentines and Ghibellines. Castruccio had the secret intention of becoming the master of all Tuscany by the aid of these men and of his own forces; and in order to gain greater weight in affairs, he entered into a league with Messer Matteo Visconti, the Prince of Milan, and organized for him the forces of his city and the country districts. As Lucca had five gates, he divided his own country districts into five parts, which he supplied with arms, and enrolled the men under captains and ensigns, so that he could quickly bring into the field twenty thousand soldiers, without those whom he could summon to his assistance from Pisa.

While he surrounded himself with these forces and allies, it happened that Messer Matteo Visconti was attacked by the Guelphs of Piacenza, who had driven out the Ghibellines with the assistance of a Florentine army and the King Ruberto. Messer Matteo called upon Castruccio to invade the Florentines in their own territories, so that, being attacked at home, they should be compelled to draw their army out of Lombardy in order to defend themselves. Castruccio invaded the Valdarno, and seized Fucecchio and San Miniato, inflicting immense damage upon the country. Whereupon the Florentines recalled their army, which had scarcely reached Tuscany, when Castruccio was forced by other necessities to return to Lucca.

There resided in the city of Lucca the Poggio family, who were so powerful that they could not only elevate Castruccio, but even advance him to the dignity of prince; and it appearing to them they had not received such rewards for their services as they deserved, they incited other families to rebel and to drive Castruccio out of Lucca. They found their opportunity one morning, and arming themselves, they set upon the lieutenant whom Castruccio had left to maintain order and killed him. They endeavored to raise the people in revolt, but Stefano di Poggio, a peaceable old man who had taken no hand in the rebellion, intervened and compelled them by his authority to lay down their arms; and he offered to be their mediator with Castruccio to obtain from him what they desired. Therefore they laid down their arms with no greater intelligence than they had taken them up. Castruccio, having heard the news of what had happened at Lucca, at once put Pagolo Guinigi in command of the army, and with a troop of cavalry set out for home. Contrary to his expectations, he found the rebellion at an end, yet he posted his men in the most advantageous places throughout the city. As it appeared to Stefano that Castruccio ought to be very much obliged to him, he sought him out, and without saying anything on his own behalf, for he did not recognize any need for doing so, he begged Castruccio to pardon the other members of his family by reason of their youth, their former friendships, and the obligations that Castruccio was under to their house. To this Castruccio graciously responded, and begged Stefano to reassure himself, declaring that it gave him more pleasure to find the tumult at an end than it had ever caused him anxiety to hear of its inception. He encouraged Stefano to bring his family to him, saying that he thanked God for having given him the opportunity of showing his clemency and liberality. Upon the word of Stefano and Castruccio they surrendered, and with Stefano were immediately thrown into prison and put to death. Meanwhile the Florentines had recovered San Miniato, whereupon it seemed advisable to Castruccio to make peace, as it did not appear to him that he was sufficiently secure at Lucca to leave him. He approached the Florentines with the proposal of a truce, which they readily entertained, for they were weary of the war, and desirous of getting rid of the expenses of it. A treaty was concluded with them for two years, by which both parties agreed to keep the conquests they had made. Castruccio, thus released from this trouble, turned his attention to affairs in Lucca, and in order that he should not again be subject to the perils from which he had just escaped, he, under various pretenses and reasons, first wiped out all those who by their ambition might aspire to the principality—not sparing one of them, but depriving them of country and property, and those whom he had in his hands of life also, stating that he had found by experience that none of them were to be trusted. Then for his further security he raised a fortress in Lucca with the stones of the towers of those whom he had killed or hunted out of the state.

While Castruccio made peace with the Florentines, and strengthened his position in Lucca, he neglected no opportunity, short of open war, of increasing his importance elsewhere. It appeared to him that if he could get possession of Pistoia, he would have one foot in Florence, which was his great desire. He, therefore, in various ways made friends with the mountaineers, and worked matters so in Pistoia that both parties confided their secrets to him. Pistoia was divided, as it always had been, into the Bianchi and Neri parties; the head of the Bianchi was Bastiano di Possente, and of the Neri, Jacopo da Gia. Each of these men held secret communications with Castruccio, and each desired to drive the other out of the city; and, after many threats, they came to blows. Jacopo fortified himself at the Florentine gate, Bastiano at that of the Lucchese side of the city; both trusted more in Castruccio than in the Florentines, because they believed that Castruccio was far more ready and willing to fight than the Florentines, and they both sent to him for assistance. He gave promises to both, saying to Bastiano that he would come in person, and to Jacopo that he would send his pupil, Pagolo Guinigi. At the appointed time he sent forward Pagolo by way of Pisa, and went himself direct to Pistoia; at midnight both of them met outside the city, and both were admitted as friends. Thus the two leaders entered, and at a signal given by Castruccio, one killed Jacopo da Gia, and the other Bastiano di Possente, and both took prisoners or killed the partisans of either faction. Without further opposition Pistoia passed into the hands of Castruccio, who, having forced the Signoria to leave the palace, compelled the people to yield obedience to him, making them many promises and remitting their old debts. The countryside flocked to the city to see the new prince, and all were filled with hope and quickly settled down, influenced in a great measure by his great valor.

About this time great disturbances arose in Rome, owing to the dearness of living that was caused by the absence of the pontiff at Avignon. The German governor, Enrico, was much blamed for what happened—murders and tumults following each other daily, without his being able to put an end to them. This caused Enrico much anxiety lest the Romans should call in Ruberto, the King of

Naples, who would drive the Germans out of the city, and bring back the pope. Having no nearer friend to whom he could apply for help than Castruccio, he sent to him, begging him not only to give him assistance, but also to come in person to Rome. Castruccio considered that he ought not to hesitate to render the emperor this service, because he believed that he himself would not be safe if at any time the emperor ceased to hold Rome. Leaving Pagolo Guinigi in command at Lucca, Castruccio set out for Rome with six hundred horsemen, where he was received by Enrico with the greatest distinction. In a short time the presence of Castruccio obtained such respect for the emperor that, without bloodshed or violence, good order was restored, chiefly by reason of Castruccio having sent by sea from the country round Pisa large quantities of corn, and thus removed the source of the trouble. When he had chastised some of the Roman leaders, and admonished others, voluntary obedience was rendered to Enrico. Castruccio received many honors, and was made a Roman senator. This dignity was assumed with the greatest pomp, Castruccio being clothed in a brocaded toga, which had the following words embroidered on its front: "I am what God wills." While on the back was: "What God desires shall be."

During this time the Florentines, who were much enraged that Castruccio should have seized Pistoia during the truce, considered how they could tempt the city to rebel, to do which they thought would not be difficult in his absence. Among the exiled Pistoians in Florence were Baldo Cecchi and Jacopo Baldini, both men of leading and ready to face danger. These men kept up communications with their friends in Pistoia, and with the aid of the Florentines entered the city by night, and after driving out some of Castruccio's officials and partisans, and killing others, they restored the city to its freedom. The news of this greatly angered Castruccio, and taking leave of Enrico, he pressed on in great haste to Pistoia. When the

Florentines heard of his return, knowing that he would lose no time, they decided to intercept him with their forces in the Val di Nievole, under the belief that by doing so they would cut off his road to Pistoia. Assembling a great army of the supporters of the Guelph cause, the Florentines entered the Pistoian territories. On the other hand, Castruccio reached Montecarlo with his army; and having heard where the Florentines' lay, he decided not to encounter it in the plains of Pistoia, nor to await it in the plains of Pescia, but, as far as he possibly could, to attack it boldly in the Pass of Serravalle. He believed that if he succeeded in this design, victory was assured, although he was informed that the Florentines had thirty thousand men, while he had only twelve thousand. Although he had every confidence in his own abilities and the valor of his troops, yet he hesitated to attack his enemy in the open lest he should be overwhelmed by numbers. Serravalle is a castle between Pescia and Pistoia, situated on a hill that blocks the Val di Nievole, not in the exact pass, but about a bowshot beyond; the pass itself is in places narrow and steep, while in general it ascends gently, but is still narrow, especially at the summit where the waters divide, so that twenty men side by side could hold it. The lord of Serravalle was Manfred, a German, who, before Castruccio became lord of Pistoia, had been allowed to remain in possession of the castle, it being common to the Lucchese and the Pistoians, and unclaimed by either—neither of them wishing to displace Manfred as long as he kept his promise of neutrality, and came under obligations to no one. For these reasons, and also because the castle was well fortified, he had always been able to maintain his position. It was here that Castruccio had determined to fall upon his enemy, for here his few men would have the advantage, and there was no fear lest, seeing the large masses of the hostile force before they became engaged, they should not stand. As soon as this trouble with Florence arose, Castruccio saw the immense advantage that possession of this castle would give him, and having an intimate friendship with a resident in the castle, he managed matters so with him that four hundred of his men were to be admitted into the castle the night before the attack on the Florentines, and the castellan put to death.

Castruccio, having prepared everything, had now to encourage the Florentines to persist in their desire to carry the seat of war away from Pistoia into the Val di Nievole; therefore he did not move his army from Montecarlo. Thus the Florentines hurried on until they reached their encampment under Serravalle, intending to cross the hill on the following morning. In the meantime, Castruccio had seized the castle at night, had also moved his army from Montecarlo, and marching from there at midnight in dead silence, had reached the foot of Serravalle: thus he and the Florentines commenced the ascent of the hill at the same time in the morning. Castruccio sent forward his infantry by the main road, and a troop of four hundred horsemen by a path on the left toward the castle. The Florentines sent forward four hundred cavalry ahead of their army that was following, never expecting to find Castruccio in possession of the hill, nor were they aware of his having seized the castle. Thus it happened that the Florentine horsemen mounting the hill were completely taken by surprise when they discovered the infantry of Castruccio, and so close were they upon it they had scarcely time to pull down their visors. It was a case of unready soldiers being attacked by ready, and they were assailed with such vigor that with difficulty they could hold their own, although some few of them got through. When the noise of the fighting reached the Florentine camp below, it was filled with confusion. The cavalry and infantry became inextricably mixed: the captains were unable to get their men either backward or forward, owing to the narrowness of the pass, and amid all this tumult no one knew what ought to be done or what could be done. In a short time the cavalry who were engaged with the enemy's infantry were scattered or killed without having made any effective defense because of their unfortunate position, although in sheer desperation they had offered a stout resistance. Retreat had been impossible, with the mountains on both flanks, while in front were their enemies, and in the rear their friends. When Castruccio saw that his men were unable to strike a decisive blow at the enemy and put them to flight, he sent one thousand infantrymen round by the castle, with orders to join the four hundred horsemen he had previously dispatched there, and commanded the whole force to fall upon the flank of the enemy. These orders they carried out with such fury that the Florentines could not sustain the attack, but gave way, and were soon in full retreat—conquered more by their unfortunate position than by the valor of their enemy. Those in the rear turned toward Pistoia, and spread through the plains, each man seeking only his own safety. The defeat was complete and very sanguinary. Many captains were taken prisoner, among whom were Bandini dei Rossi, Francesco Brunelleschi, and Giovanni della Tosa, all Florentine noblemen, with many Tuscans and Neapolitans who fought on the Florentine side, having been sent by King Ruberto to assist the Guelphs. Immediately the Pistoians heard of this defeat they drove out the friends of the Guelphs, and surrendered to Castruccio. He was not content with occupying Prato and all the castles on the plains on both sides of the Arno, but marched his army into the plain of Peretola, about two miles from Florence. Here he remained many days, dividing the spoils, and celebrating his victory with feasts and games, holding horse races, and foot races for men and women. He also struck medals in commemoration of the defeat of the Florentines. He endeavored to corrupt some of the citizens of Florence, who were to open the city gates at night; but the conspiracy was discovered, and the participators in it taken and beheaded, among whom were Tommaso Lupacci and Lambertuccio Frescobaldi. This defeat caused the Florentines great anxiety, and despairing of preserving their liberty, they sent envoys to King Ruberto of Naples, offering him the dominion of their city; and he, knowing of what immense importance the maintenance of the Guelph cause was to him, accepted it. He agreed with the Florentines to receive from them a yearly tribute of two hundred thousand florins, and he sent his son Carlo to Florence with four thousand horsemen.

Shortly after this the Florentines were relieved in some degree of the pressure of Castruccio's army, owing to his being compelled to leave his positions before Florence and march on Pisa, in order to suppress a conspiracy that had been raised against him by Benedetto Lanfranchi, one of the first men in Pisa, who could not endure that his fatherland should be under the dominion of the Lucchese. He had formed this conspiracy, intending to seize the citadel, kill the partisans of Castruccio, and drive out the garrison. As, however, in a conspiracy paucity of numbers is essential to secrecy, so for its execution a few are not sufficient, and in seeking more adherents to his conspiracy Lanfranchi encountered a person who revealed the design to Castruccio. This betrayal cannot be passed by without severe reproach to Bonifacio Cerchi and Giovanni Guidi, two Florentine exiles who were suffering their banishment in Pisa. Thereupon Castruccio seized Benedetto and put him to death, and beheaded many other noble citizens, and drove their families into exile. It now appeared to Castruccio that both Pisa and Pistoia were thoroughly disaffected; he employed much thought and energy upon securing his position there, and this gave the Florentines their opportunity to reorganize their army, and to await the coming of Carlo, the son of the King of Naples. When Carlo arrived they decided to lose no more time, and assembled a great army of more than thirty thousand infantry and ten thousand cavalry—having called to their aid every Guelph there was in Italy. They consulted whether they should attack Pistoia or Pisa first, and decided that it would be better to march on the latter—a course, owing to the recent conspiracy, more likely to succeed, and of more advantage to them, because they believed that the surrender of Pistoia would follow the acquisition of Pisa.

In the early part of May 1328, the Florentines put in motion this army and quickly occupied Lastra, Signa, Montelupo, and Empoli, passing from there on to San Miniato. When Castruccio heard of the enormous army that the Florentines were sending against him, he was in no degree alarmed, believing that the time had now arrived when Fortune would deliver the empire of Tuscany into his hands, for he had no reason to think that his enemy would make a better fight, or had better prospects of success, than at Pisa or Serravalle. He assembled twenty thousand foot soldiers and four thousand horsemen, and with this army went to Fucecchio, while he sent Pagolo Guinigi to Pisa with five thousand infantry. Fucecchio has a stronger position than any other town in the Pisan district, owing to its situation between the rivers Arno and Gusciana and its slight elevation above the surrounding plain. Moreover, the enemy could not hinder its being victualled unless they divided their forces, nor could they approach it from the direction of either Lucca or Pisa, nor could they get through to Pisa, or attack Castruccio's forces except at a disadvantage. In one case they would find themselves placed between his two armies, the one under his own command and the other under Pagolo, and in the other case they would have to cross the Arno to get to close quarters with the enemy, an undertaking of great hazard. In order to tempt the Florentines to take this latter course, Castruccio withdrew his men from the banks of the river and placed them under the walls of Fucecchio, leaving a wide expanse of land between them and the river.

The Florentines, having occupied San Miniato, held a council of war to decide whether they should attack Pisa or the army of Castruccio, and, having weighed the difficulties of both courses, they decided upon the latter. The river Arno was at that time low enough to be fordable, yet the water reached to the shoulders of the infantrymen and to the saddles of the horsemen. On the morning of June 10, 1328, the Florentines commenced the battle by ordering forward a number of cavalry and ten thousand infantry. Castruccio, whose plan of action was fixed, and who well knew what to do, at once attacked the Florentines with five thousand infantry and three thousand horsemen, not allowing them to issue from the river before he charged them; he also sent one thousand light infantry up the riverbank, and the same number down the Arno. The infantry of the Florentines were so much impeded by their arms and the water that they were not able to mount the banks of the river, while the cavalry had made the passage of the river more difficult for the others, by reason of the few who had crossed having broken up the bed of the river, and this being deep with mud, many of the horses rolled over with their riders and many of them had stuck so fast that they could not move. When the Florentine captains saw the difficulties their men were meeting, they withdrew them and moved higher up the river, hoping to find the riverbed less treacherous and the banks more adapted for landing. These men were met at the bank by the forces that Castruccio had already sent forward, who, being light armed with bucklers and javelins in their hands, let fly with tremendous shouts into the faces and bodies of the cavalry. The horses, alarmed by the noise and the wounds, would not move forward, and trampled each other in great confusion. The fight between the men of Castruccio and those of the enemy who succeeded in crossing was sharp and terrible; both sides fought with the utmost desperation and neither would yield. The soldiers of Castruccio fought to drive the others back into the river, while the Florentines strove to get a footing on land in order to make room for the others pressing forward, who if they could but get out of the water would be able to fight, and in this obstinate conflict they were urged on by their captains. Castruccio shouted to his men that these were the same enemies whom they had before conquered at Serravalle, while the Florentines reproached each other that the many should be overcome by the few. At length Castruccio, seeing how long the battle had lasted, and that both his men and the enemy were utterly exhausted, and that both sides had many killed and wounded, pushed forward another body of infantry to take up a position at the rear of those who were fighting; he then commanded these latter to open their ranks as if they intended to retreat, and one part of them to turn to the right and another to the left. This cleared a space of which the Florentines at once took advantage, and thus gained possession of a portion of the battlefield. But when these tired soldiers found themselves at close quarters with Castruccio's reserves they could not stand against them and at once fell back into the river. The cavalry of either side had not as yet gained any decisive advantage over the other, because Castruccio, knowing his inferiority in this arm, had commanded his leaders only to stand on the defensive against the attacks of their adversaries, as he hoped that when he had overcome the infantry he would be able to make short work of the cavalry. This fell out as he had hoped, for when he saw the Florentine army driven back across the river he ordered the remainder of his infantry to attack the cavalry of the enemy. This they did with lance and javelin, and, joined by their own cavalry, fell upon the enemy with the greatest fury and soon put him to flight. The Florentine captains, having seen the difficulty their cavalry had met with in crossing the river, had attempted to make their infantry cross lower down the river, in order to attack the flanks of Castruccio's army. But here, also, the banks were steep and already lined by the men of Castruccio, and this movement was quite useless. Thus the Florentines were so completely defeated at all points that scarcely a third of them escaped, and Castruccio was again covered with glory. Many captains were taken prisoner, and Carlo, the son of King Ruberto, with Michelagnolo Falconi and Taddeo degli Albizzi, the Florentine commissioners, fled to Empoli. If the spoils were great, the slaughter was infinitely greater, as might be expected in such a battle. Of the Florentines there fell twenty thousand, two hundred and thirty-one men, while Castruccio lost one thousand, five hundred and seventy men.

But Fortune growing envious of the glory of Castruccio took away his life just at the time when she should have preserved it, and thus ruined all those plans that for so long a time he had worked to carry into effect, and in the successful prosecution of which nothing but death could have stopped him. Castruccio was in the thick of the battle the whole of the day; and when the end of it came, although fatigued and overheated, he stood at the gate of Fucecchio to welcome his men on their return from victory and personally thank them. He was also on the watch for any attempt of the enemy to retrieve the fortunes of the day, he being of the opinion that it was the duty of a good general to be the first man in the saddle and the last out of it. Here Castruccio stood exposed to a wind that often rises at midday on the banks of the Arno, and that is often very unhealthy; from this he took a chill, of which he thought nothing, as he was accustomed to such troubles, but it was the cause of his death. On the following night he was attacked with high fever, which increased so rapidly that the doctors saw it must prove fatal. Castruccio, therefore, called Pagolo Guinigi to him, and addressed him as follows:

"If I could have believed that Fortune would have cut me off in the midst of the career that was leading to that glory that all my successes promised, I should have labored less, and I should have left thee, if a smaller state, at least with fewer enemies and perils, because I should have been content with the governorships of Lucca and Pisa. I should neither have subjugated the Pistoians, nor outraged the Florentines with so many injuries. But I would have made both these peoples my friends, and I should have lived, if no longer, at least more peacefully, and have left you a state without a doubt smaller, but one more secure and established on a surer foundation. But Fortune, who insists upon having the arbitrament of human affairs, did not endow me with sufficient judgment to recognize this from the first, nor the time to surmount it. Thou hast heard, for many have told thee, and I have never concealed it, how I entered the house of thy father whilst yet a boy—a stranger to all those ambitions that every generous soul should feel—and how I was brought up by him, and loved as though I had been born of his blood; how under his governance I learned to be valiant and capable of availing myself of all that fortune of which thou hast been witness. When thy good father came to die, he committed thee and all his possessions to my care, and I have brought thee up with that love, and increased thy estate with that care, which I was bound to show. And in order that thou shouldst not only possess the estate that thy father left, but also that which my fortune and abilities have gained, I have never married, so that the love of children should never deflect my mind from that gratitude that I owed to the children of thy father. Thus I leave thee a vast estate, of which I am well content, but I am deeply concerned, inasmuch as I leave it thee unsettled and insecure. Thou hast the city of Lucca on thy hands, which will never rest contented under thy government. Thou hast also Pisa, where the men are of nature changeable and unreliable, who, although they may be sometimes held in subjection, yet they will ever disdain to serve under a Lucchese. Pistoia is also disloyal to thee, she being eaten up with factions and deeply incensed against thy family by reason of the wrongs recently inflicted upon them. Thou hast for neighbors the offended Florentines, injured by us in a thousand ways, but not utterly destroyed, who will hail the news of my death with more delight than they would the acquisition of all Tuscany. In the emperor and in the princes of Milan thou canst place no reliance, for they are far distant, slow, and their help is very long in coming. Therefore, thou hast no hope in anything but in thine own abilities, and in the memory of my valor, and in the prestige that this latest victory has brought thee; which, as thou knowest how to use it with prudence, will assist thee to come to terms with the Florentines, who, as they are suffering under this great defeat, should be inclined to listen to thee. And whereas I have sought to make them my enemies, because I believed that war with them would conduce to my power and glory, thou hast every inducement to make friends of them, because their alliance will bring thee advantages and security. It is of the greatest important in this world that a man should know himself, and the measure of his own strength and means; and he who knows that he has not a genius for fighting must learn how to govern by the arts of peace. And it will be well for thee to rule thy conduct by my counsel, and to learn in this way to enjoy what my life work and dangers have gained; and in this thou wilt easily succeed when thou hast learned to believe that what I have told thee is true. And thou wilt be doubly indebted to me, in that I have left thee this realm and have taught thee how to keep it."

After this there came to Castruccio those citizens of Pisa, Pistoia, and Lucca who had been fighting at his side, and while recommending Pagolo to them, and making them swear obedience to him as his successor, he died. He left a happy memory to those who had known him, and no prince of those times was ever loved with such devotion as he was. His obsequies were celebrated with every sign of mourning, and he was buried in San Francesco at Lucca. Fortune was not so friendly to Pagolo Guinigi as she had been to Castruccio, for he had not the abilities. Not long after the death of Castruccio, Pagolo lost Pisa, and then Pistoia, and only with difficulty held on to Lucca. This latter city continued in the family of Guinigi until the time of the great-grandson of Pagolo.

From what has been related here it will be seen that Castruccio was a man of exceptional abilities, measured not only by men of his own time, but also by those of an earlier date. In stature he was above the ordinary height, and perfectly proportioned. He was of a gracious presence, and he welcomed men with such urbanity that those who spoke with him rarely left him displeased. His hair was inclined to be red, and he wore it cut short above the ears, and, whether it rained or snowed, he always went without a hat. He was delightful among friends, but terrible to his enemies, just to his subjects, ready to play false with the unfaithful, and willing to overcome by fraud those whom he desired to subdue, because he was wont to say that it was the victory that brought the glory, not the methods of achieving it. No one was bolder in facing danger, none more prudent in extricating himself. He was accustomed to say that men ought to attempt everything and fear nothing, that God is a lover of strong men, because one always sees that the weak are chastised by the strong. He was also wonderfully sharp or biting though courteous in his answers; and as he did not look for any indulgence in this way of speaking from others, so he was not angered with others who did not show it to him. It has often happened that he has listened quietly when others have spoken sharply to him, as on the following occasions. He had caused a ducat to be given for a partridge, and was taken to task for doing so by a friend, to whom Castruccio had said: "You would not have given more than a penny." "That is true," answered the friend. Then Castruccio said to him: "A ducat is much less to me." Having about him a flatterer on whom he had spat to show that he scorned him, the flatterer said to him: "Fisherman are willing to let the waters of the sea saturate them in order that they may take a few little fishes, and I allow myself to be wetted by spittle that I may catch a whale"; and this was not only heard by Castruccio with patience but rewarded. When told by a priest that it was wicked for him to live so sumptuously,

Castruccio said: "If that be a vice then you should not fare so splendidly at the feasts of our saints." Passing through a street he saw a young man as he came out of a house of ill fame blush at being seen by Castruccio, and said to him: "Thou shouldst not be ashamed when thou comest out, but when thou goest into such places." A friend gave him a very curiously tied knot to undo and was told: "Fool, do you think that I wish to untie a thing that gave so much trouble to fasten?" Castruccio said to one who professed to be a philosopher: "You are like the dogs who always run after those who will give them the best to eat," and was answered: "We are rather like the doctors who go to the houses of those who have the greatest need of them." Going by water from Pisa to Leghorn, Castruccio was much disturbed by a dangerous storm that sprang up, and was reproached for cowardice by one of those with him, who said that he did not fear anything. Castruccio answered that he did not wonder at that, since every man valued his soul for what it was worth. Being asked by one what he ought to do to gain estimation, he said: "When thou goest to a banquet take care that thou dost not seat one piece of wood upon another." To a person who was boasting that he had read many things, Castruccio said: "He knows better than to boast of remembering many things." Someone bragged that he could drink much without becoming intoxicated. Castruccio replied: "An ox does the same." Castruccio was acquainted with a girl with whom he had intimate relations, and being blamed by a friend who told him that it was undignified for him to be taken in by a woman, he said: "She has not taken me in, I have taken her." Being also blamed for eating very dainty foods, he answered: "Thou dost not spend as much as I do?" and being told that it was true, he continued: "Then thou art more avaricious than I am gluttonous." Being invited by Taddeo Bernardi, a very rich and splendid citizen of Luca, to supper, he went to the house and was shown by Taddeo into a chamber hung with silk and paved with fine stones representing flowers and foliage of the most beautiful coloring. Castruccio gathered some saliva in his mouth and spat it out upon Taddeo, and seeing him much disturbed by this, said to him: "I knew not where to spit in order to offend thee less." Being asked how Caesar died he said: "God willing I will die as he did." Being one night in the house of one of his gentlemen where many ladies were assembled, he was reproved by one of his friends for dancing and amusing himself with them more than was usual in one of his station, so he said: "He who is considered wise by day will not be considered a fool at night." A person came to demand a favor of Castruccio, and thinking he was not listening to his plea threw himself on his knees to the ground, and being sharply reproved by Castruccio, said: "Thou art the reason of my acting thus for thou hast thy ears in thy feet," whereupon he obtained double the favor he had asked. Castruccio used to say that the way to hell was an easy one, seeing that it was in a downward direction and you travelled blindfolded. Being asked a favor by one who used many superfluous words, he said to him: "When you have another request to make, send someone else to make it." Having been wearied by a similar man with a long oration who wound up by saying: "Perhaps I have fatigued you by speaking so long," Castruccio said: "You have not, because I have not listened to a word you said." He used to say of one who had been a beautiful child and who afterward became a fine man, that he was dangerous, because he first took the husbands from the wives and now he took the wives from their husbands. To an envious man who laughed, he said: "Do you laugh because you are successful or because another is unfortunate?" While he was still in the charge of Messer Francesco Guinigi, one of his companions said to him: "What shall I give you if you will let me give you a blow on the nose?" Castruccio answered: "A helmet." Having put to death a citizen of Lucca who had been instrumental in raising him to power, and being told that he had done wrong to kill one of his old friends, he answered that people deceived themselves; he had only killed a new enemy. Castruccio praised greatly those men who intended to take a wife and then did not do so, saying that they were like men who said they would go to sea, and then refused when the time came. He said that it always struck him with surprise that while men in buying an earthen or glass vase would sound it first to learn if it were good, yet in choosing a wife they were content with only looking at her. He was once asked in what manner he would wish to be buried when he died, and answered: "With the face turned downward, for I know when I am gone this country will be turned upside down." On being asked if it had ever occurred to him to become a friar in order to save his soul, he answered that it had not, because it appeared strange to him that Fra Lazerone should go to Paradise and Uguccione della Faggiuola to the Inferno. He was once asked when a man should eat to preserve his health, and replied: "If the man be rich let him eat when he is hungry; if he be poor, then when he can." Seeing one of his gentlemen make a member of his family lace him up, he said to him: "I pray God that you will let him feed you also." Seeing that someone had written upon his house in Latin the words: "May God preserve this house from the wicked," he said, "The owner must never go in." Passing through one of the streets he saw a small house with a very large door, and remarked: "That house will fly through the door." He was having a discussion with the ambassador of the King of Naples concerning the property of some banished nobles, when a dispute arose between them, and the ambassador asked him if he had no fear of the king. "Is this king of yours a bad man or a good one?" asked Castruccio, and was told that he was a good one, whereupon he said, "Why should you suggest that I should be afraid of a good man?"

I could recount many other stories of his sayings both witty and weighty, but I think that the above will be sufficient testimony to his high qualities. He lived forty-four years, and was in every way a prince. And as he was surrounded by many evidences of his good fortune, so he also desired to have near him some memorials of his bad fortune; therefore the manacles with which he was chained in prison are to be seen to this day fixed up in the tower of his residence, where they were placed by him to testify forever to his days of adversity. As in his life he was inferior neither to Philip of Macedon, the father of Alexander, nor to Scipio of Rome, so he died in the same year of his age as they did, and he would doubtless have excelled both of them had Fortune decreed that he should be born, not in Lucca, but in Macedonia or Rome.

Discourses on the First Decade of Titus Livius

Translated from the Italian
by Ninian Hill Thomson

Excerpts from Book I

PREFACE

A LBEIT THE JEALOUS TEMPER of mankind, ever more disposed to censure than to praise the work of others, has constantly made the pursuit of new methods and systems no less perilous than the search after unknown lands and seas; nevertheless, prompted by that desire that nature has implanted in me, fearlessly to undertake whatsoever I think offers a common benefit to all, I enter on a path that, being hitherto untrodden by any, though it involve me in trouble and fatigue, may yet win me thanks from those who judge my efforts in a friendly spirit. And although my feeble discernment, my slender experience of current affairs, and imperfect knowledge of ancient events, render these efforts of mine defective and of no great utility, they may at least open the way to some other, who, with better parts and sounder reasoning and judgment, shall carry out my design; whereby, if I gain no credit, at all events I ought to incur no blame.

When I see antiquity held in such reverence that, to omit other instances, the mere fragment of some ancient statue is often bought at a great price, in order that the purchaser may keep it by him to adorn his house, or to have it copied by those who take delight in this art; and how these, again, strive with all their skill to imitate it in their various works; and when, on the other hand, I find those noble labors that history shows to have been wrought on behalf of the monarchies and republics of old times, by kings, captains, citizens, lawgivers, and others who have toiled for the good of their country, rather admired than followed, nay, so absolutely renounced by everyone that not a trace of that antique worth is now left among us, I cannot but at once marvel and grieve at this inconsistency; and all the more because I perceive that, in civil disputes between citizens, and in the bodily disorders into which men fall, recourse is always had to the decisions and remedies pronounced or prescribed by the ancients.

For the civil law is no more than the opinions delivered by the ancient jurisconsults, which, being reduced to a system, teach the jurisconsults of our own times how to determine; while the healing art is simply the recorded experience of the old physicians, on which our modern physicians found their practice. And yet, in giving laws to a commonwealth, in maintaining states and governing kingdoms, in organizing armies and conducting wars, in dealing with subject nations, and in extending a state's dominions, we find no prince, no republic, no captain, and no citizen who resorts to the example of the ancients.

This I persuade myself is due not so much to the feebleness to which the present methods of education have brought the world, or to the injury that a pervading apathy has wrought in many provinces and cities of Christendom, as to the want of a right intelligence of history, which renders men incapable in reading it to extract its true meaning or to relish its flavor. Whereupon it happens that by far the greater number of those who read history take pleasure in following the variety of incidents that it presents, without a thought to imitate them; judging such imitation to be not only difficult but impossible, as though the heavens, the sun, the elements, and man himself were no longer the same as they formerly were as regards motion, order, and power.

Desiring to rescue men from this error, I have thought fit to note down with respect to all those books of Titus Livius that have escaped the malignity of Time, whatever seems to me essential to a right understanding of ancient and modern affairs, so that any who shall read these remarks of mine may reap from them that profit for the sake of which a knowledge of history is to be sought. And although the task be arduous, still, with the help of those at whose instance I assumed the burden, I hope to carry it forward so far that another shall have no long way to go to bring it to its destination.

I

Of the Beginnings of Cities in General, and in Particular of That of Rome

N O ONE WHO READS how the city of Rome had its beginning, who were its founders, and what its ordinances and laws, will marvel that so much excellence was maintained in it through many ages, or that it grew afterward to be so great an empire.

And, first, as touching its origin, I say that all cities have been founded either by the people of the country in which they stand, or by strangers. Cities have their origins in the former of these two ways when the inhabitants of a country find that they cannot live securely if they live dispersed in many and small societies, each of them unable, whether from its situation or its slender numbers, to stand alone against the attacks of its enemies, on whose approach there is no time left to unite for defense without abandoning many strongholds, and thus becoming an easy prey to the invader. To escape which dangers, whether of their own motion or at the instance of some of greater authority among them, they restrict themselves to dwell together in certain places, which they think will be more convenient to live in and easier to defend.

Among many cities taking their origin in this way were Athens and Venice, the former of which, for reasons like those just now mentioned, was built by a scattered population under the direction of Theseus. To escape the wars that, on the decay of the Roman Empire daily renewed in Italy by the arrival of fresh hordes of Barbarians, numerous refugees, sheltering in certain little islands in a corner of the Adriatic Sea, gave beginning to Venice, where, without any recognized leader to direct them, they agreed to live together under such laws as they thought best suited to maintain them. And by reason of the prolonged tranquility that their position secured, they being protected by the narrow sea and by the circumstance that the tribes who then harassed Italy had no ships wherewith to molest them, they were able from very small beginnings to attain to that greatness they now enjoy.

In the second case, namely of a city being founded by strangers, the settlers are either wholly independent, or they are controlled by others, as where colonies are sent forth either by a prince or by a republic, to relieve their countries of an excessive population, or to defend newly acquired territories that it is sought to secure at small cost. Of this sort many cities were settled by the Romans, and in all parts of their dominions. It may also happen that such cities are founded by a prince merely to add to his renown, without any intention on his part to dwell there, as Alexandria was built by Alexander the Great. Cities like these, not having had their beginning in freedom, seldom make such progress as to rank among the chief towns of kingdoms.

The city of Florence belongs to that class of towns that has not been independent from the first, for whether we ascribe its origin to the soldiers of Sylla, or, as some have conjectured, to the mountaineers of Fiesole (who, emboldened by the long peace that prevailed throughout the world during the reign of Octavianus, came down to occupy the plain on the banks of the Arno), in either case, it was founded under the auspices of Rome nor could, at first, make other progress than was permitted by the grace of the sovereign state.

The origin of cities may be said to be independent when a people, either by themselves or under some prince, are constrained by famine, pestilence, or war to leave their native land and seek a new habitation. Settlers of this sort either establish themselves in cities that they find ready to their hand in the countries of which they take possession, as did Moses, or they build new ones, as did Aeneas. It is in this last case that the merits of a founder and the good fortune of the city founded are best seen, and this good fortune will be more or less remarkable according to the greater or less capacity of him who gives the city its beginning.

The capacity of a founder is known in two ways: by his choice of a site, or by the laws that he frames. And since men act either of necessity or from choice, and merit may seem greater where choice is more restricted, we have to consider whether it may not be well to choose a sterile district as the site of a new city, in order that the inhabitants, being constrained to industry, and less corrupted by ease, may live in closer union, finding less cause for division in the poverty of their land—as was the case in Ragusa, and in many other cities built in similar situations. Such a choice would certainly be the wisest and the most advantageous, could men be content to enjoy what is their own without seeking to lord it over others. But since to be safe they must be strong, they are compelled to avoid these barren districts, and to plant themselves in more fertile regions, where, the fruitfulness of the soil enabling them to increase and multiply, they may defend themselves against any who attack them, and overthrow any who would withstand their power.

And as for that languor that the situation might breed, care must be had that hardships that the site does not enforce shall be enforced by the laws, and that the example of those wise nations be imitated who, inhabiting most fruitful and delightful countries, and such as were likely to rear a listless and effeminate race, unfit for all manly exercises, in order to obviate the mischief wrought by the amenity and relaxing influence of the soil and climate, subjected all who were to serve as soldiers to the severest training; whereupon it came that better soldiers were raised in these countries than in others by nature rugged and barren. Such, of old, was the kingdom of the Egyptians, which, though of all lands the most bountiful, yet, by the severe training that its laws enforced, produced most valiant soldiers, who, had their names not been lost in antiquity, might be thought to deserve more praise than Alexander the Great and many besides, whose memory is still fresh in men's minds. And even in recent times, anyone contemplating the kingdom of the Soldan, and the military order of the Mamclukes before they were destroyed by Selim the Grand Turk, must have seen how carefully they trained their soldiers in every kind of warlike exercise, showing thereby how much they dreaded that indolence to which their genial soil and climate might have disposed them, unless neutralized by strenuous laws. I say, then, that it is a prudent choice to found your city in a fertile region when the effects of that fertility are duly balanced by the restraint of the laws.

When Alexander the Great thought to add to his renown by founding a city, Dinocrates the architect came and showed him how he might build it on Mount Athos, which not only offered a strong position, but could be handled that the city built there might present a semblance of the human form, which would be a thing strange and striking, and worthy of so great a monarch. But on Alexander asking how the inhabitants were to live, Dinocrates answered that he had not thought of that. Whereupon, Alexander laughed, and leaving Mount Athos as it stood, built Alexandria, where the fruitfulness of the soil, and the vicinity of the Nile and the sea, might attract many to take up their abode.

To him, therefore, who inquires into the origin of Rome, if he assigns its beginning to Aeneas, it will seem to be of those cities that were founded by strangers if to Romulus, then of those founded by the natives of the country. But in whichever class we place it, it will be seen to have had its beginning in freedom, and not in subjection to another state. It will be seen, too, as hereafter shall be noted, how strict was the discipline that the laws instituted by Romulus, Numa, and its other founders made compulsory upon it; so that neither its fertility, the proximity of the sea, the number of its victories, nor the extent of its dominion could for many centuries corrupt it, but, on the contrary, maintained it replete with such virtues as were never matched in any other commonwealth.

And because the things done by Rome, and which Titus Livius has celebrated, were effected at home or abroad by public or by private wisdom, I shall begin by treating, and noting the consequences of those things done at home in accordance with the public voice, which seem most to merit attention, and to this object the whole of this first Book or first Part of my Discourses shall be directed.

II

Of the Various Kinds of Government; and to Which of Them the Roman Commonwealth Belonged

I FORGO ALL DISCUSSION concerning those cities that at the outset have been dependent upon others, and shall speak only of those that from their earliest beginnings have stood entirely clear of all foreign control, being governed from the first as pleased themselves, whether as republics or as princedoms.

These as they have had different origins, so likewise have had different laws and institutions. For to some at their very first commencement, or not long after, laws have been given by a single legislator, and all at one time, like those given by Lycurgus to the Spartans, while to others they have been given at different times, as need rose or accident determined, as in the case of Rome. That republic, indeed, may be called happy whose lot has been to have a founder so prudent as to provide for it laws under which it can continue to live securely, without need to amend them, as we find Sparta preserving hers for eight hundred years, without deterioration and without any dangerous disturbance. On the other hand, some measure of unhappiness attaches to the state that, not having yielded itself once for all into the hands of a single wise legislator, is obliged to recast its institutions for itself; and of such states, by far the most unhappy is that which is furthest removed from a sound system of government, by which I mean that its institutions lie wholly outside the path that might lead it to a true and perfect end. For it is scarcely possible that a state in this position can ever, by any chance, set itself to rights, whereas another whose institutions are imperfect, if it have made a good beginning and such as admits of its amendment, may in the course of events arrive at perfection. It is certain, however, that such states can never be reformed without great risk, for, as a rule, men will accept no new law altering the institutions of their state unless the necessity for such a change be demonstrated, and since this necessity cannot arise without danger, the state may easily be overthrown before the new order of things is established. In proof whereof we may instance the republic of Florence, which was reformed in the year 1502, in consequence of the affair of Arezzo, but was ruined in 1512, in consequence of the affair of Prato.

Desiring, therefore, to discuss the nature of the government of Rome, and to ascertain the accidental circumstances that brought it to its perfection, I say, as has been said before by many who have written of governments, that of these there are three forms, known by the names Monarchy, Aristocracy, and Democracy, and that those who give its institutions to a state have recourse to one or other of these three, according as it suits their purpose. Other, and, as many have thought, wiser teachers, will have it that there are altogether six forms of government, three of them utterly bad, the other three good in themselves, but so readily corrupted that they too are apt to become hurtful. The good are the three above named; the bad, three others dependent upon these, and each so like that to which it is related that it is easy to pass imperceptibly from the one to the other. For a Monarchy readily becomes a Tyranny, an Aristocracy an Oligarchy, while a Democracy tends to degenerate into Anarchy. So that if the founder of a state should establish any one of these three forms of government, he establishes it for a short time only, since no precaution he may take can prevent it from sliding into its contrary, by reason of the close resemblance that, in this case, the virtue bears to the vice.

These diversities in the form of government spring up among men by chance. For in the beginning of the world, its inhabitants, being few in number, for a time lived scattered after the fashion of beasts; but afterward, as they increased and multiplied, gathered themselves into societies, and, the better to protect themselves, began to seek who among them was the strongest and of the highest courage, to whom, making him their head, they tendered obedience. Next arose the knowledge of such things as are honorable and good, as opposed to those that are bad and shameful. For observing that when a man wronged his benefactor, hatred was universally felt for the one and sympathy for the other, and that the ungrateful were blamed, while those who showed gratitude were honored, and reflecting that the wrongs they saw done to others might be done to themselves, to escape these they resorted to making laws and fixing punishments against any who should transgress them, and in this way grew the recognition of justice. Whereupon it came that afterward, in choosing their rulers, men no longer looked about for the strongest, but for him who was the most prudent and the most just.

But, presently, when sovereignty grew to be hereditary and no longer elective, hereditary sovereigns began to degenerate from their ancestors, and, quitting worthy courses, took up the notion that princes had nothing to do but to surpass the rest of the world in sumptuous display and wantonness, and whatever else ministers to pleasure, so that the prince coming to be hated, and therefore to feel fear, and passing from fear to infliction of injuries, a tyranny soon sprang up. Forthwith there began movements to overthrow the prince, and plots and conspiracies against him undertaken not by those who were weak, or afraid for themselves, but by such as being conspicuous for their birth, courage, wealth, and station, could not tolerate the shameful life of the tyrant. The multitude, following the lead of these powerful men, took up arms against the prince and, he being got rid of, obeyed these others as their liberators—who, on their part, holding in hatred the name of sole ruler, formed themselves into a government and at first, while the recollection of past tyranny was still fresh, observed the laws they themselves made, and postponing personal advantage to the common welfare, administered affairs both publicly and privately with the utmost diligence and zeal. But this government passing, afterward, to their descendants who, never having been taught in the school of Adversity, knew nothing of the vicissitudes of Fortune, these not choosing to rest content with mere civil equality, but abandoning themselves to avarice, ambition, and lust, converted, without respect to civil rights what had been a government of the best into a government of the few, and so very soon met with the same fate as the tyrant.

For the multitude loathing its rulers, lent itself to any who ventured, in whatever way, to attack them; when some one man speedily arose who with the aid of the people overthrew them. But the recollection of the tyrant and of the wrongs suffered at his hands being still fresh in the minds of the people, who therefore felt no desire to restore the monarchy, they had recourse to a popular government, which they established on such a footing that neither king nor nobles had any place in it. And because all governments inspire respect at the first, this government also lasted for a while, but not for long, and seldom after the generation that brought it into existence had died out. For, suddenly, liberty passed into license, wherein neither private worth nor public authority was respected, but, everyone living as he liked, a thousand wrongs were done daily. Whereupon, whether driven by necessity, or on the suggestion of some wiser man among them and to escape anarchy, the people reverted to a monarchy, from which, step by step, in the manner and for the causes already assigned, they came round once more to license. For this is the circle revolving within which all states are and have been governed; although in the same state the same forms of government rarely repeat themselves, because hardly any state can have such vitality as to pass through such a cycle more than once, and still together. For it may be expected that in some sea of disaster, when a state must always be wanting prudent counsels and in strength, it will become subject to some neighboring and better-governed state; though assuming this not to happen, it might well pass for an indefinite period from one of these forms of government to another.

I say, then, that all these six forms of government are pernicious— the three good kinds from their brief duration, the three bad from their inherent badness. Wise legislators therefore, knowing these defects, and avoiding each of these forms in its simplicity, have made choice of a form which shares in the qualities of all the first three, and which they judge to be more stable and lasting than any of these separately. For where we have a monarchy, an aristocracy, and a democracy existing together in the same city, each of the three serves as a check upon the other.

Among those who have earned special praise by devising a consti-tution of this nature, was Lycurgus, who so framed the laws of Sparta as to assign their proper functions to kings, nobles, and commons, and in this way established a government, which, to his great glory and to the peace and tranquility of his country, lasted for more than eight hundred years. The contrary, however, happened in the case of Solon, who, by the turn he gave to the institutions of Athens, created there a purely democratic government, of such brief duration that he himself lived to witness the beginning of the despotism of Pisistratus. And although, forty years later, the heirs of Pisistratus were driven out, and Athens recovered her freedom, nevertheless because she reverted to the same form of government as had been established by Solon, she could maintain it for only a hundred years more, for though to preserve it many ordinances were passed for repressing the ambition of the great and the turbulence of the people, against which Solon had not provided, still, since neither the monarchic nor the aristocratic element was given a place in her constitution, Athens, as compared with Sparta, had but a short life.

But let us now turn to Rome, which city, although she had no Lycurgus to give her from the first such a constitution as would preserve her long in freedom, through a series of accidents, caused by the contests between the commons and the senate, obtained by chance what the foresight of her founders failed to provide. So that Fortune, if she bestowed not her first favors on Rome, bestowed her second—because, although the original institutions of this city were defective, still they lay not outside the true path that could bring them to perfection. For Romulus and the other kings made many and good laws, and such as were not incompatible with freedom; but because they sought to found a kingdom and not a commonwealth, when the city became free many things were found wanting that in the interest of liberty it was necessary to supply, since these kings had not supplied them. And although the kings of Rome lost their sovereignty, in the manner and for the causes mentioned above, nevertheless those who drove them out, by at once creating two consuls to take their place, preserved in Rome the regal authority while banishing from it the regal throne, so that as both senate and consuls were included in that republic, it in fact possessed two of the elements above enumerated, to wit, the monarchic and the aristocratic.

It then only remained to assign its place to the popular element, and the Roman nobles growing insolent from causes that shall be noticed hereafter, the commons against them, when, not to lose the whole of their power, they were forced to concede a share to the people, while with the share that remained, the senate and consuls retained so much authority that they still held their own place in the republic. In this way the tribunes of the people came to be created, after whose creation the stability of the state was much augmented, since each the three forms of government had now its due influence allowed it. And such was the good fortune of Rome that although her government passed from the kings to the nobles, and from these to the people, by the steps and for the reasons noticed above, still the entire authority of the kingly element was not sacrificed to strengthen the authority of the nobles, nor were the nobles divested of their authority to bestow it on the commons; but three, blending together, made up a perfect state, which perfection, as shall be fully shown in the next two chapters, was reached through the dissensions of the commons and the senate.

IV

That the Dissensions between the Senate and Commons of Rome Made Rome Free and Powerful

T OUCHING THOSE TUMULTS that prevailed in Rome from the extinction of the Tarquins to the creation of the tribunes the discussion of which I have no wish to avoid, and as to certain other matters of a like nature, I desire to say something in opposition to the opinion of many who assert that Rome was a turbulent city, and had fallen into utter disorder, that had not her good fortune and military prowess made amends for other defects, she would have been inferior to every other republic.

I cannot indeed deny that the good fortune and the armies of Rome were the causes of her empire, yet it certainly seems to me that those holding this opinion fail to perceive that in a state where there are good soldiers there must be good order, and, generally speaking, good fortune. And looking to the other circumstances of this city, I affirm that those who condemn these dissensions between the nobles and the commons condemn what was the prime cause of Rome becoming free, and give more heed to the tumult and uproar wherewith these dissensions were attended than to the good results that followed from them, not reflecting that while in every republic there are two conflicting factions, that of the people and that of the nobles, it is in this conflict that all laws favorable to freedom have their origin, as may readily be seen to have been the case in Rome. For from the time of the Tarquins to that of the Gracchi, a period of over three hundred years, the tumults in Rome seldom gave occasion to punishment by exile, and very seldom to bloodshed. So that we cannot truly declare those tumults to have been disastrous, or that republic to have been disorderly, which during all that time, on account of her internal broils, banished no more than eight or ten of her citizens, put very few to death, and rarely inflicted money penalties. Nor can we reasonably pronounce that city ill-governed wherein we find so many instances of virtue, for virtuous actions have their origin in right training, right training in wise laws, and wise laws in these very tumults that many would thoughtlessly condemn. For he who looks well to the results of these tumults will find that they did not lead to banishments, nor to violence hurtful to the common good, but to laws and ordinances beneficial to the public liberty. And should any object that the behavior of the Romans was extravagant and outrageous—that for the assembled people to be heard shouting against the senate, the senate against the people; for the whole commons to be seen rushing wildly through the streets, closing their shops, and quitting the town, were things that might well affright him even who only reads of them—it may be answered that the inhabitants of all cities, more especially of cities that seek to make use of the people in matters of importance, have their own ways of giving expression to their wishes; among which the city of Rome had the custom that when its people sought to have a law passed they followed one or another of those courses mentioned above, or else refused to be enrolled as soldiers when, to pacify them, something of their demands had to be conceded. But the demands of a free people are hurtful to freedom, since they originate either in being oppressed, or in the fear that they are about to be so. When this fear is groundless, it finds its remedy in public meetings, wherein some worthy person may come forward and show the people by argument that they are deceiving themselves. For though they are ignorant, the people are not therefore, as Cicero says, incapable of being taught the truth, but are readily convinced when it is told to them by one in whose honesty they can trust.

We should, therefore, be careful how we censure the government of Rome, and should reflect that all the great results effected by that republic could not have come about without good cause. And if the popular tumults led the creation of the tribunes, they merit all praise, since these magistrates not only gave its due influence to the popular voice in the government, but also acted as the guardians of Roman freedom, as shall be clearly shown in the following chapter.

VI

*Whether It Was Possible in Rome
to Contrive Such a Government as
Would Have Composed the Differences
between the Commons and the Senate*

I HAVE SPOKEN ABOVE of the effects produced in Rome by the controversies between the commons and the senate. Now, as these lasted down to the time of the Gracchi, when they brought about the overthrow of freedom, some may think it matter for regret that Rome should not have achieved the great things she did, without being torn by such disputes. Wherefore, it seems to me worthwhile to consider whether the government of Rome could ever have been constituted in such a way as to prevent such controversies.

In making this inquiry we must first look to those republics that have enjoyed freedom for a great while, undisturbed by any violent contentions or tumults, and see what their government was, and whether it would have been possible to introduce it into Rome. Of such republics we have an example in ancient times in Sparta, in modern times in Venice, both of which states I have already made mention. Sparta created for herself a government consisting of a king and a limited senate. Venice has made no distinction in the titles of her rulers, all qualified to take part in her government being classed under the one designation of "Gentlemen," an arrangement due rather to chance than to the foresight of those who gave this state its constitution. For many persons, from causes already noticed, seeking shelter on these rocks on which Venice now stands, after they had so multiplied that if they were to continue to live together it became necessary for them to frame laws, established a form of government; and assembling often in their councils to consult for the interests of their city, when it seemed to them that their numbers were sufficient for political existence, they closed the entrance to civil rights against all who came afterward to live there, not allowing them to take any part in the management of affairs. And when in course of time there came to be many citizens excluded from the government, to add to the importance of the governing body, they named these "Gentlemen" (*gentiluomini*), the others "Plebeians" (*popolani*). And this distinction could grow up and maintain itself without causing disturbance; for as at the time of its origin, whosoever then lived in Venice was made one of the governing body, none had reason to complain, while those who came to live there afterward, finding the government in a completed form, had neither ground nor opportunity to object. No ground, because nothing was taken from them, and no opportunity, because those in authority kept them under control, and never employed them in affairs in which they could acquire importance. Besides which, they who came later to dwell in Venice were not so numerous as to destroy all proportion between the governors and the governed, the number of the "Gentlemen" being as great as, or greater than that of the "Plebeians." For these reasons, therefore, it was possible for Venice to make her constitution what it is, and to maintain it without divisions.

Sparta, again, being governed, as I have said, by a king and a limited senate, was able to maintain herself for the long period she did, because, from the country being thinly inhabited and further influx of population forbidden, and from the laws of Lycurgus (the observance whereof removed all ground of disturbance) being held in high esteem, the citizens were able to continue long in unity. For

Lycurgus having by his laws established in Sparta great equality as to property, but less equality as to rank, there prevailed there an equal poverty; and the commons were less ambitious, because the offices of the state, which were held to their exclusion, were confined to a few, and because the nobles never by harsh treatment aroused in them any desire to usurp these offices. And this was due to the Spartan kings, who, being appointed to that dignity for life, and placed in the midst of this nobility, had no stronger support to their authority than in defending the people against injustice. Whereupon it resulted that as the people neither feared nor coveted the power that they did not possess, the conflicts that might have arisen between them and the nobles were escaped, together with the causes that would have led to them, and in this way they were able to live long united. But of this unity in Sparta there were two chief causes: one, the fewness of its inhabitants, which allowed of their being governed by a few; the other, that by denying foreigners admission into their country, the people had less occasion to become corrupted, and never so increased in numbers as to prove troublesome to their few rulers.

Weighing all those circumstances, we see that to have kept Rome in the same tranquility wherein these republics were kept, one of two courses must have been followed by her legislators; for either, like the Venetians, they must have refrained from employing the commons in war, or else, like the Spartans, they must have closed their country to foreigners. Whereas, in both particulars, they did the opposite, arming the commons and increasing their number, and thus affording endless occasions for disorder. And had the Roman commonwealth grown to be more tranquil, this inconvenience would have resulted, that it must at the same time have grown weaker, since the road would have been closed to that greatness to which it came, for in removing the causes of her tumults, Rome must have interfered with the causes of her growth.

And he who looks carefully into the matter will find that in all human affairs, we cannot rid ourselves of one inconvenience without running into another. So that if you would have your people numerous and warlike, to the end that with their aid you may establish a great empire, you will have them of such a sort as you cannot afterward control at your pleasure; while should you keep them few and unwarlike, to the end that you may govern them easily, you will be unable, should you extend your dominions, to preserve them, and will become so contemptible as to be the prey of any who attack you. For which reason in all our deliberations we ought to consider where we are likely to encounter least inconvenience, and accept that as the course to be preferred, since we shall never find any line of action entirely free from disadvantage.

Rome might, therefore, following the example of Sparta, have created a king for life and a senate of limited numbers, but desiring to become a great empire, she could not, like Sparta, have restricted the number of her citizens. So that to have created a king for life and a limited senate had been of little service to her.

Were anyone, therefore, about to found a wholly new republic, he would have to consider whether he desired it to increase as Rome did in territory and dominion, or to continue within narrow limits. In the former case he would have to shape its constitution as nearly as possible on the pattern of the Roman, leaving room for dissensions and popular tumults, for without a great and warlike population no republic can ever increase, or increasing maintain itself. In the second case he might give his republic a constitution like that of Venice or Sparta, but since extension is the ruin of such republics, the legislator would have to provide in every possible way against the state that he had founded making any additions to its territories. For these, when superimposed upon a feeble republic, are sure to be fatal to it: as we see to have been the case with Sparta and Venice, the former of which, after subjugating nearly all Greece, on sustaining a trifling reverse, betrayed the insufficiency of her foundations, for when, after the revolt of Thebes under Pelopidas, other cities also rebelled, the Spartan kingdom was utterly overthrown. Venice in like manner, after gaining possession of a great portion of Italy (most of it not by her arms but by her wealth and subtlety), when her strength was put to the proof, lost all in one pitched battle.

I can well believe, then, that to found a republic that shall long endure, the best plan may be to give it internal institutions like those of Sparta or Venice; placing it in a naturally strong situation, and so fortifying it that none can expect to get the better of it easily, yet, at the same time, not making it so great as to be formidable to its neighbors, since by taking these precautions, it might long enjoy its independence. For there are two causes that lead to wars being made against a republic: one, your desire to be its master, the other the fear lest it should master you—both of which dangers the precaution indicated will go far to remove. For if, as we are to assume, this republic be well prepared for defense, and consequently difficult of attack, it will seldom or never happen that anyone will form the design to attack it, and while it keeps within its own boundaries, and is seen from experience not to be influenced by ambition, no one will be led, out of fear for himself, to make war upon it, more particularly when its laws and constitution forbid its extension. And were it possible to maintain things in this equilibrium, I veritably believe that herein would be found the true form of political life, and the true tranquility of a republic. But all human affairs being in movement, and incapable of remaining as they are, they must either rise or fall, and to many conclusions to which we are not led by reason, we are brought by necessity. So that when we have given institutions to a state on the footing that it is to maintain itself without enlargement, should necessity require its enlargement, its foundations will be cut from below it, and its downfall quickly ensue. On the other hand, were a republic so favored by Heaven as to lie under no necessity of making war, the result of this ease would be to make it effeminate and divided, which two evils together, and each by itself, would ensure its ruin. And since it is impossible, as I believe, to bring about an equilibrium, or to adhere strictly to the mean path, we must, in arranging our republic, consider what is the more honorable course for it to take, and so contrive that even if necessity compel its enlargement, it may be able to keep what it gains.

But returning to the point first raised, I believe it necessary for us to follow the method of the Romans and not that of the other republics, for I know of no middle way. We must, consequently, put up with those dissensions that arise between commons and senate, looking on them as evils that cannot be escaped if we would arrive at the greatness of Rome.

In connection with the arguments here used to prove that the authority of the tribunes was essential in Rome to the guardianship of freedom, we may naturally go on to show what advantages result to a republic from the power of impeachment, which, together with others, was conferred upon the tribunes—a subject to be noticed in the following chapter.

VII

That to Preserve Liberty in a State There Must Exist the Right to Accuse

T
O THOSE SET FORWARD in a commonwealth as guardians of public freedom, no more useful or necessary authority can be given than the power to accuse, either before the people, or before some council or tribunal, those citizens who in any way have offended against the liberty of their country.

A law of this kind has two effects most beneficial to a state: first, that the citizens, from fear of being accused, do not engage in attempts hurtful to the state, or doing so, are put down at once and without respect of persons; and next, that a vent is given for the escape of all those evil humors that, from whatever cause, gather in cities against particular citizens, for unless an outlet be duly provided for these by the laws, they flow into irregular channels and overwhelm the state. There is nothing, therefore, that contributes so much to the stability and permanence of a state, as to take care that the fermentation of these disturbing humors be supplied by operation of law with a recognized outlet. This might be shown by many examples, but by none so clearly as by that of Coriolanus related by Livius, where he tells us that at a time when the Roman nobles were angry with the plebeians (thinking that the appointment of tribunes for their protection had made them too powerful), it happened that Rome was visited by a grievous famine, to meet which the senate sent to Sicily for corn. But

Coriolanus, hating the commons, sought to persuade the senate that now was the time to punish them, and to deprive them of the authority that they had usurped to the prejudice of the nobles, by withholding the distribution of corn, and so suffering them to perish of hunger. Which advice of his coming to the ears of the people, kindled them to such fury against him that they would have slain him as he left the senate house had not the tribunes cited him to appear and answer before them to a formal charge.

In respect of this incident I repeat what I have just now said, how useful and necessary it is for republics to provide by their laws a channel by which the displeasure of the multitude against a single citizen may find a vent. For when none such is regularly provided, recourse will be had to irregular channels, and these will assuredly lead to much worse results. For when a citizen is borne down by the operation or the ordinary laws, even though he be wronged, little or no disturbance is occasioned to the state: the injury he suffers not being wrought by private violence, nor by foreign force, which are the causes of the overthrow of free institutions, but by public authority and in accordance with public ordinances, which, having definite limits set them, are not likely to pass beyond these so as to endanger the commonwealth. For proof of which I am content to rest on this old example of Coriolanus, since all may see what a disaster it would have been for Rome had he been violently put to death by the people. For, as between citizen and citizen, a wrong would have been done affording ground for fear, fear would have sought defense, defense have led to faction, faction to divisions in the state, and these to its ruin. But the matter being taken up by those whose office it was to deal with it, all the evils that must have followed had it been left in private hands were escaped.

In Florence, on the other hand, and in our own days, we have seen what violent commotions follow when the people cannot show their displeasure against particular citizens in a form recognized by the laws, in the instance of Francesco Valori, at one time looked upon as the foremost citizen of our republic. But many thinking him ambitious, and likely from his high spirit and daring to overstep the limits of civil freedom, and there being no way to oppose him save by setting up an adverse faction, the result was that, apprehending irregular attacks, he sought to gain partisans for his support, while his opponents, on their side, having no course open to them of which the laws approved, resorted to courses of which the laws did not approve, and, at last, to open violence. And as his influence had to be attacked by unlawful methods, these were attended by injury not to him only, but to many other noble citizens—whereas, could he have been met by constitutional restraints, his power might have been broken without injury to any save himself. I might also cite from our Florentine history the fall of Piero Soderini, which had no other cause than there not being in our republic any law under which powerful and ambitious citizens can be impeached. For to form a tribunal by which a powerful citizen is to be tried, eight judges only are not enough; the judges must be numerous, because a few will always do the will of a few. But had there been proper methods for obtaining redress, the people either would have impeached Piero if he was guilty, and thus have given vent to their displeasure without calling in the Spanish army, or, if he was innocent, would not have ventured, through fear of being accused themselves, to have taken proceedings against him. So that in either case the bitter spirit that was the cause of all the disorder would have had an end. Wherefore, when we find one of the parties in a state calling in a foreign power, we may safely conclude that it is because the defective laws of that state provide no escape for those malignant humors that are natural to men, which can best be done by arranging for an impeachment before a sufficient number of judges, and by giving countenance to this procedure. This was so well contrived in Rome that in spite of the perpetual struggle maintained between the commons and the senate, neither the senate nor the commons, nor any single citizen, ever sought redress at the hands of a foreign power—for having a remedy at home, there was no need to seek one abroad.

Although the examples above cited be proof sufficient of what I affirm, I desire to adduce one other, recorded by Titus Livius in his history, where he relates that a sister of Aruns having been violated by a Lucumo of Clusium, the chief of the Etruscan towns, Aruns being unable, from the interest of her ravisher, to avenge her, betook himself to the Gauls who ruled in the province we now name Lombardy, and besought them to come with an armed force to Clusium, showing them how with advantage to themselves they might avenge his wrongs. Now, had Aruns seen that he could have had redress through the laws of his country, he never would have resorted to these Barbarians for help.

But as the right to accuse is beneficial in a republic, so calumny, on the other hand, is useless and hurtful, as in the following chapter I shall proceed to show.

VIII

That Calumny Is as Hurtful in a Commonwealth as the Power to Accuse Is Useful

S
UCH WERE THE SERVICES rendered to Rome by Furius Camillus in rescuing her from the oppression of the Gauls, that no Roman, however high his degree or station, held it derogatory to yield place to him, save only Manlius Capitolinus, who could not brook such glory and distinction being given to another. For he thought that in saving the Capitol, he had himself done as much as Camillus to preserve Rome, and that in respect of his other warlike achievements he was no whit behind him. So that, bursting with jealousy, and unable to remain at rest by reason of the other's renown, and seeing no way to sow discord among the Fathers, he set himself to spread abroad sinister reports among the commons, throwing out, among other charges, that the treasure collected to be given to the Gauls, but which, afterward, was withheld, had been embezzled by certain citizens, and if recovered might be turned to public uses in relieving the people from taxes or from private debts. These assertions so prevailed with the commons that they began to hold meetings and to raise what tumults they liked throughout the city. But this displeasing the senate, and the matter appearing to them grave and dangerous, they appointed a dictator to inquire into it, and to restrain the attacks of Manlius. The dictator, forthwith,

caused Manlius to be cited before him, and these two were thus brought face to face in the presence of the whole city, the dictator surrounded by the nobles, and Manlius by the commons. The latter, being desired to say with whom the treasure of which he had spoken was to be found, since the senate were as anxious to know this as the commons, made no direct reply, but answered evasively that it was needless to tell them what they already knew. Whereupon the dictator ordered him to prison.

In this passage we are taught how hateful a thing is calumny in all free states, as, indeed, in every society, and how we must neglect no means that may serve to check it. And there can be no more effective means for checking calumny than by affording ample facilities for impeachment, which is as useful in a commonwealth as the other is pernicious. And between them there is this difference, that calumny needs neither witness nor circumstantial proof to establish it, so that any man may be calumniated by any other, but not impeached, since impeachment demands that there be substantive charges made, and trustworthy evidence to support them. Again, it is before the magistrates, the people, or the courts of justice that men are impeached, but in the streets and market places that they are calumniated. Calumny, therefore, is most rife in that state wherein impeachment is least practiced, and the laws least favor it. For which reasons the legislator should so shape the laws of his state that it shall be possible therein to impeach any of its citizens without fear or favor, and, after duly providing for this, should visit calumniators with the sharpest punishments. Those punished will have no cause to complain, since it was in their power to have impeached openly where they have secretly calumniated. Where this is not seen to, grave disorders will always ensue. For calumnies sting without disabling, and those who are stung, being more moved by hatred of their detractors than by fear of the things they say against them, seek revenge.

This matter, as we have said, was well arranged for in Rome, but has always been badly regulated in our city of Florence. And as the Roman ordinances with regard to it were productive of much good, so the want of them in Florence has bred much mischief. For anyone reading the history of our city may perceive how many calumnies have at all times been aimed against those of its citizens who have taken a leading part in its affairs. Thus, of one it would be said that he had plundered the public treasury, of another that he had failed in some enterprise because he had been bribed, of a third that this or the other disaster had originated in his ambition. Hence hatred sprung up on every side, and hatred growing to division, these led to factions, and these again to ruin. But had there existed in Florence some procedure whereby citizens might have been impeached, and calumniators punished, numberless disorders that have taken there would have been prevented. For citizens who were impeached, whether con-demned or acquitted, would have had no power to injure the state, and they would have been impeached far seldomer than they have been calumniated, for calumny, as I have said already, is an easier matter than impeachment.

Some, indeed, have made use of calumny as a means for raising themselves to power, and have found their advantage in traducing eminent citizens who withstood their designs, for by taking the part of the people, and confirming them in their ill-opinion of these great men, they made them their friends. Of this, though I could give many instances, I shall content myself with one. At the siege of Lucca the Florentine army was commanded by Messer Giovanni Guicciardini, as its commissary, through whose bad generalship or ill-fortune the town was not taken. But whatever the cause of this failure, Messer Giovanni had the blame, and the rumor ran that he had been bribed by the people of Lucca. Which calumny being fostered by his enemies, brought Messer Giovanni to very verge of despair; and though to clear himself he would willingly have given himself up to the Captain of Justice he found he could not, there being no provision in the laws of the republic that allowed of his doing so. Hence arose the bitterest hostility between the friends of Messer Giovanni, who were mostly of the old nobility (*grandi*), and those who sought to reform the government of Florence; and from this and the like causes, the affair grew to such dimensions as to bring about the downfall of our republic.

Manlius Capitolinus, then, was a calumniator, not an accuser; and in their treatment of him the Romans showed how calumniators should be dealt with—by which I mean that they should be forced to become accusers, and if their accusation be proved true, should be rewarded, or at least not punished, but if proved false should be punished as Manlius was.

XI

Of the Religion of the Romans

THOUGH ROME HAD ROMULUS for her first founder, and as a daughter owed him her being and nurture, nevertheless, when the institutions of Romulus were seen by Heaven to be insufficient for so great a state, the Roman senate were moved to choose Numa Pompilius as his successor, that he might look to all matters that Romulus had neglected. He finding the people fierce and turbulent, and desiring with the help of the peaceful arts to bring them to order and obedience, called in the aid of religion as essential to the maintenance of civil society, and gave it such a form that for many ages God was nowhere so much feared as in that republic. The effect of this was to render easy any enterprise in which the senate or great men of Rome thought fit to engage. And whosoever pays heed to an infinity of actions performed, sometimes by the Roman people collectively, often by single citizens, will see that, esteeming the power of God beyond that of man, they dreaded far more to violate their oath than to transgress the laws, as is clearly shown by the examples of Scipio and of Manlius Torquatus. For after the defeat of the Romans by Hannibal at Cannae, many citizens together resolved, in their terror and dismay, to abandon Italy and seek refuge in Sicily. But Scipio, getting word of this, went among them, and menacing them with his naked sword, made them swear never to abandon their country. Again, when Lucius Manlius was accused by the tribune Marcus Pomponius, before the day fixed for trial, Titus Manlius, afterward named Torquatus, son to Lucius, went to seek this Marcus, and threatening him with death if he did not withdraw the charge against his father, compelled him to swear compliance; and he, through fear, having sworn, kept his oath. In the first of these two instances, therefore, citizens whom love of their country and its laws could not have retained in Italy, were kept there by the oath forced upon them; and in the second, the tribune Marcus, to keep his oath, laid aside the hatred he bore the father, and overlooked the injury done him by the son, and his own dishonor. And this from no other cause than the religion that Numa had impressed upon this city.

And it will be plain to anyone who carefully studies Roman history how much religion helped in disciplining the army, in uniting the people, in keeping good men good, and putting bad men to shame; so that had it to be decided to which prince, Romulus or Numa, Rome owed the greater debt, I think the balance must turn in favor of Numa—for when religion is once established you may readily bring in arms, but where you have arms without religion it is not easy afterward to bring in religion. We see, too, that while Romulus in order to create a senate, and to establish his other ordinances civil and military, needed no support from Divine authority, this was very necessary to Numa, who feigned to have intercourse with a Nymph by whose advice he was guided in counselling the people. And this, because desiring to introduce in Rome new and untried institutions, he feared that his own authority might not achieve his end. Nor, indeed, has any attempt ever been made to introduce unusual laws among a people without resorting to Divine authority, since without such sanction they never would have been accepted. For the wise recognize many things to be good that do not bear such reasons on the face of them as command their acceptance by others; wherefore, wise men who would obviate these difficulties have recourse to Divine aid. Thus did Lycurgus, thus Solon, and thus have done many besides who have had the same end in view.

The Romans, accordingly, admiring the prudence and virtues of Numa, assented to all the measures that he recommended. This, however, is to be said, that the circumstance of these times being deeply tinctured with religious feeling, and of the men with whom he had to deal being rude and ignorant, gave Numa better facility to carry out his plans, as enabling him to mold his subjects readily to any new impression. And, doubtless, he who should seek at the present day to form a new commonwealth would find the task easier among a race of simple mountaineers than among the dwellers in cities where society is corrupt, as the sculptor can more easily carve a fair statue from a rough block, than from the block that has been badly shaped out by another. But taking all this into account, I maintain that the religion introduced by Numa was one of the chief causes of the prosperity of Rome, since it gave rise to good ordinances, which in turn brought with them good fortune, and with good fortune, happy issues to whatsoever was undertaken.

And as the observance of the ordinances of religion is the cause of the greatness of a state, so their neglect is the occasion of its decline, since a kingdom without the fear of God must either fall to pieces, or must be maintained by the fear of some prince who supplies that influence not supplied by religion. But since the lives of princes are short, the life of this prince, also, and with it his influence, must soon come to an end; so it happens that a kingdom that rests wholly on the qualities of its prince, lasts for a brief time only, because these qualities, terminating with his life, are rarely renewed in his successor. For as Dante wisely says:

"Seldom through the boughs doth human worth renew itself; for such the will of Him who gives it, that to Him we may ascribe it."*

It follows, therefore, that the safety of a commonwealth or kingdom lies not in its having a ruler who governs it prudently while he lives, but in having one who so orders things that, when he dies, the state may still maintain itself. And though it is easier to impose new institutions or a new faith on rude and simple men, it is not therefore impossible to persuade their adoption by men who are civilized, and who do not think themselves rude. The people of Florence do not esteem themselves rude or ignorant, and yet were persuaded by the Friar Girolamo Savonarola that he spoke with God. Whether in this he said truth or no, I take not on me to pronounce, since of so great a man we must speak with reverence—but this I do say, that very many believed him without having witnessed anything extraordinary to warrant their belief, his life, his doctrines, the matter whereof he treated, being sufficient to enlist their faith.

Let no man, therefore, lose heart from thinking that he cannot do what others have done before him, for, as I said in my Preface, men are born, and live, and die, always in accordance with the same rules.

---

* *L'umana probitate: e questo vuole Quei che la dà, perchè da lui si chiami. Purg.* vii. 121–123.

XVII

That a Corrupt People Obtaining Freedom Can Hardly Preserve It

I BELIEVE THAT if her kings had not been expelled, Rome must very soon have become a weak and inconsiderable state. For seeing to what a pitch of corruption these kings had come, we may conjecture that if two or three more like reigns had followed, and the taint spread from the head to the members, so soon as the latter became infected, cure would have been hopeless. But from the head being removed while the trunk was still sound, it was not difficult for the Romans to return to a free and constitutional government.

It may be assumed, however, as most certain, that a corrupted city living under a prince can never recover its freedom, even were the prince and all his line to be exterminated. For in such a city it must necessarily happen that one prince will be replaced by another, and that things will never settle down until a new lord be established; unless, indeed, the combined goodness and valor of some one citizen should maintain freedom, which, even then, will endure only for his lifetime, as happened twice in Syracuse, first under the rule of Dion, and again under that of Timoleon, whose virtues while they lived kept their city free, but on whose death it fell once more under a tyranny.

But the strongest example that can be given is that of Rome, which on the expulsion of the Tarquins was able at once to seize on liberty and to maintain it; yet, on the deaths of Caesar, Caligula, and

Nero, and on the extinction of the Julian line, was not only unable to establish her freedom, but did not even venture a step in that direction. Results so opposite arising in one and the same city can only be accounted for by this, that in the time of the Tarquins the Roman people were not yet corrupted, but in these later times had become utterly corrupt. For on the first occasion, nothing more was needed to prepare and determine them to shake off their kings than that they should be bound by oath to suffer no king ever again to reign in Rome; whereas, afterward, the authority and austere virtue of Brutus, backed by all the legions of the East, could not rouse them to maintain their hold of that freedom which he, following in the footsteps of the first Brutus, had won for them—and this because of the corruption wherewith the people had been infected by the Marian faction, whereof Caesar becoming head, was able so to blind the multitude that it saw not the yoke under which it was about to lay its neck.

Though this example of Rome be more complete than any other, I desire to instance likewise, to the same effect, certain peoples well known in our own days, and I maintain that no change, however grave or violent, could ever restore freedom to Naples or Milan, because in these states the entire body of the people has grown corrupted. And so we find that Milan, although desirous to return to a free form of government, on the death of Filippo Visconti, had neither the force nor the skill needed to preserve it.

Most fortunate, therefore, was it for Rome that her kings grew corrupt soon, so as to be driven out before the taint of their corruption had reached the vitals of the city. For it was because these were sound that the endless commotions that took place in Rome, so far from being hurtful, were, from their object being good, beneficial to the commonwealth. From which we may draw this inference, that where the body of the people is still sound, tumults and other like disorders do little hurt, but that where it has become corrupted, laws, however well devised, are of no advantage, unless imposed by someone whose paramount authority causes them to be observed until the community be once more restored to a sound and healthy condition.

Whether this has ever happened I know not, nor whether it ever can happen. For we see, as I have said a little way back, that a city that owing to its pervading corruption has once begun to decline, if it is to recover at all, must be saved not by the excellence of the people collectively, but of some one man then living among them, on whose death it at once relapses into its former plight—as happened with Thebes, in which the virtue of Epaminondas made it possible while he lived to preserve the form of a free government, but which fell again on his death into its old disorders, the reason being that hardly any ruler lives so long as to have time to accustom to right methods a city that has long been accustomed to wrong. Wherefore, unless things be put on a sound footing by some one ruler who lives to a very advanced age, or by two virtuous rulers succeeding one another, the city upon their death at once falls back into ruin, or, if it be preserved, must be so by incurring great risks, and at the cost of much blood. For the corruption I speak of is wholly incompatible with a free government, because it results from an inequality that pervades the state and can only be removed by employing unusual and very violent remedies, such as few are willing or know how to employ, as in another place I shall more fully explain.

XVIII

*How a Free Government Existing in
a Corrupt City May Be Preserved,
or Not Existing May Be Created*

I THINK IT NEITHER out of place, nor inconsistent with what has been said above, to consider whether a free government existing in a corrupt city can be maintained, or, not existing, can be introduced. And on this head I say that it is very difficult to bring about either of these results, and next to impossible to lay down rules as to how it may be done, because the measures to be taken must vary with the degree of corruption that prevails.

Nevertheless, since it is well to reason things out, I will not pass this matter by, but will assume, in the first place, the case of a very corrupt city, and then take the case of one in which corruption has reached a still greater height; but where corruption is universal, no laws or institutions will ever have force to restrain it. Because as good customs stand in need of good laws for their support, so laws, that they may be respected, stand in need of good customs. Moreover, the laws and institutions established in a republic at its beginning, when men were good, are no longer suitable when they have become bad; but while the laws of a city are altered to suit its circumstances, its institutions rarely or never change, and so it results that the intro- duction of new laws is of no avail, because the institutions, remaining unchanged, corrupt them.

And to make this plainer, I say that in Rome it was first of all the institutions of the state, and next the laws as enforced by the magistrates, which kept the citizens under control. The institutions of the state consisted in the authority of the people, the senate, the tribunes, and the consuls; in the methods of choosing and appointing magistrates; and in the arrangements for passing laws. These institutions changed little, if at all, with circumstances. But the laws by which the people were controlled, as for instance the law relating to adultery, the sumptuary laws, the law as to canvassing at elections, and many others, were altered as the citizens grew more and more corrupted. Hence, the institutions of the state remaining the same although from the corruption of the people no longer suitable, amendments in the laws could not keep men good, though they might have proved very useful if at the time when they were made the institutions had likewise been reformed.

That its original institutions are no longer adapted to a city that has become corrupted is plainly seen in two matters of great moment, I mean in the appointment of magistrates and in the passing of laws. For the Roman people conferred the consulship and other great offices of their state on none save those who sought them, which was a good institution at first, because then none sought these offices save those who thought themselves worthy of them, and to be rejected was held disgraceful, so that, to be deemed worthy, all were on their best behavior. But in a corrupted city this institution grew to be most mischievous. For it was no longer those of greatest worth, but those who had most influence, who sought the magistracies, while all who were without influence, however deserving, refrained through fear. This untoward result was not reached all at once, but like other similar results, by gradual steps. For after subduing Africa and Asia, and reducing nearly the whole of Greece to submission, the Romans became perfectly assured of their freedom, and seemed to themselves no longer to have any enemy whom they had cause to fear. But this security and the weakness of their adversaries led them in conferring the consulship, no longer to look to merit, but only to favor, selecting for the office those who knew best how to pay court to them, not those who knew best how to vanquish their enemies. And afterward, instead of selecting those who were best liked, they came to select those who had most influence, and in this way, from the imperfection of their institutions, good men came to be wholly excluded.

Again, as to making laws, any of the tribunes and certain others of the magistrates were entitled to submit laws to the people, but before these were passed it was open to every citizen to speak either for or against them. This was a good system so long as the citizens were good, since it is always well that every man should be able to propose what he thinks may be of use to his country, and that all should be allowed to express their views with regard to his proposal; so that the people, having heard all, may resolve on what is best. But when the people grew depraved, this became a very mischievous institution, for then it was only the powerful who proposed laws, and these not in the interest of public freedom but of their own authority, and because, through fear, none durst speak against the laws they proposed, the people were either deceived or forced into voting their own destruction.

In order, therefore, that Rome after she had become corrupted might still preserve her freedom, it was necessary that, as in the course of events she had made new laws, so likewise she should frame new institutions, since different institutions and ordinances are needed in a corrupt state from those that suit a state that is not corrupted, for where the matter is wholly dissimilar, the form cannot be similar.

But since old institutions must either be reformed all at once, as soon as they are seen to be no longer expedient, or else gradually, as the imperfection of each is recognized, I say that each of these two courses is all but impossible. For to effect a gradual reform requires a sagacious man who can discern mischief while it is still remote and in the germ. But it may well happen that no such person is found in a city—or that, if found, he is unable to persuade others of what he is himself persuaded. For men used to living in one way are loath to leave it for another, especially when they are not brought face to face with the evil against which they should guard, and only have it indicated to them by conjecture. And as for a sudden reform of institutions that are seen by all to be no longer good, I say that defects that are easily discerned are not easily corrected, because for their correction it is not enough to use ordinary means, these being in themselves insufficient, but recourse must be had to extraordinary means, such as violence and arms, and, as a preliminary, you must become prince of the city, and be able to deal with it at your pleasure. But since the restoration of a state to new political life presupposes a good man, and to become prince of a city by violence presupposes a bad man, it can, consequently, very seldom happen that, although the end be good, a good man will be found ready to become a prince by evil ways, or that a bad man having become a prince will be disposed to act virtuously, or think of turning to good account his ill-acquired authority.

From all these causes comes the difficulty, or rather the impossibility, which a corrupted city finds in maintaining an existing free government, or in establishing a new one. So that had we to establish or maintain a government in that city, it would be necessary to give it a monarchical, rather than a popular form, in order that men too arrogant to be restrained by the laws might in some measure be kept in check by a power almost absolute, since to attempt to make them good otherwise would be a very cruel or a wholly futile endeavor. This, as I have said, was the method followed by Cleomenes; and if he, that he might stand alone, put to death the Ephori, and if Romulus, with a like object, put to death his brother and Titus Tatius the Sabine, and if both afterward made good use of the authority they thus acquired, it is nevertheless to be remembered that it was because neither Cleomenes nor Romulus had to deal with so corrupt a people as that of which I am now speaking, that they were able to effect their ends and to give a fair color to their acts.

XIX

*After a Strong Prince a Weak
Prince May Maintain Himself:
But after One Weak Prince No
Kingdom Can Stand a Second*

WHEN WE CONTEMPLATE the excellent qualities of Romulus, Numa, and Tullus, the first three kings of Rome, and note the methods that they followed, we recognize the extreme good fortune of that city in having her first king fierce and warlike, her second peaceful and religious, and her third, like the first, of a high spirit and more disposed to war than to peace. For it was essential for Rome that, almost at the outset of her career, a ruler should be found to lay the foundations of her civil life; but, after that had been done, it was necessary that her rulers should return to the virtues of Romulus, since otherwise the city must have grown feeble, and become a prey to her neighbors.

And here we may note that a prince who succeeds to another of superior valor may reign on by virtue of his predecessor's merits, and reap the fruits of his labors, but if he live to a great age, or if he be followed by another who is wanting in the qualities of the first, that then the kingdom must necessarily dwindle. Conversely, when two consecutive princes are of rare excellence, we commonly find them achieving results that win for them enduring renown. David, for example, not only surpassed in learning and judgment, but was so valiant in arms that, after conquering and subduing all his neighbors, he left to his young son Solomon a tranquil state, which the latter, though unskilled in the arts of war, could maintain by the arts of peace, and thus happily enjoy the inheritance of his father's valor. But Solomon could not transmit this inheritance to his son Rehoboam, who, neither resembling his grandfather in valor, nor his father in good fortune, with difficulty made good his right to a sixth part of the kingdom. In like manner Bajazet, sultan of the Turks, though a man of peace rather than of war, was able to enjoy the labors of Mahomet his father, who, like David, having subdued his neighbors, left his son a kingdom so safely established that it could easily be retained by him by peaceful arts. But had Selim, son to Bajazet, been like his father, and not like his grandfather, the Turkish monarchy must have been overthrown; as it is, he seems likely to outdo the fame of his grandsire.

I affirm it to be proved by these examples that after a valiant prince a feeble prince may maintain himself, but that no kingdom can stand when two feeble princes follow in succession, unless, as in the case of France, it be supported by its ancient ordinances. By feeble princes, I mean such as are not valiant in war. And, to put the matter shortly, it may be said that the great valor of Romulus left Numa a period of many years within which to govern Rome by peaceful arts; that after Numa came Tullus, who renewed by his courage the fame of Romulus; and that he in turn was succeeded by Ancus, a prince so gifted by nature that he could equally avail himself of the methods of peace or war; who setting himself at first to pursue the former, when he found that his neighbors judged him to be effeminate, and therefore held him in slight esteem, understood that to preserve Rome he must resort to arms and resemble Romulus rather than Numa. From whose example every ruler of a state may learn that a prince like Numa will hold or lose his power according as fortune and circumstances befriend him, but that the prince who resembles

Romulus, and like him is fortified with foresight and arms, will hold his state whatever befall, unless deprived of it by some stubborn and irresistible force. For we may reckon with certainty that if Rome had not had for her third king one who knew how to restore her credit by deeds of valor, she could not, or at any rate not without great difficulty, have afterward held her ground, nor could ever have achieved the great exploits she did.

And for these reasons Rome, while she lived under her kings, was in constant danger of destruction through a king who might be weak or bad.

XXVII

That Men Seldom Know How to
Be Wholly Good or Wholly Bad

WHEN IN THE YEAR 1505, Pope Julius II went to
Bologna to expel from that city the family of the
Bentivogli, who had been princes there for over a hundred years, it was also in his mind, as a part of the general design he
had planned against all those lords who had usurped Church lands,
to remove Giovanpagolo Baglioni, tyrant of Perugia. And coming to
Perugia with this intention and resolve, of which all men knew, he
would not wait to enter the town with a force sufficient for his protection, but entered it unattended by troops, although Giovanpagolo
was there with a great company of soldiers whom he had assembled
for his defense. And thus, urged on by that impetuosity that stamped
all his actions, accompanied only by his bodyguard, he committed
himself into the hands of his enemy, whom he forthwith carried away
with him, leaving a governor behind to hold the town for the Church.
All prudent men who were with the pope remarked on his temerity,
and on the pusillanimity of Giovanpagolo; nor could they conjecture
why the latter had not, to his eternal glory, availed himself of this
opportunity for crushing his enemy, and at the same time enriching
himself with plunder, the pope being attended by the whole College
of Cardinals with all their luxurious equipage. For it could not be
supposed that he was withheld by any promptings of goodness or

scruples of conscience, because in the breast of a profligate living in incest with his sister, and who to obtain the princedom had put his nephews and kinsmen to death, no virtuous impulse could prevail. So that the only inference to be drawn was that men know not how to be splendidly wicked or wholly good, and shrink in consequence from such crimes as are stamped with an inherent greatness or disclose a nobility of nature. For which reason Giovanpagolo, who thought nothing of incurring the guilt of incest, or of murdering his kinsmen, could not, or more truly durst not, avail himself of a fair occasion to do a deed that all would have admired; which would have won for him a deathless fame as the first to teach the prelates how little those who live and reign as they do are to be esteemed; and which would have displayed a greatness far transcending any infamy or danger that could attach to it.

XLIV

That the Multitude Is Helpless
Without a Head: And that We
Should Not with the Same Breath
Threaten and Ask Leave

WHEN VIRGINIA DIED by her father's hand, the commons of Rome withdrew under arms to the Sacred Hill. Whereupon the senate sent messengers to demand by what sanction they had deserted their commanders and assembled there in arms. And in such reverence was the authority of the senate held that the commons, lacking leaders, durst make no reply. "Not," says Titus Livius, "that they were at a loss what to answer, but because they had none to answer for them"—words that clearly show how helpless a thing is the multitude when without a head.

This defect was perceived by Virginius, at whose instance twenty military tribunes were appointed by the commons to be their spokesmen with the senate, and to negotiate terms; who, having asked that Valerius and Horatius might be sent to them, to whom their wishes would be made known, these declined to go until the decemvirs had laid down their office. When this was done, and Valerius and Horatius came to the hill where the commons were assembled, the latter demanded that tribunes of the people should be appointed; that in future there should be an appeal to the people from the magistrates of whatever degree; and that all the decemvirs should be given up to them to be burned alive. Valerius and Horatius approved the first two demands, but rejected the last as inhuman, telling the commons that "they were rushing into that very cruelty that they themselves had condemned in others," and counselling them to say nothing about the decemvirs, but to be satisfied to regain their own power and authority, since thus the way would be open to them for obtaining every redress.

Here we see plainly how foolish and unwise it is to ask a thing and with the same breath to say, "I desire this that I may inflict an injury." For we should never declare our intention beforehand, but watch for every opportunity to carry it out. So that it is enough to ask another for his weapons, without adding, "With these I purpose to destroy you," for when once you have secured his weapons, you can use them afterward as you please.

Excerpts from Book III

II

That on Occasion It Is
Wise to Feign Folly

NEVER DID ANY MAN by the most splendid achievements gain for himself so great a name for wisdom and prudence as is justly due to Junius Brutus for feigning to be a fool. And although Titus Livius mentions one cause only as having led him to assume this part, namely, that he might live more securely and look after his patrimony, yet on considering his behavior we may believe that in counterfeiting folly it was also his object to escape notice, and so find better convenience to overthrow the kings, and to free his country whenever an occasion offered. That this was in his mind is seen first of all from the interpretation he gave to the oracle of Apollo, when, to render the gods favorable to his designs, he pretended to stumble, and secretly kissed his mother earth; and, again, from this, that on the death of Lucretia, though her father, her husband, and others of her kinsmen were present, he was the first to draw the dagger from her wound, and bind the bystanders by oath never more to suffer king to reign in Rome.

From his example all who are discontented with their prince are taught, first of all, to measure, and to weigh their strength, and if they find themselves strong enough to disclose their hostility and proclaim open war, then to take that course as at once the nobler and less dangerous; but, if too weak to make open war, then sedulously to court the favor of the prince, using to that end all such methods as they may judge needful, adapting themselves to his pleasures, and showing delight in whatever they see him delight in. Such an intimacy, in the first place, enables you to live securely, and permits you, without incurring any risk, to share the happy fortunes of the prince, while it affords you every facility for carrying out your plans. Some, no doubt, will tell you that you should not stand so near the prince as to be involved in his downfall; nor yet at such a distance that when he falls you shall be too far off to use the occasion for rising on his ruin. But although this mean course, could we only follow it, would certainly be the best, yet, since I believe it to be impracticable, we must resort to the methods above indicated, and either keep altogether aloof, or else cleave closely to the prince. Whosoever does otherwise, if he be of great station, lives in constant peril; nor will it avail him to say, "I concern myself with nothing; I covet neither honors nor preferment; my sole wish is to live a quiet and peaceful life." For such excuses, though they be listened to, are not accepted; nor can any man of great position, however much and sincerely he desire it, elect to live this life of tranquility since his professions will not be believed, so that although he might be contented to be let alone, others will not suffer him to be so. Wherefore, like Brutus, men must feign folly, and to play the part effectively, and so as to please their prince, must say, do, see, and praise things contrary to their inclinations.

But now, having spoken of the prudence shown by Brutus when he sought to recover the freedom of Rome, let us next speak of the severity that he used to maintain it.

VI

Of Conspiracies

I T WOULD BE AN OMISSION not to say something on the
subject of conspiracies, these being a source of much danger
both to princes and to private men. For we see that many more
princes have lost their lives and states through these than in open
warfare, power to wage open war upon a prince being conceded to
few, whereas power to conspire against him is denied to none. On the
other hand, since conspiracies are attended at every stage by difficulties and dangers, no more hazardous or desperate undertakings can
be engaged in by any private citizen, and so while many conspiracies
are planned, few achieve their object. Wherefore, to put princes on
their guard against these dangers, and to make subjects more cautious how they take part in them, and rather learn to live content
under whatever government fortune has assigned them, I shall treat
of them at length, without omitting any noteworthy circumstance
that may serve for the instruction of either. Though, indeed, this is a
golden sentence of Cornelius Tacitus, wherein he says that "the past
should have our reverence, the present our obedience, and that we
should wish for good princes, but put up with any."* For assuredly
whosoever does otherwise is likely to bring ruin both on himself
and on his country.

---

* Tac. *Hist.* iv. 8.

But, to go deeper into the matter, we have first of all to examine against whom conspiracies are directed, and we shall find that men conspire either against their country or their prince, and it is of these two kinds of conspiracy that at present I desire to speak. For of conspiracies that have as their object the surrender of cities to enemies who are besieging them, and of all others contrived for like ends, I have already said enough.

First, then, I shall treat of those conspiracies that are directed against a prince, and begin by inquiring into their causes, which are manifold, but of which one is more momentous than all the rest: I mean, the being hated by the whole community. For it may reasonably be assumed that when a prince has drawn upon himself this universal hatred, he must also have given special offense to particular men, which they will be eager to avenge. And this eagerness will be augmented by the feeling of general ill-will that the prince is seen to have incurred. A prince ought, therefore, to avoid this load of public hatred. How he is to do so I need not stop here to explain, having discussed the matter already in another place, but if he can guard against this, offense given to particular men will expose him to but few attacks. One reason being that there are few men who think so much of an injury done to them as to run great risks to revenge it; another, that assuming them to have both the disposition and the courage to avenge themselves, they are restrained by the universal favor that they see entertained toward the prince.

Injuries are either to a man's life, to his property, or to his honor. As regards the first, they who threaten injuries to life incur more danger than they who actually inflict them; or rather, while great danger is incurred in threatening, none at all is incurred from inflicting such injuries. For the dead are past thinking of revenge, and those who survive, for the most part leave such thoughts to the dead. But he whose life is threatened, finding himself forced by necessity either to do or to suffer, becomes a man most dangerous to the prince, as shall be fully explained hereafter.

After menaces to life, injuries to property and honor stir men more than any others, and of these a prince has most to beware. For he can never strip a man so bare of his possessions as not to leave him some weapon wherewith to redress his wrongs, nor ever so far dishonor him as to quell the stubborn spirit that prompts revenge. Of all dishonors those done to the women of a household are the worst; after which come such personal indignities as nerved the arm of Pausanias against Philip of Macedon, and of many another against other princes; and, in our own days, it was no other reason that moved Giulio Belanti to conspire against Pandolfo, lord of Siena, than that Pandolfo, who had given him his daughter to wife, afterward took her from him, as presently shall be told. Chief among the causes that led the Pazzi to conspire against the Medici was the law passed by the latter depriving them of the inheritance of Giovanni Bonromei.

Another most powerful motive to conspire against a prince is the desire men feel to free their country from a usurper. This impelled Brutus and Cassius to conspire against Caesar, and countless others against such tyrants as Phalaris, Dionysius, and the like. Against this humor no tyrant can guard, except by laying down his tyranny, which, as none will do, few escape an unhappy end. Whence the verses of Juvenal:

> "Few tyrants die a peaceful death, and few
> The kings who visit Proserpine's dread lord,
> Unscathed by wounds and blood."*

---

* *Ad generum Cereris sine caede et vulnere pauci Descendunt reges, et sicca morte tiranni.* Juv. *Sat.* x. 112.

Great, as I have said already, are the dangers that men run in conspiring, for at all times they are in peril, whether in contriving, in executing, or after execution. And since in conspiracies either many are engaged, or one only (for although it cannot properly be said of one man that he conspires, there may exist in him the fixed resolve to put the prince to death), it is only the solitary plotter who escapes the first of these three stages of danger. For he runs no risk before executing his design, since as he imparts it to none, there is none to bring it to the ear of the prince. A deliberate resolve like this may be conceived by a person in any rank of life, high or low, base or noble, and whether or not he be the familiar of his prince. For everyone must, at some time or other, have leave to speak to the prince, and whoever has this leave has opportunity to accomplish his design. Pausanias, of whom we have made mention so often, slew Philip of Macedon as he walked between his son and his son-in-law to the temple, surrounded by a thousand armed guards. Pausanias indeed was noble, and known to the prince, but Ferdinand of Spain was stabbed in the neck by a poor and miserable Spaniard, and though the wound was not mortal, it sufficed to show that neither courage nor opportunity were wanting to the would-be assassin. A Dervish, or Turkish priest, drew his scimitar on Bajazet, father of the Sultan now reigning, and if he did not wound him, it was from no lack either of daring or of opportunity. And I believe that there are many who in their minds desire the deed, no punishment or danger attending the mere wish, though there be but few who dare do it. For since few or none who venture escape death, few are willing to go forward to certain destruction.

But to pass from these solitary attempts to those in which several are engaged, I affirm it to be shown by history that all such plots have been contrived by men of great station, or by those who have been on terms of close intimacy with the prince, since no others, not being downright madmen, would ever think of conspiring. For men of humble rank, and such as are not the intimates of their prince, are neither fed by the hopes nor possessed of the opportunities essential for such attempts. Because, in the first place, men of low degree will never find any to keep faith with them, none being moved to join in their schemes by those expectations that encourage men to run great risks; wherefore, so soon as their design has been imparted to two or three, they are betrayed and ruined. Or, assuming them fortunate enough to have no traitor of their number, they will be so hampered in the execution of their plot by the want of easy access to the prince, that they are sure to perish in the mere attempt. For if even men of great position, who have ready access to the prince, succumb to the difficulties that I shall presently notice, those difficulties must be infinitely increased in the case of men who are without these advantages. And because when life and property are at stake men are not utterly reckless, on perceiving themselves to be weak they grow cautious, and though cursing the tyrant in their hearts, are content to endure him, and to wait until someone of higher station than they comes forward to redress their wrongs. So that should we ever find these weaklings attempting anything, we may commend their courage rather than their prudence.

We see, however, that the great majority of conspirators have been persons of position and the familiars of their prince, and that their plots have been as often the consequence of excessive indulgence as of excessive injury, as when Perennius conspired against Commodus, Plautianus against Severus, and Sejanus against Tiberius—all of whom had been raised by their masters to such wealth, honors, and dignities that nothing seemed wanting to their authority save the imperial name. That they might not lack this also, they fell to conspiring against their prince, but in every instance their conspiracies had the end that their ingratitude deserved.

The only instance in recent times of such attempts succeeding is the conspiracy of Jacopo IV d'Appiano against Messer Piero Gambacorti, lord of Pisa. For Jacopo, who had been bred and brought up by Piero, and loaded by him with honors, deprived him of his state. Similar to this, in our own days, was the conspiracy of Coppola against King Ferdinand of Aragon. For Coppola had reached such a pitch of power that he seemed to himself to have everything but sovereignty; in seeking to obtain that he lost his life; though if any plot entered into by a man of great position could be expected to succeed, this certainly might, being contrived, as we may say, by another king, and by one who had the amplest opportunities for its accomplishment. But that lust of power that blinds men to dangers darkened the minds of those to whom the execution of the scheme was committed, who, had they only known how to add prudence to their villainy, could hardly have missed their aim.

The prince, therefore, who would guard himself against plots ought more to fear those men to whom he has been too indulgent than those to whom he has done great wrongs. For the latter lack opportunities that the former have in abundance, and the moving cause is equally strong in both, lust of power being at least as strong a passion as lust of revenge. Wherefore, a prince should entrust his friends with so much authority only as leaves a certain interval between his position and theirs, so that between the two something is still left to desire. Otherwise it will be strange if he does not fare like those princes who have been named above.

But to return from this digression, I say that having shown it to be necessary that conspirators should be men of great station, and such as have ready access to the prince, we have next to consider what have been the results of their plots, and to trace the causes that have made them succeed or fail. Now, as I have said already, we find that conspiracies are attended by danger at three stages: before, during, and after their execution; for which reason very few of them have had a happy issue, it being next to impossible to surmount all these different dangers successfully. And to begin with those that are incurred beforehand, and which are graver than all the rest, I say that he must be both very prudent and very fortunate who, when contriving a conspiracy, does not suffer his secret to be discovered.

Conspiracies are discovered either by disclosures made or by conjecture. Disclosures are made through the treachery or folly of those to whom you communicate your design. Treachery is to be looked for, because you can impart your plans only to such persons as you believe ready to face death on your behalf, or to those who are discontented with the prince. Of men whom you can trust thus implicitly, one or two may be found, but when you have to open your designs to many, they cannot all be of this nature, and their goodwill toward you must be extreme if they are not daunted by the danger and by fear of punishment. Moreover men commonly deceive themselves in respect of the love that they imagine others bear them, nor can ever be sure of it until they have put it to the proof. But to make proof of it in a matter like this is very perilous; and even if you have proved it already, and found it true in some other dangerous trial, you cannot assume that there will be the same fidelity here, since this far transcends every other kind of danger. Again, if you gauge a man's fidelity by his discontent with the prince, you may easily deceive yourself; for so soon as you have taken this discontented man into your confidence, you have supplied him with the means whereby he may become contented; so that either his hatred of the prince must be great indeed, or your influence over him extraordinary, if it keep him faithful. Hence it comes that so many conspiracies have been discovered and crushed in their earliest stage, and that when the secret is preserved among many accomplices for any length of time, it is looked on as a miracle, as in the case of the conspiracy of Piso against Nero, and, in our own days, in that of the Pazzi against Lorenzo and Giuliano de' Medici—which last, though more than fifty persons were privy to it, was not discovered until it came to be carried out.

Conspiracies are disclosed through the imprudence of a conspirator when he talks so indiscreetly that some servant, or other person not in the plot, overhears him—as happened with the sons of Brutus, who, when treating with the envoys of Tarquin, were overheard by a slave, who became their accuser—or else through your own weakness in imparting your secret to some woman or boy whom you love, or to some other such light person, as when Dymnus, who was one of those who conspired with Philotas against Alexander the Great, revealed the plot to Nicomachus, a youth whom he loved, who at once told Cebalinus, and Cebalinus the king.

Of discoveries by conjecture we have an instance in the conspiracy of Piso against Nero, for Scaevinus, one of the conspirators, the day before he was to kill Nero, made his will, liberated all his slaves and gave them money, and bade Milichus, his freedman, sharpen his old rusty dagger, and have bandages ready for binding up wounds. From all which preparations Milichus conjecturing what work was in hand, accused Scaevinus before Nero, whereupon Scaevinus was arrested, and with him Natalis, another of the conspirators, who the day before had been seen to speak with him for a long time in private; and when the two differed in their account of what then passed between them, they were put to the torture and forced to confess the truth. In this way the conspiracy was brought to light, to the ruin of all concerned.

Against these causes of the discovery of conspiracies it is impossible so to guard as that either through treachery, want of caution, or levity the secret shall not be found out, whenever more than three or four persons are privy to it. And whenever more than one conspirator is arrested, the plot is certain to be detected, because no two persons can perfectly agree in a false account of what has passed between them. If only one be taken, should he be a man of resolute courage, he may refuse to implicate his comrades, but they on their part must have no less courage, to stay quiet where they are, and not betray themselves by flight—for if courage be absent anywhere, whether in him who is taken or in those still at large, the conspiracy is revealed. And what is related by Titus Livius as having happened in the conspiracy against Hieronymus, tyrant of Syracuse, is most extraordinary, namely, that on the capture of one of the conspirators, named Theodorus, he, with great fortitude, withheld the names of all his accomplices, and accused friends of the tyrant, while his companions, on their part, trusted so completely in his courage that not one of them quitted Syracuse or showed any sign of fear.

All these dangers, therefore, which attend the contrivance of a plot, must be passed through before you come to its execution; or if you would escape them, you must observe the following precautions. Your first and surest, nay, to say truth, your only safeguard, is to leave your accomplices no time to accuse you, for which reason you must impart the affair to them only at the moment when you mean it to be carried out, and not before. Those who have followed this course have wholly escaped the preliminary dangers of conspiracies, and, generally speaking, the others also; indeed, I may say that they have all succeeded, and that it is open to every prudent man to act as they did. It will be enough to give two instances of plots effected in this way. Nelematus, unable to endure the tyranny of Aristotimus, despot of Epirus, assembling many of his friends and kinsmen in his house, exhorted them to free their country, and when some of them asked for time to consider and mature their plans, he bade his slaves close the doors, and told those assembled that unless they swore to go at once and do as he directed he would make them over to Aristotimus as prisoners. Alarmed by his threats, they bound themselves by a solemn oath, and going forth at once and without delay, successfully carried out his bidding. A certain Magus having fraudulently usurped the throne of Persia, Ortanes, a grandee of that realm, discovering the fraud, disclosed it to six others of the chief nobility, telling them that it behooved them to free the kingdom from the tyranny of this impostor. And when some among them asked for time, Darius, who was one of the six summoned by Ortanes, stood up and said, "Either we go at once to do this deed, or I go to the Magus to accuse you all." Whereupon, all rising together, without time given to any to change his mind, they went forth and succeeded in effecting their end. Not unlike these instances was the plan taken by the Aetolians to rid themselves of Nabis, the Spartan tyrant, to whom, under pretense of succoring him, they sent Alasamenes, their fellow citizen, with two hundred foot soldiers and thirty horsemen. For they imparted their real design to Alasamenes only, charging the rest, under pain of exile, to obey him in whatever he commanded. Alasamenes repaired to Sparta, and never divulged his commission till the time came for executing it, and so succeeded in putting Nabis to death.

It was, therefore, by the precautions they observed that the persons of whom I have just now spoken escaped all those perils that attend the contrivance of conspiracies, and any following their example may expect the like good fortune. And that all may learn to do as they did I shall notice the case of Piso, of which mention has before been made. By reason of his rank, his reputation, and the intimate terms on which he lived with Nero, who trusted him without reserve, and would often come to his garden to sup with him, Piso was able to gain the friendship of many persons of spirit and courage, and well fitted in every way to take part in his plot against the emperor, which, under these circumstances, might easily have been carried out. For when Nero came to his garden, Piso could readily have communicated his design to those friends of his, and with suitable words have encouraged them to do what, in fact, they would not have had time to withdraw from, and was certain to succeed. And were we to examine all similar attempts, it would be seen that there are few that might not have been effected in the manner shown. But since most men are very ignorant of practical affairs, they commit the gravest blunders, especially in matters that lie, as this does, a little way out of the beaten track.

Wherefore, the contriver of a plot ought never, if he can help it, to communicate his design until the moment when it is to be executed; or if he must communicate it, then to some one man only, with whom he has long been intimate, and whom he knows to be moved by the same feelings as himself. To find one such person is far easier than to find several, and, at the same time, involves less risk, for though this one man play you false, you are not left altogether without resource, as you are when your accomplices are numerous. For I have heard it shrewdly said that to one man you may impart anything, since, unless you have been led to commit yourself by writing, your denial will go as far as his assertion. Shun writing, therefore, as you would a rock, for there is nothing so damning as a letter under your own hand.

Plautianus, desiring to procure the deaths of the Emperor Severus and his son Caracalla, entrusted the business to the tribune Saturninus, who, being more disposed to betray than obey Plautianus, but at the same time afraid that, if it came to laying a charge, Plautianus might be believed sooner than he, asked him for a written authority, that his commission might be credited. Blinded by ambition, Plautianus complied, and forthwith was accused by Saturninus and found guilty; whereas, but for that written warrant, together with other corroborating proofs, he must have escaped by his bold denial of the charge. Against the testimony of a single witness, you have thus some defense, unless convicted by your own handwriting, or by other circumstantial proof against which you must guard. A woman, named Epicharis, who had formerly been a mistress of Nero, was privy to Piso's conspiracy, and thinking it might be useful to have the help of a certain captain of triremes whom Nero had among his bodyguards, she acquainted him with the plot, but not with the names of the plotters. This fellow, turning traitor, and accusing Epicharis to Nero, so stoutly did she deny the charge that Nero, confounded by her effrontery, let her go.

In imparting a plot to a single person there are, therefore, two risks: one, that he may come forward of his own accord to accuse you; the other, that if arrested on suspicion, or on some proof of his guilt, he may, on being convicted, in the hope to escape punishment, betray you. But in neither of these dangers are you left without a defense, since you may meet the one by ascribing the charge to the malice of your accuser, and the other by alleging that the witness his been forced by torture to say what is untrue. The wisest course, however, is to impart your design to none, but to act like those who have been mentioned above; or if you impart it, then to one only: for although even in this course there be a certain degree of danger, it is far less than when many are admitted to your confidence.

A case nearly resembling that just now noticed is where an emergency, so urgent as to leave you no time to provide otherwise for your safety, constrains you to do to a prince what you see him minded to do to you. A necessity of this sort leads almost always to the end desired, as two instances may suffice to show. Among the closest friends and intimates of the Emperor Commodus were two captains of the praetorian guards, Letus and Electus, while among the most favored of his distresses was a certain Martia. But because these three often reproved him for his manner of living, as disgraceful to himself and to his station, he resolved to rid himself of them, and so wrote their names, along with those of certain others whom he meant should be put to death the next night, in a list that he placed under the pillow of his bed. But on his going to bathe, a boy, who was a favorite of his, while playing about his room and on his bed, found the list, and coming out of the chamber with it in his hand, was met by Martia, who took it from him, and on reading it and finding what it contained, sent for Letus and Electus. And all three, recognizing the danger in which they stood, resolved to be beforehand with the tyrant, and losing no time, murdered him that very night.

The Emperor Caracalla, being with his armies in Mesopotamia, had with him Macrinus, who was more of a statesman than a soldier, as his prefect. But because princes who are not themselves good are always afraid lest others treat them as they deserve, Caracalla wrote to his friend Maternianus in Rome to learn from the astrologers whether any man had ambitious designs upon the empire, and to send him word. Maternianus, accordingly, wrote back that such designs were entertained by Macrinus. But this letter, ere it reached the emperor, fell into the hands of Macrinus, who, seeing when he read it that he must either put Caracalla to death before further letters arrived from Rome, or else die himself, committed the business to a centurion, named Martialis, whom he trusted, and whose brother had been slain by Caracalla a few days before, who succeeded in killing the emperor.

We see, therefore, that an urgency that leaves no room for delay has almost the same results as the method already noticed as followed by Nelematus of Epirus. We see, too, what I remarked almost at the outset of this Discourse, that the threats of princes expose them to greater danger than the wrongs they actually inflict, and lead to more active conspiracies: and, therefore, that a prince should be careful not to threaten, since men are either to be treated kindly or else got rid of, but never brought to such a pass that they have to choose between slaying and being slain.

As to the dangers attending the execution of plots, these result either from some change made in the plan, or from a failure in courage on the part of him who is to carry it out; or else from some mistake he falls into through want of foresight, or from his not giving the affair its finishing stroke, as when some are left alive whom it was meant to put to death. Now, nothing causes so much disturbance and hindrance in human affairs as to be forced, at a moment's notice and without time allowed for reflection, to vary your plan of action and adopt a different one from that fixed on at the first. And if such changes cause confusion anywhere, it is in matters appertaining to war, and in enterprises of the kind we are now speaking of; for in such affairs as these, there is nothing so essential as that men be prepared to do the exact thing entrusted to them. But when men have for many days together turned their whole thoughts to doing a thing in a certain way and in a certain order, and the way and order are suddenly altered, it is impossible but that they should be disconcerted and the whole scheme ruined. For which reason, it is far better to do everything in accordance with the preconcerted plan, though it is seen to be attended with some disadvantages, than, in order to escape these, to involve yourself in an infinity of dangers. And this will happen when you depart from your original design without time given to form a new one. For when time is given you may manage as you please.

The conspiracy of the Pazzi against Lorenzo and Giuliano de' Medici is well known. The scheme agreed on was to give a banquet to the Cardinal S. Giorgio, at which the brothers should be put to death. To each of the conspirators a part was assigned: to one the murder, to another the seizure of the palace, while a third was to ride through the streets and call on the people to free themselves. But it so chanced that at a time when the Pazzi, the Medici, and the cardinal were all assembled in the cathedral church of Florence to hear High Mass, it became known that Giuliano would not be present at the banquet; whereupon the conspirators, laying their heads together, resolved to do in church what they were to have done elsewhere. This, however, deranged the whole scheme. For Giovambattista of Montesecco would have no hand in the murder if it was to be done in a church, and the whole distribution of parts had in consequence to be changed; when, as those to whom the new parts were assigned had no time allowed them to nerve their minds to their new tasks, they managed matters so badly that they were overpowered in their attempt.

Courage fails a conspirator either from his own poorness of spirit or from his being overcome by some feeling of reverence. For such majesty and awe attend the person of a prince that it may well happen that he softens or dismays his executioners. When Caius Marius was taken by the people of Minturnum, the slave sent in to slay him, overawed by the bearing of the man, and by the memories that his name called up, became unnerved, and powerless to perform his office. And if this influence was exercised by one who was a prisoner, and in chains, and overwhelmed by adverse fortune, how much more must reverence be inspired by a prince who is free and uncontrolled, surrounded by his retinue and by all the pomp and splendor of his station, whose dignity confounds, and whose graciousness conciliates.

Certain persons conspiring against Sitalces, king of Thrace, fixed a day for his murder, and assembled at the place appointed, whither the king had already come. Yet none of them raised a hand to harm him, and all departed without attempting anything against him or knowing why they refrained, each blaming the others. And more than once the same folly was repeated, until the plot getting wind, they were taken and punished for what they might have done, yet durst not do.

Two brothers of Alfonso, Duke of Ferrara, conspired against him, employing as their tool a certain priest named Giennes, a singing man in the service of the duke. He, at their request, repeatedly brought the duke into their company, so that they had full opportunity to make away with him. Yet neither of them ever ventured to strike the blow; till at last, their scheme being discovered, they paid the penalty of their combined cowardice and temerity. Such irresolution can only have arisen from their being overawed by the majesty of the prince, or touched by his graciousness.

In the execution of conspiracies, therefore, errors and mishaps arise from a failure of prudence or courage to which all are subject, when, losing self-control, they are led in their bewilderment to do and say what they ought not. That men are thus confounded, and thrown off their balance, could not be better shown than in the words of Titus Livius, where he describes the behavior of Alasamenes the Aetolian, at the time when he resolved on the death of Nabis the Spartan, of whom I have spoken before. For when the time to act came, and he had disclosed to his followers what they had to do, Livius represents him as "collecting his thoughts that had grown confused by dwelling on so desperate an enterprise." For it is impossible for anyone, though of the most steadfast temper and used to the sight of death and to handle deadly weapons, not to be perturbed at such a moment. For which reason we should on such occasions choose for our tools those who have had experience in similar affairs, and trust no others though reputed of the truest courage. For in these grave undertakings, no one who is without such experience, however bold and resolute, is to be trusted.

The confusion of which I speak may cause you either to drop your weapon from your hand, or to use words that will have the same results. Quintianus being commanded by Lucilla, sister of Commodus, to slay him, lay in wait for him at the entrance of the amphitheater, and rushing upon him with a drawn dagger, cried out, "The senate sends you this"—which words caused him to be seized before his blow descended. In like manner Messer Antonio of Volterra, who as we have elsewhere seen was told off to kill Lorenzo de' Medici, exclaimed as he approached him, "Ah traitor!" and this exclamation proved the salvation of Lorenzo and the ruin of that conspiracy.

For the reasons now given, a conspiracy against a single ruler may readily break down in its execution; but a conspiracy against two rulers is not only difficult, but so hazardous that its success is almost hopeless. For to effect like actions, at the same time, in different places, is well-nigh impossible; nor can they be effected at different times, if you would not have one counteract another. So that if conspiracy against a single ruler be imprudent and dangerous, to conspire against two is in the last degree foolhardy and desperate. And were it not for the respect in which I hold the historian, I could not credit as possible what Herodian relates of Plautianus, namely, that he committed to the centurion Saturninus the task of slaying single-handed both Severus and Caracalla, they dwelling in different places; for the thing is so opposed to reason that on no other authority could I be induced to accept it as true.

Certain young Athenians conspired against Diocles and Hippias, tyrants of Athens. Diocles they slew; but Hippias, making his escape, avenged him. Chion and Leonidas of Heraclea, disciples of Plato, conspired against the despots Clearchus and Satirus. Clearchus fell, but Satirus survived and avenged him. The Pazzi, of whom we have spoken so often, succeeded in murdering Giuliano only. From such conspiracies, therefore, as are directed against more heads than one, all should abstain, for no good is to be got from them, whether for ourselves, for our country, or for anyone else. On the contrary, when those conspired against escape, they become harsher and more insufferable than before, as, in the examples given, Florence, Athens, and Heraclea had cause to know. True it is that the conspiracy contrived by Pelopidas for the liberation of his country had to encounter every conceivable hindrance, and yet had the happiest end. For Pelopidas had to deal not with two tyrants only, but with ten; and so far from having their confidence, could not, being an outlaw, even approach them. And yet he succeeded in coming to Thebes, in putting the tyrants to death, and in freeing his country. But whatever he did was done with the aid of one of the counsellors of the tyrants, a certain Charon, through whom he had all facilities for executing his design. Let none, however, take this case as a pattern; for that it was in truth a desperate attempt, and its success a marvel, was and is the opinion of all historians, who speak of it as a thing altogether extraordinary and unexampled.

The execution of a plot may be frustrated by some groundless alarm or unforeseen mischance occurring at the very moment when the scheme is to be carried out. On the morning on which Brutus and his confederates were to slay Caesar, it so happened that Caesar talked for a great while with Cneus Pompilius Lenas, one of the conspirators; which some of the others observing, were in terror that Pompilius was divulging the conspiracy to Caesar; whose life they would therefore have attempted then and there, without waiting his arrival in the senate house, had they not been reassured by seeing that when the conference ended he showed no sign of unusual emotion. False alarms of this sort are to be taken into account and allowed for, all the more that they are easily raised. For he who has not a clear conscience is apt to assume that others are speaking of him. A word used with a wholly different purpose may throw his mind off its balance and lead him to fancy that reference is intended to the matter he is engaged on, and cause him either to betray the conspiracy by flight, or to derange its execution by anticipating the time fixed. And the more there are privy to the conspiracy, the likelier this is to happen.

As to the mischances that may befall, since these are unforeseen, they can only be instanced by examples that may make men more cautious. Giulio Belanti of Siena, of whom I have spoken before, from the hate he bore Pandolfo Petrucci, who had given him his daughter to wife and afterward taken her from him, resolved to murder him, and thus chose his time. Almost every day Pandolfo went to visit a sick kinsman, passing the house of Giulio on the way, who, remarking this, took measures to have his accomplices ready in his house to kill Pandolfo as he passed. Wherefore, placing the rest armed within the doorway, one he stationed at a window to give the signal of Pandolfo's approach. It so happened however, that as he came nigh the house, and after the lookout had given the signal, Pandolfo fell in with a friend who stopped him to converse; when some of those with him, going on in advance, saw and heard the gleam and clash of weapons, and so discovered the ambuscade; whereby Pandolfo was saved, while Giulio with his companions had to fly from Siena. This plot accordingly was marred, and Giulio's schemes balked, in consequence of a chance meeting. Against such accidents, since they are out of the common course of things, no provision can be made. Still it is very necessary to take into account all that may happen, and devise what remedies you can.

It now only remains for us to consider those dangers that follow after the execution of a plot. These in fact resolve themselves into one, namely, that some should survive who will avenge the death of the murdered prince. The part of avenger is likely to be assumed by a son, a brother, or other kinsman of the deceased, who in the ordinary course of events might have looked to succeed to the princedom. And such persons are suffered to live, either from inadvertence, or from some of the causes noted already, as when Giovann' Andrea of Lampognano, with the help of his companions, put to death the Duke of Milan. For the son and two brothers of the duke, who survived him, were able to avenge his death. In cases like this, indeed, the conspirators may be held excused, since there is nothing they can do to help themselves. But when from carelessness and want of due caution someone is allowed to live whose death ought to have been secured, there is no excuse. Certain conspirators, after murdering the lord, Count Girolamo of Forli, made prisoners of his wife and of his children, who were still very young. By thinking they could not be safe unless they got possession of the citadel, which the governor refused to surrender, they obtained a promise from Madonna Caterina, for so the countess was named, that on their permitting her to enter the citadel she would cause it to be given up to them, her children in the meantime remaining with them as hostages. On which undertaking they suffered her to enter the citadel. But no sooner had she got inside than she fell to upbraid them from the walls with the murder of her husband, and to threaten them with every kind of vengeance; and to show them how little store she set upon her children, told them scoffingly that she knew how others could be got. In the end, the rebels having no leader to advise them, and perceiving too late the error into which they had been betrayed, had to pay the penalty of their rashness by perpetual banishment.

But of all the dangers that may follow on the execution of a plot, none is so much or so justly to be feared as that the people should be well affected to the prince whom you have put to death. For against this danger conspirators have no resource that can ensure their safety. Of this we have example in the case of Caesar, who as he had the love of the Roman people was by them avenged; for they it was who, by driving out the conspirators from Rome, were the cause that all of them, at different times and in different places, came to violent ends.

Conspiracies against their country are less danger for those who take part in them than conspiracies against princes, since there is less risk beforehand, and though there be the same danger in their execution, there is none afterward. Beforehand, the risks are few, because a citizen may use means for obtaining power without betraying his wishes or designs to any, and unless his course be arrested, his designs are likely enough to succeed—nay, though laws be passed to restrain him, he may strike out a new path. This is to be understood of a commonwealth that has to some degree become corrupted, for in one wherein there is no taint of corruption, there being no soil in which evil seed can grow, such designs will never suggest themselves to any citizen.

In a commonwealth, therefore, a citizen may by many means and in many ways aspire to the princedom without risking destruction, both because republics are slower than princes are to take alarm, are less suspicious and consequently less cautious, and because they look with greater reverence upon their great citizens, who are in this way rendered bolder and more reckless in attacking them. Anyone who has read Sallust's account of the conspiracy of Catiline must remember how, when that conspiracy was discovered, Catiline not only remained in Rome, but even made his appearance in the senate house, where he was suffered to address the senate in the most insulting terms—so scrupulous was that city in protecting the liberty of all its citizens. Nay, even after he had left Rome and placed himself at the head of his army, Lentulus and his other accomplices would not have been imprisoned had not letters been found upon them clearly establishing their guilt. Hanno, the foremost citizen of Carthage, aspiring to absolute power, on the occasion of the marriage of a daughter contrived a plot for administering poison to the whole senate and so making himself prince. The scheme being discovered, the senate took no steps against him beyond passing a law to limit the expense of banquets and marriage ceremonies. So great was the respect they paid to his quality.

True, the execution of a plot against your country is attended with greater difficulty and danger, since it seldom happens that, in conspiring against so many, your own resources are sufficient by themselves; for it is not everyone who, like Caesar, Agathocles, or Cleomenes, is at the head of an army, so as to be able at a stroke, and by open force, to make himself master of his country. To such as these, doubtless, the path is safe and easy enough; but others who have not such an assembled force ready at their command must effect their ends either by stratagem and fraud, or with the help of foreign troops. Of such stratagems and frauds we have an instance in the case of Pisistratus the Athenian, who after defeating the Megarians and thereby gaining the favor of his fellow citizens, showed himself to them one morning covered with wounds and blood, declaring that he had been thus outraged through the jealousy of the nobles, and asking that he might have an armed guard assigned for his protection. With the authority that this lent him, he easily rose to such a pitch of power as to become tyrant of Athens. In like manner Pandolfo Petrucci, on his return with the other exiles to Siena, was appointed the command of the public guard, as a mere office of routine that others had declined. Very soon, however, this armed force gave him so much importance that he became the supreme ruler of the state. And many others have followed other plans and methods, and in the course of time, and without incurring danger, have achieved their aim.

Conspirators against their country, whether trusting to their own forces or to foreign aid, have had more or less success in proportion as they have been favored by Fortune. Catiline, of whom we spoke just now, was overthrown. Hanno, who has also been mentioned, failing to accomplish his object by poison, armed his partisans to the number of many thousands, but both he and they came to an ill end. On the other hand, certain citizens of Thebes conspiring to become its tyrants, summoned a Spartan army to their assistance, and usurped the absolute control of the city. In short, if we examine all the conspiracies that men have engaged in against their country, we shall find that few or none have been quelled in their inception, but that all have either succeeded, or broken down in their execution. Once executed, they entail no further risks beyond those implied in the nature of a princedom. For the man who becomes a tyrant incurs all the natural and ordinary dangers in which a tyranny involves him, and has no remedies against them save those of which I have already spoken.

This is all that occurs to me to say on the subject of conspiracies. If I have noticed those that have been carried out with the sword rather than those wherein poison has been the instrument, it is because, generally speaking, the method of proceeding is the same in both. It is true, nevertheless, that conspiracies that are to be carried out by poison are, by reason of their uncertainty, attended by greater danger. For since fewer opportunities offer for their execution, you must have an understanding with persons who can command opportunities. But it is dangerous to have to depend on others. Again, many causes may hinder a poisoned draft from proving mortal, as when the murderers of Commodus, on his vomiting the poison given him, had to strangle him.

Princes, then, have no worse enemy than conspiracy, for when a conspiracy is formed against them, it either carries them off or discredits them: since, if it succeeds, they die; while, if it be discovered, and the conspirators be put to death themselves, it will always be believed that the whole affair has been trumped up by the prince that he might glut his greed and cruelty with the goods and blood of those whom he has made away with. Let me not, however, forget to warn the prince or commonwealth against whom a conspiracy is directed, that on getting word of it, and before taking any steps to punish it, they endeavor, as far as they can, to ascertain its character, and after carefully weighing the strength of the conspirators with their own, on finding it preponderate, never suffer their knowledge of the plot to appear until they are ready with a force sufficient to crush it. For otherwise, to disclose their knowledge will only give the signal for their destruction. They must strive therefore to seem unconscious of what is going on, for conspirators who see themselves detected are driven forward by necessity and will stick at nothing. Of this precaution we have an example in Roman history, when the officers of the two legions, who, as has already been mentioned, were left behind to defend the Capuans from the Samnites, conspired together against the Capuans. For on rumors of this conspiracy reaching Rome, Rutilius the new consul was charged to see to it; who, not to excite the suspicions of the conspirators, publicly gave out that by order of the senate the Capuan legions were continued in their station. The conspirators, believing this and thinking they would have ample time to execute their plans, made no effort to hasten matters, but remained at their ease, until they found that the consul was moving one of the two legions to a distance from the other. This, arousing their suspicion, led them to disclose their designs and endeavor to carry them out.

Now, we could have no more instructive example than this in whatever way we look at it. For it shows how slow men are to move in those matters wherein time seems of little importance, and how active they become when necessity urges them. Nor can a prince or commonwealth desiring for their own ends to retard the execution of a conspiracy use any more effectual means to do so than by artfully holding out to the conspirators some special opportunity as likely soon to present itself—awaiting which, and believing they have time and to spare for what they have to do, they will afford that prince or commonwealth all the leisure needed to prepare for their punishment. Whosoever neglects these precautions hastens his own destruction, as happened with the Duke of Athens, and with Guglielmo de' Pazzi. For the duke, who had made himself tyrant of Florence, on learning that he was being conspired against, without further inquiry into the matter, caused one of the conspirators to be seized, whereupon the rest at once armed themselves and deprived him of his government. Guglielmo, again, being commissary in the Val di Chiana in the year 1501, and learning that a conspiracy was being hatched in Arezzo to take the town from the Florentines and give it over to the

Vitelli, repaired thither with all haste; and without providing himself with the necessary forces or giving a thought to the strength of the conspirators, on the advice of the bishop, his son, had one of them arrested. Which becoming known to the others, they forthwith rushed to arms, and taking the town from the Florentines, made Guglielmo their prisoner. Where, however, conspiracies are weak, they may and should be put down without scruple or hesitation.

Two methods, somewhat opposed to one another, which have occasionally been followed in dealing with conspiracies, are in no way to be commended. One of these was that adopted by the Duke of Athens, of whom I have just now spoken, who to have it thought that he confided in the goodwill of the Florentines, caused a certain man who gave information of a plot against him, to be put to death. The other was that followed by Dion the Syracusan, who, to sound the intentions of one whom he suspected, arranged with Calippus, whom he trusted, to pretend to get up a conspiracy against him. Neither of these tyrants reaped any advantage from the course he followed. For the one discouraged informers and gave heart to those who were disposed to conspire, the other prepared an easy road to his own death, or rather was prime mover in a conspiracy against himself. As the event showed. For Calippus having free leave to plot against Dion, plotted to such effect that he deprived him at once of his state and life.

IX

That to Enjoy Constant Good Fortune We Must Change with the Times

I HAVE REPEATEDLY noted that the good or bad fortune of men depends on whether their methods of acting accord with the character of the times. For we see that in what they do some men act impulsively, others warily and with caution. And because, from inability to preserve the just mean, they in both of these ways overstep the true limit, they commit mistakes in one direction or the other. He, however, will make fewest mistakes, and may expect to prosper most, who, while following the course to which nature inclines him, finds, as I have said, his method of acting in accordance with the times in which he lives.

All know that in his command of the Roman armies, Fabius Maximus displayed a prudence and caution very different from the audacity and hardihood natural to his countrymen; and it was his good fortune that his methods suited with the times. For Hannibal coming into Italy in all the flush of youth and recent success, having already by two defeats stripped Rome of her best soldiers and filled her with dismay, nothing could have been more fortunate for that republic than to find a general able, by his deliberateness and caution, to keep the enemy at bay. Nor, on the other hand, could Fabius have fallen upon times better suited to the methods that he used, and by which he crowned himself with glory. That he acted in accordance with his natural bent, and not from a reasoned choice, we may gather from this, that when Scipio, to bring the war to an end, proposed to pass with his army into Africa, Fabius, unable to depart from his characteristic methods and habits, strenuously opposed him; so that had it rested with him, Hannibal might never have left Italy. For he perceived not that the times had changed, and that with them it was necessary to change the methods of prosecuting the war. Had Fabius, therefore, been King of Rome, he might well have caused the war to end unhappily, not knowing how to accommodate his methods to the change in the times. As it was, he lived in a commonwealth in which there were many citizens, and many different dispositions— and which, as it produced a Fabius, excellent at a time when it was necessary to protract hostilities, so also afterward gave birth to a Scipio, at a time suited to bring them to a successful close.

And hence it comes that a commonwealth endures longer, and has a more sustained good fortune than a princedom, because from the diversity in the characters of its citizens, it can adapt itself better than a prince can to the diversity of times. For, as I have said before, a man accustomed to follow one method will never alter it, so when times change and longer accord with his method, he will be ruined. Piero Soderini, of whom I have already spoken, was guided in all his actions by patience and gentleness, and he and his country prospered while the times were in harmony with these methods. But, afterward, when a time came when it behooved him to have done with patience and gentleness, he knew not how to drop them, and was ruined together with his country. Pope Julius II, throughout the whole of his pontificate, was governed by impulse and passion, and because the times were in perfect accord, all his undertakings prospered. But had other times come requiring other qualities, he could not have escaped destruction, since he could not have changed his methods nor his habitual line of conduct.

As to why such changes are impossible, two reasons may be given. One is that we cannot act in opposition to the bent of our nature. The other, that when a man has been very successful while following a particular method, he can never be convinced that it is for his advantage to try some other. And hence it results that a man's fortunes vary, because times change and he does not change with them. So, too, with commonwealths, which, as we have already shown at length, are ruined from not altering their institutions to suit the times. And commonwealths are slower to change than princes are, changes costing them more effort, because occasions must be waited for which shall stir the whole community, and it is not enough that a single citizen alters his method of acting.

But since I have made mention of Fabius Maximus, who wore out Hannibal by keeping him at bay, I think it opportune to consider in the following chapter whether a general who desires to engage his enemy at all risks can be prevented by that enemy from doing so.

XIV

Of the Effect Produced in Battle
by Strange and Unexpected
Sights or Sounds

THAT THE DISORDER occasioned by strange and unexpected sights or sounds may have momentous consequences in combat might be shown by many instances, but by none better than by what befell in the battle fought between the Romans and the Volscians, when Quintius, the Roman general, seeing one wing of his army begin to waver, shouted aloud to his men to stand firm, for the other wing was already victorious. Which words of his giving confidence to his own troops and striking the enemy with dismay won him the battle. But if a cry like this produces great effect on a well-disciplined army, far greater must be its effect on one that is ill disciplined and disorderly. For by such a wind the whole mass will be moved, as I shall show by a well-known instance happening in our own times.

A few years ago the city of Perugia was split into the two factions of the Baglioni and the Oddi, the former holding the government, the latter being in exile. The Oddeschi, however, with the help of friends, having got together an armed force that they lodged in villages of their own near Perugia, obtained, by the favor of some of their party, an entrance into the city by night, and moving forward without discovery, came as far as the public square. And as all the streets of Perugia are barred with chains drawn across them at their corners, the Oddeschi had in front of them a man who carried an iron hammer wherewith to break the fastenings of the chains so that horsemen might pass. When the only chain remaining unbroken was that which closed the public square, the alarm having now been given, the hammerman was so impeded by the crowd pressing behind him that he could not raise his arm to strike freely. Whereupon, to get more room for his work, he called aloud to the others to stand back; and the word *back* passing from rank to rank those furthest off began to run, and, presently, the others also, with such precipitancy, that they fell into utter disorder. In this way, and from this trifling circumstance, the attempt of the Oddeschi came to nothing.

Here we may note that discipline is needed in an army, not so much to enable it to fight according to a settled order, as that it may not be thrown into confusion by every insignificant accident. For a tumultuary host is useless in war, simply because every word, or cry, or sound, may throw it into a panic and cause it to fly. Wherefore it behooves a good captain to provide that certain fixed persons shall receive his orders and pass them on to the rest, and to accustom his soldiers to look to these persons, and to them only, to be informed what his orders are. For whenever this precaution is neglected the gravest mishaps are constantly seen to ensue.

As regards strange and unexpected sights, every captain should endeavor while his army is actually engaged with the enemy to effect some such feint or diversion as will encourage his own men and dismay his adversary since this of all things that can happen is the likeliest to ensure victory. In evidence whereof we may cite the example of Cneius Sulpitius, the Roman dictator, who, when about to give battle to the Gauls, after arming his sutlers and camp followers, mounted them on mules and other beasts of burden, furnished them with spears and banners to look like cavalry, and placing them behind a hill, ordered them on a given signal, when the fight was at the hottest, to appear and show themselves to the enemy. All which being carried out as he had arranged, threw the Gauls into such alarm that they lost the battle.

A good captain, therefore, has two things to see to: first, to contrive how by some sudden surprise he may throw his enemy into confusion; and next, to be prepared should the enemy use a like stratagem against him to discover and defeat it, as the stratagem of Semiramis was defeated by the King of India. For Semiramis seeing that this king had elephants in great numbers, to dismay him by showing that she, too, was well supplied, caused the skins of many oxen and buffaloes to be sewn together in the shape of elephants and placed upon camels and sent to the front. But the trick being detected by the king, turned out not only useless but hurtful to its contriver. In a battle that the dictator Mamercus fought against the people of Fidenae, the latter, to strike terror into the minds of the Romans, contrived that while the combat raged a number of soldiers should issue from Fidenae bearing lances tipped with fire, thinking that the Romans, disturbed by so strange a sight, would be thrown into confusion.

We are to note, however, with regard to such contrivances, that if they are to serve any useful end, they should be formidable as well as seem so, for when they menace a real danger, their weak points are not so soon discerned. When they have more of pretense than reality, it will be well either to dispense with them altogether, or, resorting to them, to keep them, like the muleteers of Sulpitius, in the background, so that they are not too readily found out. For any weakness inherent in them is soon discovered if they are brought near, when, as happened with the elephants of Semiramis and the fiery spears of the men of Fidenae, they do harm rather than good. For although by this last-mentioned device the Romans at the first were somewhat disconcerted, so soon as the dictator came up and began to chide them, asking if they were not ashamed to fly like bees from smoke, and calling on them to turn on their enemy, and "with her own flames efface that Fidenae whom their benefits could not conciliate," they took courage; so that the device proved of no service to its contrivers, who were vanquished in the battle.

XV

That One and Not Many Should Head
an Army: And Why It Is Harmful
to Have More Leaders than One

T HE MEN OF FIDENAE rising against the colonists whom
the Romans had settled among them, and putting them
to the sword, the Romans to avenge the insult appointed
four tribunes with consular powers: one of whom they retained
to see to the defense of Rome, while the other three were sent
against the Fidenati and the Veientines. But these three falling out
among themselves, and being divided in their counsels, returned
from their mission with discredit though not with loss. Of which
discredit they were themselves the cause. That they sustained no
loss was due to the valor of their soldiers But the senate perceiving the source of the mischief, to the end that one man might put
to rights what three had thrown into confusion, resorted to the
appointment of a dictator.

Here we see the disadvantage of having several leaders in one army
or in a town that has to defend itself. And the case could not be put in
clearer words than by Titus Livius, where he says, "The three tribunes
with consular authority gave proof how hurtful it is in war to have
many leaders, for each forming a different opinion, and each abiding
by his own, they threw opportunities in the way of their enemies."
And though this example suffice by itself to show the disadvantage

in war of divided commands, to make the matter still plainer I shall cite two further instances, one ancient and one modern.

In the year 1500, Louis XII of France, after recovering Milan, sent troops to restore Pisa to the Florentines, Giovambattista Ridolfi and Luca d'Antonio Albizzi going with them as commissaries. Now, because Giovambattista had a great name, and was older than Luca, the latter left the whole management of everything to him; and although he did not show his jealousy of him by opposing him, he betrayed it by his silence, and by being so careless and indifferent about everything, that he gave no help in the business of the siege either by word or deed, just as though he had been a person of no account. But when, in consequence of an accident, Giovambattista had to return to Florence, all this was changed; for Luca, remaining in sole charge, behaved with the greatest courage, prudence, and zeal, all which qualities had been hidden while he held a joint command. Further to bear me out I shall again borrow the words of Titus Livius, who, in relating how when Quintius and Agrippa his colleague were sent by the Romans against the Aequians, Agrippa contrived that the conduct of the war should rest with Quintius, observes, "Most wholesome is it that in affairs of great moment, supreme authority be vested in one man." Very different, however, is the course followed by the republics and princes of our own days, who, thinking to be better served, are used to appoint several captains or commissioners to fill one command, a practice giving rise to so much confusion that were we seeking for the causes of the overthrow of the French and Italian armies in recent times, we should find this to be the most active of any.

Rightly, therefore, may we conclude that in sending forth an army upon service, it is wiser to entrust it to one man of ordinary prudence, than to two of great parts but with a divided command.

XIX

Whether Indulgence or Severity Be More Necessary for Controlling a Multitude

THE ROMAN REPUBLIC was distracted by the feuds of the nobles and commons. Nevertheless, on war breaking out, Quintius and Appius Claudius were sent forth in command of Roman armies. From his harshness and severity to his soldiers, Appius was so ill obeyed by them that after sustaining what almost amounted to a defeat, he had to resign his command. Quintius, on the contrary, by kindly and humane treatment, kept his men obedient and returned victorious to Rome. From this it might seem that to govern a large body of men it is better to be humane than haughty, and kindly rather than severe.

And yet Cornelius Tacitus, with whom many other authors are agreed, pronounces a contrary opinion where he says, "In governing a multitude it avails more to punish than to be compliant."* If it be asked how these opposite views can be reconciled, I answer that you exercise authority either over men used to regard you as their equal, or over men who have always been subject to you. When those over

---

* "*In multitudine regenda plus poena quam obsequium valet.*" But compare *Annals,* III. 55, "*Obsequium inde in principem et æmulandi amoi validioi quam poena ex legibus et metus.*"

whom you exercise authority are your equals, you cannot trust wholly to punishment or to that severity of which Tacitus speaks. And since in Rome itself the commons had equal weight with the nobles, none appointed their captain for a time only, could control them by using harshness and severity. Accordingly we find that those Roman captains who gained the love of their soldiers and were considerate of them, often achieved greater results than those who made themselves feared by them in an unusual degree, unless, like Manlius Torquatus, these last were endowed with consummate valor. But he who has to govern subjects such as those of whom Tacitus speaks, to prevent their growing insolent and trampling upon him by reason of his too great easiness, must resort to punishment rather than to compliance. Still, to escape hatred, punishment should be moderate in degree, for to make himself hated is never for the interest of any prince. And to escape hatred, a prince has chiefly to guard against tampering with the property of any of his subjects, for where nothing is to be gained by it, no prince will desire to shed blood, unless, as seldom happens, constrained to do so by necessity. But where advantage is to be gained thereby, blood will always flow, and neither the desire to shed it nor causes for shedding it will ever be wanting, as I have fully shown when discussing this subject in another treatise.

Quintius therefore was more deserving of praise than Appius. Nevertheless the opinion of Tacitus, duly restricted and not understood as applying to a case like that of Appius, merits approval. But since I have spoken of punishment and indulgence, it seems not out of place to show how a single act of humanity availed more than arms with the citizens of Falerii.

XXVI

How Women Are a Cause
of the Ruin of States

A FEUD BROKE OUT in Ardea touching the marriage of an heiress, whose hand was sought at the same time by two suitors, the one of plebeian, the other of noble birth. For her father being dead, her guardian wished her to wed the plebeian, her mother the noble. And so hot grew the dispute that resort was had to arms, the whole nobility siding with their fellow noble, and all the plebeians with the plebeian. The latter faction, being worsted, left the town, and sent to the Volscians for help, whereupon the nobles sought help from Rome. The Volscians were first in the field, and on their arrival encamped round Ardea. The Romans, coming up later, shut in the Volscians between themselves and the town, and, reducing them by famine, forced them to surrender at discretion. They then entered Ardea, and putting all the ringleaders in this dispute to the sword, composed the disorders of the city.

In connection with this affair there are several points to be noted. And in the first place we see how women have been the occasion of many divisions and calamities in states, and have wrought great harm to rulers, as when, according to our historian, the violence done to Lucretia drove the Tarquins from their kingdom, and that done to Virginia broke the power of the decemvirs. And among the chief causes that Aristotle assigns for the downfall of tyrants are the wrongs done by them to their subjects in respect of their women, whether by adultery, rape, or other like injury to their honor, as has been sufficiently noticed in the chapter wherein we treated "of Conspiracies."

I say, then, that neither absolute princes nor the rulers of free states should underrate the importance of this matter, but take heed to the disorders that it may breed and provide against them while remedies can still be used without discredit to themselves or to their governments. And this should have been done by the rulers of Ardea, who, by suffering the rivalry between their citizens to come to a head, promoted their divisions, and when they sought to reunite them had to summon foreign help, than which nothing sooner leads to servitude.

But now let us turn to another subject that merits attention, namely, the means whereby divided cities may be reunited; and of this I propose to speak in the following chapter.

XXIX

That the Faults of a People
Are Due to Its Prince

L ET NO PRINCE complain of the faults committed by a people under his control, since these must be ascribed either to his negligence or to his being himself blemished by similar defects. And were anyone to consider what peoples in our own times have been most given to robbery and other like offenses, he would find that they have only copied their rulers, who have themselves been of a like nature. Romagna, before those lords who ruled it were driven out by Pope Alexander VI, was a nursery of all the worst crimes, the slightest occasion giving rise to wholesale rapine and murder. This resulted from the wickedness of these lords, and not, as they asserted, from the evil disposition of their subjects. For these princes being poor, yet choosing to live as though they were rich, were forced to resort to cruelties innumerable and practiced in divers ways, and, among other shameful devices contrived by them to extort money, they would pass laws prohibiting certain acts, and then be the first to give occasion for breaking them. Nor would they chastise offenders until they saw many involved in the same offense, when they fell to punishing not from any zeal for the laws that they had made, but out of greed to realize the penalty. From which flowed many mischiefs, and more particularly this, that the people being impoverished, but not corrected, sought to make good their injuries at the expense of others weaker than themselves. And thus there sprang up all those evils spoken of above, whereof the prince is the true cause.

The truth of what I say is confirmed by Titus Livius, where he relates how the Roman envoys, who were conveying the spoils of the Veientines as an offering to Apollo, were seized and brought on shore by the corsairs of the Lipari islands in Sicily; when Timasitheus, the prince of these islands, on learning the nature of the offering, its destination, and by whom sent, though himself of Lipari, behaved as a Roman might, showing his people what sacrilege it would be to intercept such a gift, and speaking to such purpose that by general consent the envoys were suffered to proceed upon their voyage, taking all their possessions with them. With reference to which incident the historian observes: "The multitude, who always take their color from their ruler, were filled by Timasitheus with a religious awe." And to like purport we find it said by Lorenzo de' Medici:

> "A prince's acts his people imitate;
> For on their lord the eyes of all men wait."*

---

* *E quel che fa il signer, fanno poi molti;*
  Chè nel signer son tutti gli occhi volti.
      (*La Rappresentazione di San Giovanni e Paolo*)

XXXI

That Strong Republics and Valiant Men Preserve through Every Change the Same Spirit and Bearing

AMONG OTHER HIGH SAYINGS that our historian ascribes to Camillus, as showing of what stuff a truly great man should be made, he puts in his mouth the words, "My courage came not with my dictatorship nor went with my exile," for by these words we are taught that a great man is constantly the same through all vicissitudes of Fortune; so that although she change, now exalting, now depressing, he remains unchanged, and retains always a mind so unmoved, and in such complete accordance with his nature as declares to all that over him Fortune has no dominion.

Very different is the behavior of those weak-minded mortals who, puffed up and intoxicated with their success, ascribe all their felicity to virtues that they never knew, and thus grow hateful and insupportable to all around them. So too the changes in their fortunes. For whenever they have to look adversity in the face, they suddenly pass to the other extreme, becoming abject and base. And thus it happens that feeble-minded princes, when they fall into difficulties, think rather of flight than of defense, because, having made bad use of their prosperity, they are wholly unprepared to defend themselves.

The same merits and defects that I say are found in individual men are likewise found in republics, whereof we have an example in the case of Rome and of Venice. For no reverse of fortune ever broke the spirit of the Roman people, nor did any success ever unduly elate them, as we see plainly after their defeat at Cannae, and after the victory they had over Antiochus. For the defeat at Cannae, although most momentous, being the third they had met with, no whit daunted them, so that they continued to send forth armies, refused to ransom prisoners as contrary to their custom, and dispatched no envoy to Hannibal or to Carthage to sue for peace; but without ever looking back on past humiliations, thought always of war, though in such straits for soldiers that they had to arm their old men and slaves. Which facts being made known to Hanno the Carthaginian, he, as I have already related, warned the Carthaginian senate not to lay too much stress upon their victory. Here, therefore, we see that in times of adversity the Romans were neither cast down nor dismayed. On the other hand, no prosperity ever made them arrogant. Before fighting the battle wherein he was finally routed, Antiochus sent messengers to Scipio to treat for an accord; when Scipio offered peace on condition that he withdrew at once into Syria, leaving all his other dominions to be dealt with by the Romans as they thought fit. Antiochus, refusing these terms, fought and was defeated, and again sent envoys to Scipio, enjoining them to accept whatever conditions the victor might be pleased to impose. But Scipio proposed no different terms from those he had offered before, saying that "the Romans, as they lost not heart on defeat, so waxed not insolent with success."

The contrary of all this is seen in the behavior of the Venetians, who thinking their good fortune due to valor of which they were devoid, in their pride addressed the French king as "Son of St. Mark," and making no account of the Church, and no longer restricting their ambition to the limits of Italy, came to dream of founding an empire like the Roman. But afterward, when their good fortune deserted them, and at Vailà they met a half-defeat at the hands of the French king, they lost their whole dominions, not altogether from revolt, but mainly by a base and abject surrender to the pope and the King of Spain. Nay, so low did they stoop as to send ambassadors to the emperor offering to become his tributaries, and to write letters to the pope, full of submission and servility, in order to move his compassion. They were brought to such abasement in four days' time by what was in reality only a half-defeat. For on their flight after the battle of Vailà only about a half of their forces were engaged, and one of their two *provveditori* escaped to Verona with twenty-five thousand men, horse and foot. So that had there been a spark of valor in Venice, or any soundness in her military system, she might easily have renewed her armies, and again confronting fortune have stood prepared either to conquer, or, if she must fall, to fall more gloriously, and at any rate might have obtained for herself more honorable terms. But a pusillanimous spirit, occasioned by the defects of her ordinances insofar as they relate to war, caused her to lose at once her courage and her dominions. And so will it always happen with those who behave like the Venetians. For when men grow insolent in good fortune, and abject in evil, the fault lies in themselves and in the character of their training, which, when slight and frivolous, assimilates them to itself; but when otherwise, makes them of another temper, and giving them better acquaintance with the world, causes them to be less disheartened by misfortunes and less elated by success.

And while this is true of individual men, it holds good also of a concourse of men living together in one republic, who will arrive at that measure of perfection that the institutions of their state permit. And although I have already said on another occasion that a good militia is the foundation of all states, and where that is wanting there can neither be good laws, nor aught else that is good, it seems to me not superfluous to say the same again, because in reading this history of Titus Livius the necessity of such a foundation is made apparent in every page. It is likewise shown that no army can be good unless it is thoroughly trained and exercised, and that this can only be the case with an army raised from your own subjects. For as a state is not and cannot always be at war, you must have the opportunity to train your army in times of peace, but this, having regard to the cost, you can only have in respect of your own subjects.

When Camillus, as already related, went forth to meet the Etruscans, his soldiers, on seeing the great army of their enemy, were filled with fear, thinking themselves too weak to withstand its onset. This untoward disposition being reported to Camillus, he showed himself to his men and by visiting their tents, and conversing with this and the other among them, was able to remove their misgivings; and, finally, without other word of command, he bade them "each do his part as he had learned and been accustomed." Now, anyone who well considers the methods followed by Camillus, and the words spoken by him to encourage his soldiers to face their enemy, will perceive that these words and methods could never have been used with an army that had not been trained and disciplined in time of peace as well as of war. For no captain can trust to untrained soldiers or look for good service at their hands; nay, though he were another Hannibal, with such troops his defeat would be certain. For, as a captain cannot be present everywhere while a battle is being fought, unless he has taken all measures beforehand to render his men of the same temper as himself, and made sure that they perfectly understand his orders and arrangements, he will inevitably be destroyed.

When a city therefore is armed and trained as Rome was, and when its citizens have daily opportunity, both singly and together, to make trial of their valor and learn what fortune can effect, it will always happen that at all times, and whether circumstances be adverse or favorable, they will remain of unaltered courage and preserve the same noble bearing. But when its citizens are unpracticed in arms, and trust not to their own valor but wholly to the arbitration of Fortune, they will change their temper as she changes, and offer always the same example of behavior as was given by the Venetians.

XXXII

Of the Methods that Some Have Used to Make Peace Impossible

T HE TOWNS OF CAERE and Velitrae, two of her own colonies, revolted from Rome in expectation of being protected by the Latins. But the Latins being routed and all hopes of help from that quarter at an end, many of the townsmen recommended that envoys should be sent to Rome to make their peace with the senate. This proposal, however, was defeated by those who had been the prime movers of the revolt, who, fearing that the whole punishment might fall on their heads, to put a stop to any talk of an adjustment, incited the multitude to take up arms and make a foray into the Roman territory.

And, in truth, when it is desired that a prince or people should banish from their minds every thought of reconciliation, there is no surer or more effectual plan than to incite them to inflict grave wrong on him with whom you would not have them be reconciled; for, then, the fear of that punishment that they will seem to themselves to have deserved will always keep them apart. At the close of the first war waged by the Romans against Carthage, the soldiers who had served under the Carthaginians in Sardinia and Sicily, upon peace being proclaimed, returned to Africa, where, being dissatisfied with their pay, they mutinied against the Carthaginians, and choosing two of their number, Mato and Spendio, to be their leaders, seized and sacked many towns subject to Carthage. The Carthaginians, being loath to use force until they had tried all other methods for bringing them to reason, sent Hasdrubal, their fellow citizen, to mediate with them, thinking that from formerly having commanded them he might be able to exercise some influence over them. But on his arrival, Spendio and Mato, to extinguish any hope these mutineers might have had of making peace with Carthage, and so leave them no alternative but war, persuaded them that their best course was to put Hasdrubal, with all the other Carthaginian citizens whom they had taken prisoner, to death. Whereupon they not only put them to death, but first subjected them to an infinity of tortures, crowning their wickedness by a proclamation to the effect that every Carthaginian who might thereafter fall into their hands should meet a like fate. This advice, therefore, and its consummation had the effect of rendering these mutineers relentless and inveterate in their hostility to the Carthaginians.

XL

That Fraud Is Fair in War

LTHOUGH IN ALL other affairs it be hateful to use fraud,
in the operations of war it is praiseworthy and glorious;
so that he who gets the better of his enemy by fraud is as
much extolled as he who prevails by force. This appears in the judgments passed by such as have written of the lives of great warriors,
who praise Hannibal and those other captains who have been most
noted for acting in this way. But since we may read of many instances
of such frauds, I shall not cite them here. This, however, I desire to
say, that I would not have it understood that any fraud is glorious that
leads you to break your plighted word, or to depart from covenants
to which you have agreed, for though to do so may sometimes gain
you territory and power, it can never, as I have said elsewhere, gain
you glory.

The fraud, then, which I here speak of is that employed against
an enemy who places no trust in you, and is wholly directed to
military operations, such as the stratagem of Hannibal at the Lake
of Thrasymene, when he feigned flight in order to draw the Roman
consul and his army into an ambuscade; or when to escape from
the hands of Fabius Maximus he fastened lights to the horns of his
oxen. Similar to the above was the deceit practiced by Pontius the
Samnite commander to inveigle the Roman army into the Caudine
Forks. For after he had drawn up his forces behind the hills, he sent

out a number of his soldiers, disguised as herdsmen, to drive great herds of cattle across the plain, who, being captured by the Romans, and interrogated as to where the Samnite army was, all of them, as they had been taught by Pontius, agreed in saying that it had gone to besiege Nocera—which being believed by the consuls, led them to advance within the Caudine Valley, where no sooner were they come than they were beset by the Samnites. And the victory thus won by a fraud would have been most glorious for Pontius had he but taken the advice of his father Herennius, who urged that the Romans should either be set at liberty unconditionally, or all be put to death; but that a mean course "which neither gains friends nor gets rid of foes" should be avoided. And this was sound advice, for, as has already been shown, in affairs of moment a mean course is always hurtful.

XLVII

That Love of His Country Should Lead a Good Citizen to Forget Private Wrongs

WHILE COMMANDING as consul against the Samnites, Manlius was wounded in a skirmish. His army being thereby endangered, the senate judged it expedient to send Papirius Cursor as dictator to supply his place. But as it was necessary that the dictator should be nominated by Fabius, the other consul, who was with the army in Etruria, and as a doubt was felt that he might refuse to nominate Papirius, who was his enemy, the senate sent two messengers to entreat him to lay aside private animosity, and make the nomination that the public interest required. Moved by love of his country Fabius did as he was asked, although by his silence, and by many other signs, he gave it to be known that compliance was distasteful. From his conduct at this juncture all who would be thought good citizens should take example.

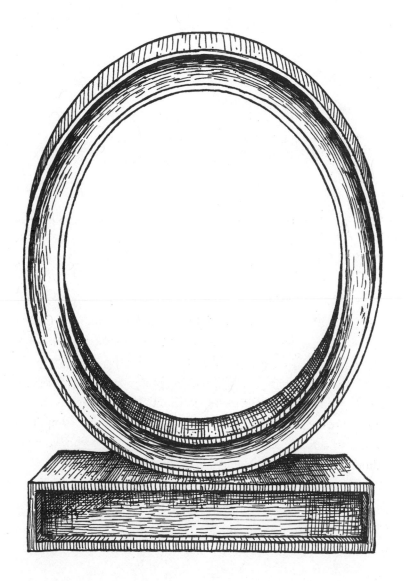

Suggestions for Further Reading

OTHER WORKS BY NICOLLÒ MACHIAVELLI

The Mandrake. Dramatists Play Service, 1978.
Florentine Histories. Princeton University Press, 1988.
The Art of War. University of Chicago Press, 2003.
The Life of Castruccio Castracani. Hesperus Classics, 2003.

BIOGRAPHIES OF MACHIAVELLI

Sebastian De Grazia. *Machiavelli in Hell*. Vintage Books USA, 1989.
Miles J. Unger. *Machiavelli: A Biography*. Simon and Schuster, 2011
Maurizio Viroli. *Niccolò's Smile*. Farrar Straus and Giroux, 1998.

CONTEXT, COMPANION, AND CRITICISM

James B. Atkinson and David Sices, eds. *Machiavelli and His Friends: Their Personal Correspondence*. Northern Illinois University Press, 1996.
Erica Benner. *Machiavelli's Ethics*. Princeton University Press, 2009.
Gisela Bock, Quentin Skinner, and Maurizio Viroli, eds. *Machiavelli and Republicanism*. Cambridge University Press, 1990.
Maurizio Viroli. *How to Read Machiavelli*. Granta Books, 2008.

A Guide for Restless Readers

1. Modern European colonization began during Machiavelli's lifetime, during which Spanish conquistadors sought to expand their empire to new continents. In what ways can Machiavelli's discussion of "new principalities" illuminate the dynamics of colonization that took place after his lifetime, and the intervention of large, powerful nations in the affairs of less powerful nations today?

2. Machiavelli's suggestions about the way princes should conduct themselves earned him a reputation for encouraging deceit, dishonesty, and even cruelty as a means of governing. To what extent do you think this "moral flexibility" is practiced by the democratic nation states that dominate the current world stage? What justifies this flexibility, and what mitigates it?

3. The twentieth century saw several freedom movements (e.g. Anti-Apartheid, Indian Independence, American Civil Rights) that successfully won their objectives by centering peaceful protest in spite of state violence. Considering Machiavelli's discussions of an armed citizenry as essential to liberty in *The Discourses*, and his emphasis on ruthlessness and forcefulness in *The Prince*, how do you think he would account for the states' choices to grant rights to peaceful groups?

4. The relationships among states look very different today than they did in Machiavelli's time. The presence of international governing and judicial bodies (e.g. the UN and the World Court), and the capacity for government atrocity to be exposed through technology and mass/social media, have changed the way states relate to one another. Do you think this has diminished the effectiveness of ruthless governance as a way of obtaining and maintaining power? Why or why not?

5. Book I of *The Discourses on Livy* extolls the virtues of the Roman Republic, which in Machiavelli's view combines the virtues of democracy, aristocracy, and monarchy, and protects them from falling into anarchy, oligarchy, or tyranny, all of which involve ruthless and violent governance. How does Machiavelli's favorable view of republics affect your understanding of what he meant by *virtù* in *The Prince*?

6. In *The Discourses*, Machiavelli claims that the contentious relationship between plebeians and patricians in the Roman Republic was essential to the preservation of liberty within the state. How do you think this dissent is viewed by and shapes the political life of people in today's democratic republics?

7. *The Prince* was written in the wake of several invasions upon Italian city-states by the Spanish, the French, and the Holy Roman Empire. Machaivelli's advice can thereby be conceived of (at least in part) as a defensive politics designed to prevent occupation by external forces. How, if at all, does this context affect your reading of Machiavelli's amoral approach to the consolidation and maintenance of power?

8. The moral values that underlie political life in today's democratic republics are mostly drawn from Enlightenment ideals that postdate Machiavelli. Considering both the stark pragmatism of

The Prince and the idealization of the Roman Republic's liberty in *The Discourses,* are there any identifiable moral values that you can draw from his works? Do any of these values seem to be antecedents of Enlightenment thought?

About the Author

NICCOLÒ MACHIAVELLI (1469–1527) was an Italian diplomat, politician, historian, philosopher, and writer of the Renaissance period. As a young Florentine envoy to the courts of France and the Italian principalities, he witnessed firsthand how people could be united under a powerful leader. This vision motivated his writing on acquiring and maintaining political power.

About the Introducer

JON LEE ANDERSON has been a staff writer for *The New Yorker* since 1998. He has covered numerous conflicts in the Middle East and Africa, reported frequently from Latin America and the Caribbean, and written profiles of Augusto Pinochet, Fidel Castro, Hugo Chávez, and Gabriel García Márquez. He is the author of several books, including *The Lion's Grave: Dispatches from Afghanistan, Che Guevara: A Revolutionary Life, Guerrillas: Journeys in the Insurgent World,* and *The Fall of Baghdad.*

About the Illustrator

Born in Mexico in 1958, EKO is an engraver and painter. His wood etchings, often erotic in nature and the focus of controversial discussion, are part of a broader tradition in Mexican folk art popularized by José Guadalupe Posada. He has collaborated on projects for *The New York Times*, the *Frankfurter Allgemeine Zeitung*, and the Spanish daily *El País*, in addition to having published numerous books in Mexico and Spain.

About the Translators

W. K. MARRIOTT (1847–1927) was a translator known for his translations of several of Machiavelli's works, and for his translation of Hermann Hesse's *Siddhartha*. His 1908 translation of *The Prince* has been reprinted in several editions and anthologies of political theory, including this one.

NINIAN HILL THOMSON (1830–1921) was a British legal scholar whose career spanned several decades and countries (Scotland, India, and England among them). Thomson spent his later years in Florence, and translated the work of both Machiavelli and Francesco Guicciardini: one of Machiavelli's contemporaries and friends. Thomson's translations are known for both their accessibility and their thoroughness.

RESTLESS CLASSICS

Don Quixote of La Mancha
MIGUEL DE CERVANTES SAAVEDRA
Introduction by Ilan Stavans

Frankenstein, or The Modern Prometheus
MARY SHELLEY
Introduction by Francine Prose

The Souls of Black Folk
W. E. B. DU BOIS
Introduction by Vann R. Newkirk III

Chekhov: Stories for Our Time
ANTON CHEKHOV
Introduction by Boris Fishman

Passing
NELLA LARSEN
Introduction by Darryl Pinckney

Night and Day
VIRGINIA WOOLF
Introduction by Lauren Groff

Robinson Crusoe
DANIEL DEFOE
Introduction by Jamaica Kincaid

Visit restlessbooks.org/classics to learn more.

RESTLESS BOOKS is an independent, nonprofit publisher devoted to championing essential voices from around the world whose stories speak to us across linguistic and cultural borders. We seek extraordinary international literature for adults and young readers that feeds our restlessness: our hunger for new perspectives, passion for other cultures and languages, and eagerness to explore beyond the confines of the familiar.

Through cultural programming, we aim to celebrate immigrant writing and bring literature to underserved communities. We believe that immigrant stories are a vital component of our cultural consciousness; they help to ensure awareness of our communities, build empathy for our neighbors, and strengthen our democracy.

Visit us at www.restlessbooks.org